P9-EML-636

THE UNITED STATES AND WEST GERMANY

1945–1973

The Royal Institute of International Affairs is an unofficial body which promotes the scientific study of international questions and does not express opinions of its own. The opinions expressed in this publication are the responsibility of the author.

The Institute gratefully acknowledges the comments and suggestions of the following, who read the manuscript on behalf of the Research Committee: Professor Max Beloff, Sir Alan Bullock, and Professor Paul Seabury.

The United States and West Germany
1945-1973

A STUDY IN ALLIANCE POLITICS

ROGER MORGAN

Published for
THE ROYAL INSTITUTE OF INTERNATIONAL AFFAIRS
and the
HARVARD CENTER FOR INTERNATIONAL AFFAIRS
by
OXFORD UNIVERSITY PRESS
LONDON
1974

Oxford University Press, Ely House, London W.1

GLASGOW NEW YORK TORONTO MELBOURNE WELLINGTON
CAPE TOWN IBADAN NAIROBI DAR ES SALAAM LUSAKA ADDIS ABABA
DELHI BOMBAY CALCUTTA MADRAS KARACHI LAHORE DACCA
KUALA LUMPUR SINGAPORE HONG KONG TOKYO

ISBN 0 19 218304 4

Printed in Great Britain by
The Eastern Press Ltd. London and Reading

CONTENTS

ACKNOWLEDGEMENTS

The foundations of this study were laid during a year which I was able to spend as a Research Associate of the Harvard University Center for International Affairs, thanks to a generous invitation from its then Director, Robert Bowie. I am deeply grateful to him, and also to my colleagues at the Center during that time, particularly Karl Kaiser, Morton Halperin and Tom Schelling, for many stimulating discussions on various aspects of my work.

A further considerable debt is owed to the many participants in the events analysed in this book, Americans, Germans and others, who kindly spared the time to give me their recollections and their judgements, of the sort which form an invaluable source for the student of recent or contemporary events. Since some of these witnesses still hold official positions I must thank them all anonymously, but none the less sincerely, for their contributions. Facilities for interviews, and for other research in the two capital cities of this story, along with much helpful information and advice, were provided by Wolfgang Wagner of the Deutsche Gesellschaft für Auswärtige Politik, Robert Osgood of the Washington Center for Foreign Policy Research, and Ken Myers of the Georgetown University Center for Strategic and International Studies. In respect of sources of a different kind, the John Foster Dulles Papers and the transcripts of interviews in the Dulles Oral History Project at Princeton University, I thank the curators for their guidance and the interviewees for permission to quote from their testimony.

The writing of the book was greatly helped by invitations to work for periods of time in ideal surroundings. My warm thanks are due to the Trustees of the Rockefeller Foundation and to Bill and Betsy Olson at the Villa Serbelloni, Bellagio; to Dick Rosecrance and George Quester at the Center for International Studies, Cornell University; and to my parents at Tingewick, Buckinghamshire.

Most useful comments on all or part of the draft have been made not only by the three readers appointed by the Chatham House Research Committee, Max Beloff, Sir Alan Bullock and Paul Seabury, but also by Alastair Buchan, Dieter Dettke, George Kennan, Bob Kleiman, Manfred Knapp, Hans-Peter Schwarz, Ian Smart, Susan Strange, and John Yochelson. I am grateful to all of them for removing errors and for their suggestions for improvements, including those with which I disagreed.

My greatest institutional debt is to the Royal Institute of International Affairs, my employer during most of the time I have been engaged on this study. The Library and Press Library have lived up to their reputation for superlatively efficient and pleasant service; I have been greatly aided by Joanna Holland's work in finding and assembling some of the material; Rena Fenteman has edited the text most rigorously, to its great benefit; I am indebted to Helen Roy for the index; and the burdens of typing successive drafts and helping with the footnotes and bibliography have been most cheerfully borne by Carola Piggott and Elizabeth McMillan.

Last and at the same time first, my deep thanks are due to my family, and particularly to my wife Annette for her intellectual contribution to this undertaking, and her willing acceptance of its inevitable inconveniences, including restrictions on her own research work.

The multiplicity of my debts to others requires me to emphasize that the responsibility for my conclusions lies solely with myself.

London R.P.M.
March 1974

NOTE ON TERMINOLOGY

In accordance with normal usage in the Western world, the German Federal Republic (established in 1949 by an amalgamation of the American, British, and French zones of occupation of 1945) is referred to in this book sometimes as 'West Germany' and sometimes as 'Germany'. The latter term is also used to refer to the country as a whole, but the meaning in each case will be clear from the context. The use of the adjective 'German' is analogous: 'German-American relations' normally means relations between the United States and the Federal Republic whereas, for instance, 'the German problem' normally means the problem of Germany as a whole.

Translations from German sources, except where otherwise indicated, have been made by the author.

ABBREVIATIONS

ABM	Anti-ballistic missile
Adenauer, *1945–1953*; *1953–1955*; *1955–1959*; *1959–1963*	Konrad Adenauer, *Erinnerungen*, vols i–iii (paperback edn, 1967–9); vol. iv (hard-cover edn, 1968). Full publication details are supplied in the Bibliography, Pt 4.
ANF	Atlantic Nuclear Force
L'Année Politique 19—	*L'Année Politique, Economique, Sociale et Diplomatique en France 19—*
CDU	Christlich-Demokratische Union
CSCE	Conference on Security and Co-operation in Europe
CSU	Christlich-Soziale Union
DOHP	Dulles Oral History Project (see Bibliography, Pt 1)
DOSB	*The Department of State Bulletin*
Dulles Papers	John Foster Dulles Papers (see Bibliography, Pt 1)
EDC	European Defence Community
EEC	European Economic Community
FAZ	*Frankfurter Allgemeine Zeitung*
FDP	Freidemokratische Partei
For. Aff.	*Foreign Affairs*
Int. Aff.	*International Affairs* (London)
Int. Org.	*International Organization*
MBFR	Mutual and Balanced Force Reductions
MLF	Multilateral Force
NPD	Nationaldemokratische Partei Deutschlands
NPG	Nuclear Planning Group
NPT	Non-Proliferation Treaty
NYT	*New York Times*
NZZ	*Neue Zürcher Zeitung*
OECD	Organization for Economic Co-operation and Development
OEEC	Organization for European Economic Co-operation
SALT	Strategic Arms Limitation Talks
SPD	Sozialdemokratische Partei Deutschlands

CHAPTER ONE

The Theme and the Approach

THIS book analyses the course of the relationship between the governments of the United States and West Germany during a period of somewhat more than a quarter of a century. It does so with two purposes in view. First, to tell as accurately and clearly as possible the story of a relationship which underwent several striking variations during the twenty-eight years separating the Unconditional Surrender of the Third Reich in May 1945 from Germany's entry into the United Nations Organization in September 1973. Secondly, to present the elements of this story in such a way as to bring out its significance as a case-study in the politics of alliance, some of whose features are likely to be found in other bilateral alliances widely separated in time and place from the particular example selected for analysis here.

Even a brief survey of the story of post-war American-German relations reveals their variety and complexity, and their interest as a case-study in the rapid fluctuations which a bilateral relationship can undergo. During the first four years after the end of hostilities in 1945, when Germany temporarily ceased to exist as a political unit and appeared only as a stake in the growing Soviet-Western conflict, the foundations were laid for the rebirth of 1949, largely under American auspices. There followed three years of increasingly close collaboration, stimulated largely by a common interest in defence against the Soviet Union, leading to the treaty of 1952 which provided for Germany's rearmament as a member of the European Defence Community. In 1952–4, during the struggle for the ratification of this agreement, US-German harmony began significantly to take the form of alignment against certain policies of other members of the Western alliance, particularly France for her delays and Britain for her aloofness from the Continent. During and after the breakdown of the EDC and the creation of Western European Union in 1954 and Germany's entry into NATO in 1955, this source of agreement remained influential, as Britain and France compromised their relations with the United States by the Suez operation, and by dissent from American policy in the Far East. It is difficult to be certain whether to attribute the continued American-German harmony of 1954–8 primarily to this 'alliance' factor, or to the close personal relationship of Dulles and Adenauer, or to Germany's record as a 'good European' when the US was firmly committed to promoting Western European unity. However, the relationship was patently very close during those years, and the factors producing something of a decline after 1958 did so only gradually: they included the advent of President de Gaulle and President Kennedy, the revival of the Soviet threat to Berlin, the development of the deadlock in missile power, and the relative increase in American concern with the Far East at the expense of Europe.

The onset of some of these factors provoked a first period of strain in US-German relations during the Berlin crisis of 1958–9, for instance when the US and the other Western allies accepted the presence of an East German delegation at the Geneva foreign ministers' conference of May 1959. Much more serious strain developed in 1961–2, when the United States, despite its firm military response to the Berlin Wall, carried diplomatic flexibility much further than the West German government welcomed. The removal of Soviet pressure by the beginning of 1963, though it might have been expected to increase the gap between the United States and Germany, in fact coincided with a striking rapprochement, inspired this time by common disagreement with the policy of France towards the Atlantic alliance. The American reaction to this policy included 'strenuous efforts to forge new United States-German links,' amounting in one view to 'the impression of a special United States-German relationship'.[1] For various reasons, including the tension provoked by the test-ban agreement of late 1963, this rapprochement was not developed further in 1964–5; by this time, US-German relations appeared to have been stabilized in a relatively harmonious condition, but no more. Before arriving at this point, however, a survey of the United States-German relationship has to consider what one observer of its Washington end called 'the fluctuations in our German policy from impatient aloofness in 1961 to ardent wooing in 1963 to a more distant policy in 1965.'[2]

Washington's 'distant policy' of 1965—whose causes included a declining fear of war in Western Europe, increasing preoccupation with Vietnam, and a worsening American balance of payments deficit—helped to contribute to the downfall of the Erhard government late in 1966. American relations with its successor, the Grand Coalition led by Kurt Georg Kiesinger and Willy Brandt, were reasonably good on the whole, although they suffered some strain from the Johnson administration's determination to achieve a nuclear non-proliferation treaty and from the wish of the Bonn government to assert a greater degree of independence from Washington.

The last-mentioned tendency became somewhat more pronounced in 1969–72, particularly during the year 1970, when the Brandt government pursued its policy of Eastern rapprochement with a vigour which occasionally aroused considerable concern in Washington. As usual, the pursuit by one ally of better relations with the presumed adversary was the main source of disharmony between the two allied capitals: the novelty of the situation at the beginning of the 1970s—in contrast to the Kennedy period ten years earlier—was that the capital whose policies occasioned controversy was now sometimes Bonn rather than Washington. However, thanks in part to effective consultation and in part to a determined removal of other sources of friction, notably the issue of offset costs for the American troops stationed in Germany, the Bonn-Washington relationship remained almost as harmonious during the period of détente under Brandt and Nixon as it had been several years earlier during the period of *immobilisme* under Adenauer and Dulles.

The second purpose of this book, the attempt to present the subject in such a way as to emphasize its paradigmatic quality as a case-study, may require more explanation. The study attempts to explain a specific historical process, and its extension over the entire post-war period appeared essential, since the nature of international politics is intrinsically a dynamic one, in which the expectations and designs of policy-makers are conditioned by their perceptions of the past. The book's approach is thus in part historical and it relies on the established methods of contemporary historiography, and the sources of information—public and (sometimes) private documents, secondary works, the press, and the oral evidence of participants or witnesses—normally available to the historian of contemporary events.[3] This material forms the basis of a narrative which attempts to recount as accurately as possible 'what actually happened,'[4] and to give enough detail to make clear the nature of the issues at stake. The narrative has deliberately been restricted in length, partly because there exists a growing literature of detailed monographs on various episodes or aspects of the subject, which are listed in the bibliography, and partly because too much detail would have obscured the second purpose of the study, the identification and clarification of the essential forces at work.

The 'essential forces' are those producing harmony or discord between the two allies in question. Writers on alliances in fact disagree widely and interestingly in their assessments of the degree of harmony to be expected among states linked in them. In the view of Charles Burton Marshall, 'Allies are political entities aligned together and capable of doing each other some good.'[5] Coral Bell asserts much more negatively that 'the brutal fact is that international politics is a system based on the gradations in the power to inflict injury, either on foe or (by default) on friend.'[6] These generalizations cannot both be true, and both may be false. The titles of a significant sample of monographs on twentieth-century alliances suggest that even if the allies concerned have done each other 'some good', their relations have also been marked, if not always, by 'injury,' at least by enough tension to involve a serious risk of it: alliances have been described characteristically as 'debatable,'[7] 'troubled,'[8] and 'unholy,'[9] while the parties to them figure as 'uneasy,'[10] 'implacable,'[11] and even 'incompatible.'[12]

Most of the writers represented in a recent anthology on the theory of alliances also emphasize their potentialities for discord and their normally transitory character, and its editors also rightly describe alliance as 'a central but intellectually much neglected aspect of international politics.'[13]

This book attempts to contribute to the construction of a theory of how alliances operate, by presenting the data of the German-American case within a rigorous framework of concepts. The purpose is to demonstrate the explanatory value of these concepts in elucidating the forces at work in the particular case analysed here, in the belief that the same method will prove valid for the study of other bilateral alliances too.[14]

The fundamental hypothesis underlying the approach employed here is that harmony or discord in a bilateral alliance may result from forces arising at any one of four distinct levels: the domestic political systems of the two parties to the alliance; the bilateral relationship between them; the multilateral alliance or grouping of which their bilateral alliance may form part; and those parts of the global international system which affect them, notably the adversary or adversaries against which their alliance is directed.

It is often difficult in practice to isolate the respective causal importance of events at these four levels of analysis. For instance, in the period of Kennedy and Adenauer, when American-German relations were marked by a considerable degree of discord, the brief sketch offered above suggests that this arose at all four levels simultaneously. Each administration contained political forces antipathetic to the other; they disagreed somewhat on specific aspects of their bilateral relations, including the question of Germany's payments towards the costs of stationing American troops there; they disagreed very sharply on some central questions of the structure of the Western alliance, notably the problem of how to deal with de Gaulle; and their dealings with the presumed adversary—particularly, Kennedy's pursuit of East-West détente on terms which gravely alarmed Adenauer—was probably the most serious irritant of all.[15]

This example suggests not merely that several sources of discord (or harmony) can operate simultaneously, but also that the lines of demarcation between the four proposed levels of analysis are to some degree arbitrary. The Kennedy and Adenauer administrations acted as they did in their bilateral relations (i.e. at the second level) in part *because* of their views about the appropriate policies for the alliance as a whole (the third level), and these policies were in turn influenced by their contrasting perceptions of how to deal with the Soviet Union (fourth level) which in turn reflected in part the kind of domestic political forces the two governments represented (first level).

Let us take another example, this time from the most recent phase of the story. The accusation by the West German opposition in the spring of 1973 that Chancellor Brandt's adviser Egon Bahr supported the abolition of NATO was clearly an instance of pressure within the German political system (first level); the accusation did, however, lead to a degree of tension in the bilateral German-American relationship (second level) and the Western alliance generally (third level)—essentially because of what it implied about German intentions towards the Soviet bloc (fourth level).[16]

The structure of this book is based on the approach just described; in particular it reflects the view that the sources of harmony or discord in a bilateral alliance can usefully be identified in the form of pressures *originating* at one or another of the four levels indicated. Each chapter deals with periods of time demarcated by recognizable turning-points, and is divided into five sections. The first of these gives a summary sketch of the major international developments of the period concerned, to remind the reader of the context within which American-German relations developed; the second section deals with the forces and pressures within the American and German domestic systems, in so far as these were relevant to the bilateral relationship; the third analyses the problems specific to the bilateral relationship itself; the fourth covers the multilateral alliance within which the bilateral one was embedded; and the fifth returns to the broader level of the whole international system, dealing particularly with the effect on the bilateral relationship of each party's dealings with their presumed adversary.

This approach, by focusing on the *pressures* and *processes* operating in successive phases of the story, may in a certain measure divert attention from the specific themes which have actually formed the *substance* of German-American relations, e.g. the problem of Berlin or the commercial frictions between the United States and the European Community. Most of these issues have, however, been extensively analysed in the large number of works already alluded to, and the present study aims not to analyse them fully, yet again, but rather to assess their respective effects on the overall state of the relationship between Washington and Bonn—a subject which has *not* so far been systematically studied.

The mode of presentation, which takes the reader through each chronological period from four different angles (five if the preliminary background survey is included), should thus direct his attention to the political salience of each major issue as a determinant of the overall state of the alliance, as well as to its intrinsic substance and the course of its development. The method also points to the important conclusion, which will be stated now and developed in more detail at the end of the study, that relations with the presumed adversary, i.e. the processes at work at the fourth level of analysis, are clearly a more important factor affecting the overall harmony of the alliance than the variables operating at any of the other three levels.

It should be clearly stated that the entities whose relations are here assessed in terms of discord or harmony are the two small groups wielding supreme authority over foreign affairs in Washington and Bonn. At various times these might include, as well as American presidents and German chancellors, certain secretaries of state or defence, finance ministers, or presidential special assistants: at all times, however, it is the leaders of *governments* whose relationship is at the centre of consideration. Various non-governmental or transnational forces of a psychological or economic character have obviously had profound effects on the relations between governments, and these factors —for instance, the fact that nearly 40 per cent of all American direct investment in the EEC in 1964 was in Germany [17]—have been kept in mind but also kept in their place. For example, Professor Robert Gilpin's confident assertion that the essence of the American-German 'special relationship' has been a perfectly straightforward trading of military security for economic gain, America defending Germany against Russia in exchange for access for American exports to the European market,[18] demands considerable modification in the light of a systematic weighing of the economic, strategic, and other factors along the lines adopted here. Again, the multifarious interactions between sub-units of the American and German national bureaucracies have been taken into account (usually in the 'internal' and 'bilateral' sections of the appropriate chapters), but only in so far as their influence on the state of relations at the top level of government could be traced with any precision.

The period of time covered by each chapter depends on the quantity of relevant material each period can offer. The ten years before 1955, the period before West Germany's recovery of sovereignty, is covered in only two chapters. In contrast, the Kennedy presidency—a short period of just under three years, but one remarkably productive of American-German discord—is also covered in two chapters. In general, the lines of division between each chapter are significant turning-points falling at roughly three-year intervals.

NOTES

1 Henry A. Kissinger, *The Troubled Partnership* (1965), p. 74.
2 Ibid. p. 235.
3 On some of the problems this entails, see the author's essay 'The Writing and Teaching of Contemporary History,' in J. L. Henderson, ed., *Since 1945: Aspects of Contemporary World History*, 2nd edn (1971).
4 Though, on the pitfalls of Ranke's prescription that historians should describe the past *wie es eigentlich gewesen*, see E. H. Carr, *What is History?* (1961), esp. pp. 3–24.
5 *The Exercise of Sovereignty* (1965), p. 223.
6 *The Debatable Alliance: an Essay in Anglo-American Relations* (1964), p. 124.
7 Ibid.
8 Kissinger, *The Troubled Partnership*; Edgar Furniss, *France, Troubled Ally* (1960).
9 Gerald Freund, *Unholy Alliance* (1957).
10 Leon D. Epstein, *Britain—Uneasy Ally* (1954).
11 Roy C. Macridis, *De Gaulle—Implacable Ally* (1966).
12 Gustav Hilger and A. G. Meyer, *The Incompatible Allies* (1953).
13 Julian R. Friedman, Christopher Bladen, and Steven Rosen, eds, *Alliance in International Politics* (1970), p. vii.
14 For a fuller exposition of the framework, including a critique of the alternative approach adopted by Professor Richard Neustadt in his *Alliance Politics* (1970), see the author's article 'Washington and Bonn: a Case Study in Alliance Politics', *Int. Aff.*, 47/3 (1971), pp. 489–502. The method is applied to another bilateral relationship in a short study of 'Anglo-French Relations Today', *The World Today*, 27/7 (1971), pp. 285–90.
15 The Kennedy period is analysed in detail in chs 6 and 7 below.
16 See ch. 11 below.
17 Kurt Blauhorn, *Ausverkauf in Germany?* 3rd edn (1967), p. 251.
18 *Int. Org.*, 25/3 (1971), pp. 413–15.

CHAPTER TWO

The Making of an Alliance 1945–1949

Background: the Post-war International System

GERMANY's unconditional surrender on 8 May 1945 marked the end of the Second World War in Europe. The signing of the North Atlantic Treaty almost four years later, on 4 April 1949, finally marked the division of Europe into the two opposing alliances of the Cold War. A considerable degree of tension between the former members of the coalition against Hitler had of course become plain, even during the earlier part of this four-year period. Before the war against Japan was ended by the use of two atomic bombs in August 1945 distinct conflicts between the interests of the allies were apparent.

The Soviet government, determined to increase its influence and to protect itself against any future aggression, used the traditional methods of power politics: the extension of its own frontiers westwards, at the expense of Finland, Poland, Germany, Czechoslovakia, and Rumania; the establishment of satellite regimes in a broad band of states covering thousands of square kilometres between itself and the nearest potential enemy, Germany; and the attempt to preserve alliances with some at least of the Western powers—though in practice the Soviet treaties with Britain, and of 1944 with France, were soon emptied of any substance.[1]

These Soviet policies naturally led to differences with the Western powers: even though Churchill had agreed, when he visited Stalin in October 1944, that the Soviet Union should have the preponderant share of influence in Bulgaria and Rumania, and a ' fifty-fifty ' share in Yugoslavia and Hungary, the Soviet attempt at the same time to extend her influence in Greece, and her pressure on Iran and Turkey slightly later, ran counter not only to the spirit but also in some cases to the letter of the Stalin-Churchill agreement. Even in Poland, where it was generally accepted as inevitable that Soviet influence would be predominant, the actual form of regime imposed by the Soviet authorities—outwardly a coalition but in reality under very firm Communist domination—provoked strong protests from the British and American governments.

President Truman, who succeeded Roosevelt in April 1945, was less optimistic than his predecessor about the prospects of understanding with the Soviet Union; but he was under strong pressure from the public and the legislature, particularly after the Republicans gained control of Congress in 1946, to reduce the size of the armed forces, and was thus in no position to commit American power to the European balance against the Soviet Union.

It was only after a series of open clashes, notably the Soviet Union's refusal to remove her forces from northern Iran until Western counter-measures and local resistance forced her to do so, that American opinion could be mobilized in favour of a more active engagement. Even then, it took Britain's virtual ultimatum to Washington of February 1947—Ernest Bevin's warning that British aid to Greece and Turkey would have to end in a matter of weeks—to bring about the ' Truman Doctrine', proclaimed on 12 March, stating America's readiness to take over a large part of the burden.

This first American commitment to the European balance of power was followed in June by the Marshall Plan, offering economic aid to the whole of Europe (the Soviet Union declined the offer, and forced her satellites to do likewise), which led by 1948 to the setting-up of the OEEC. This was only one of a number of Western organizations that symbolized the growing unity of the Western side in the developing Cold War: it was established at the same time as the Benelux Union and the European Payments Union, and—in the military field—the Brussels Treaty Organization. The Council of Europe was to follow in 1949. On the Eastern side, the years 1947–8 saw the establishment of the Cominform (the successor to the Comintern abolished in 1943), the Communist take-over in Czechoslovakia in February 1948, and the breach between Tito and Stalin later in the same year, which led to Yugoslavia's expulsion from the now increasingly consolidated Cominform.

This development of the East-West conflict in Europe came at a time when acute problems in other areas were also claiming the attention of the world's political leaders. Britain's imperial position was being eroded by the granting of independence to India, Pakistan, Ceylon, and Burma and by the weakness which forced her to abandon control of Palestine as well as support for Greece and Turkey. France and the Netherlands also had their difficulties with colonial revolts, since both Indochina and Indonesia had seen the undermining of European rule by the Japanese occupation. More significant than these colonial conflicts was the civil war in China between the Nationalists under Chiang Kai-shek and the Communists under Mao Tse-tung which broke out almost as soon as Japan had been defeated. Despite considerable help from the United States, the Nationalist regime revealed itself as unable to hold the support of the Chinese people, and by October 1949 Mao's victory was confirmed by the establishment of the Chinese People's Republic.

Meanwhile, the East-West conflict in Europe was becoming ever more acute. The Soviet Union and the Western powers now pursued increasingly irreconcilable policies in their respective zones of occupation in Germany, as will be seen,[2] and their antagonism reached a new pitch with the currency reform carried out in the three Western zones in June 1948. The attempt by the Soviet authorities to cut off West Berlin both from the reformed Western currency and from the West altogether—through a blockade lasting nearly a year—was met by the Western allies with the air-lift of supplies to West Berlin. By the time the blockade was ended in May 1949, the foundations were laid not only for the adhesion of the United States to the North Atlantic Treaty, but also for the establishment of the German Federal Republic and the German Democratic Republic by their respective foreign patrons.

Internal Politics: the Beginnings of a Rapprochement

At first sight, the internal political situations of the United States and West Germany in 1945–9 could hardly have stood in sharper contrast: on the one hand, the government of the most powerful state in the world, and, on the other, the uncoordinated strivings which led from the total political void of 1945 to the creation of the Federal Republic four years later. On closer inspection, however, the contrast appears less stark: the process of development and adjustment whereby the dispersed and powerless German politicians and administrators of 1945 formed themselves into the Bonn regime of 1949—a process leading from the rebirth of political parties and the hesitant promotion of local government by the occupying powers, through the Economic Advisory Council and the Parliamentary Council of 1948–9—appears only in degree more dramatic than the adjustments the United States had to make. A vast difference separates the moment of Truman's succession to Roosevelt in April 1945 and his administration's signature of the North Atlantic Treaty four years later.

In January 1946 Kurt Schumacher, the leader of the SPD, summarized Germany's political situation in a letter to a fellow-socialist who had emigrated to America:

> We here can see quite clearly that Germany can have no foreign policy for a long time to come, and not even any domestic policy amounting to much more than a function of the policies of the individual victorious powers. The great difficulty for us lies in the fact that the policy of the United Nations [i.e. that of the Allies] has no common denominator vis-a-vis Germany. This is why, to our misfortune, the division into zones has already taken place.[3]

Schumacher might have added that even within each of the victorious powers—and to a marked degree inside the United States—there was very little agreement about how to deal with Germany, as indeed about the future of international politics in general. In the formation of US foreign policy in the first two years after the war at least three distinct groups competed for influence: the traditional isolationists who wanted a complete withdrawal of American power from Europe now that the war was won; the liberal Left which counted on maintaining the war-time alliance with the Soviet Union as the basis of

American policy; and the 'realists' who saw as early as 1945–7 that the maintenance of the balance of power in Europe depended on a commitment of American support to its Western side.

Fortunately, from the point of view of the growth of close relations with the leaders of West Germany, it was the third of these groups that had by 1947 established a clear ascendancy in Washington. The first of the three—the isolationists—in fact lost influence very rapidly, even though many spokesmen of the Republican majority elected to Congress in 1946 still called for a reduction of the taxes needed to keep American forces in Europe. Senator Robert Taft and several others continued to hold this view, but more significant was the way in which Senator Arthur Vandenberg, an arch-isolationist before 1941 and highly influential as Chairman of the Foreign Relations Committee after the 1946 election, now underwent a spectacular conversion to the cause of American involvement in Europe.[4] The isolationists were giving way to the realists. The second main group—the liberal Left represented by Henry Wallace (Truman's Secretary of Agriculture), Henry Morgenthau (Secretary of the Treasury under Roosevelt), and up to a point the Secretary of State, J. F. Byrnes, himself—were more influential than the isolationists. They were also strongly opposed to a revival of Germany's strength, since in essence they stood for a continuation of the war-time alliance against her. The picture of a dismembered and pastoralized Germany, spelt out in the Morgenthau Plan of 1943 and published in book form in December 1945 as a contribution to the public debate on how Germany should be treated,[5] could become a reality only through collaboration between the Western allies and the Soviet Union. This was clearly understood, as several of their articles and public statements showed, by Morgenthau and other supporters of a Carthaginian peace settlement: they included Sumner Welles, former Under-Secretary of State and a close associate of Roosevelt, and also James P. Warburg, an influential banker and prolific author. The hope of continued co-operation with the Soviet Union, against any revival of German power, was embodied in official United States policy with Secretary Byrnes's offer to Moscow in July 1945 of a twenty-five-year alliance. The offer remained open until the spring of 1947, but by this time Washington's hopes for good

American-Soviet relations had declined drastically—as was demonstrated by Henry Wallace's enforced resignation from President Truman's cabinet when he made an incautious speech on the subject at the end of 1946.[6]

The decisive influence in American foreign policy thus fell to the realists, starting with Truman himself, who increasingly felt that Soviet power must be countered by that of America: as Truman irately expressed it to Byrnes at the start of 1946, 'I'm tired of babying the Soviets',[7] and the prevailing mood—building up to the commitment to Greece and Turkey in the Truman Doctrine of March 1947—became much tougher. Truman's approach to world politics was altogether more hard-headed than Roosevelt's. Other leading 'realists' were Dean Acheson (Under-Secretary of State from mid-1945 to mid-1947, Secretary of State from January 1949 onwards), General Marshall (Secretary of State from January 1947 to January 1949), and Robert Lovett (Assistant Secretary for War from 1940 to 1945, Under-Secretary of State from 1947 to 1949).

The determination of these men to build up and organize Western Europe against Soviet pressure inevitably meant more American support and brighter prospects for the Western part of Germany: in this their objectives converged with those of the men responsible for American policy on the spot in Germany—notably General Lucius Clay, the American Deputy Military Governor from 1945 to 1947, and Military Governor from 1947 to 1949—who saw the need to restore Germany's economic capacity as imperative. Byrnes's speech in Stuttgart in September 1946 laid down the lines of the new policy. Its promise of American support for Germany's economic recovery and political reconstruction marked the conversion of a man who had previously held back from supporting Germany in the hope of maintaining the war-time alliance with Russia. A corresponding shift of objective occurred on the part of Clay and others who now concentrated on the task of German reconstruction which their practical experience told them was necessary, but which they had so far carried out only hesitantly in the hope of a continuing partnership with the Soviet Union.[8]

If changes in Washington brought more power to men who saw common interests with the Germans (for any one of a variety of reasons), the new political life of Western Germany also developed in such a way that its leading figures were in close sympathy with the United States. This did not happen automatically: the very close German-American understanding achieved by Konrad Adenauer almost as soon as he became Chancellor in 1949 should not tempt us to regard Bonn's alignment with Washington as something that was automatic in terms of the situation of 1946, or even of 1947.

The strongest political party in West Germany, as the first crucial election of 1949 approached, was generally thought to be not Adenauer's Christian Democrats, but the Social Democrats under Kurt Schumacher, who would have given West Germany's foreign policy a much less unquestioningly pro-Western orientation. A German government under Schumacher would still have been basically pro-Western—Schumacher's experience of Communism made him mistrustful of neutralism or of a pro-Soviet posture—but it would have bargained much more vigorously with the Western allies for its own interests. Schumacher would not, for instance, have accepted the territorial demands made by France in the West (notably on the Saar) any more than he accepted the Soviet transfer of the lands east of the Oder-Neisse Line to Poland, and for Washington, too, he would have proved a much less amenable partner than Adenauer. For Acheson, when he met Schumacher late in 1949, the German Socialist

> combined a harsh and violent nature with nationalistic and aggressive ideas. . . . His idea of sound policy for Germany was neutrality between East and West and evacuation of all foreign troops from German soil, thus winning Soviet agreement to the reunification of Germany. . . . I told him frankly that an attempt by the Social Democratic Party to curry favor with the voters or the Russians by baiting the occupation would be given short shrift. We had all made great sacrifices to remove Hitler and nazism from Germany and bring about her admission to the community of Europe. If he believed that the occupation would tolerate an attempt to play the Western allies and the Russians off against one another, he would find himself mistaken.[9]

Although Schumacher's firm stand for German national interests can be explained both by personal and by historical factors—his own intense sufferings under the Nazis and his determination not to let the SPD be blamed as it had been in the Weimar Republic for lacking in patriotism [10]—Acheson's evidence confirms that Bonn's relations with Washington under Schumacher would have been distinctly less harmonious than they were to be under Adenauer, and also confirms why Washington, unlike London, gave unhesitating support to the latter.

The harmony of these relations also owed a good deal to Adenauer's victory, within the CDU, over the rival school of thought represented by Jakob Kaiser. Kaiser, a Catholic trade union leader who had been active in the war-time plottings against Hitler, was one of Adenauer's few serious rivals for the leadership of the CDU. Throughout 1946 and 1947, working from his political base in Berlin—his location in itself goes far to explain his attitude—he tried to induce the CDU in West Germany to adopt a distinctly socialist programme and a neutralist foreign policy: both of these, he hoped, would appease the Soviet Union and allow the reunification of a neutralized Germany. By the end of 1947, the development of the Cold War made it relatively easy for Adenauer, now assured of American support, to carry the whole CDU behind his policy of alignment with the West: Kaiser's political activities in the Soviet zone were brought to an end by the occupying power and two years later he was to accept office in Bonn as Adenauer's first Minister for all-German Affairs. A less harsh Soviet line in 1947, however, might have brought into power a neutralist West German government under Kaiser (possibly in alliance with Schumacher, though the latter, as we have noted, held much more anti-Soviet views), which would have been a very disconcerting partner for Washington.[11]

The growing sense of common purpose between the political leaders of the United States and West Germany, from 1945 onwards, was brought about not merely by Soviet policies, but also by a clearly perceived convergence of views on the main issues of Germany's future. Of these, the two central ones were the political structure of the emerging West German state, and the nature of its economic policy.

On the former point, the similarity of CDU and American views was clearly visible as soon as the question of a political structure for West Germany was seriously discussed: in contrast to the SPD and the British, both the political leadership in Washington and Germany's future rulers in Bonn strongly favoured a decentralized federal system. American constitutional principles and Adenauer's disagreeable memories of Prussian rule over the Rhineland converged in support of decentralization (this was also supported by the French, for the somewhat different reason that decentralization would delay or even obstruct German unification), and this left little doubt of what the form of the new state would in fact be.[12]

On economic policy, again, a patent harmony prevailed between Adenauer and his essentially conservative colleagues on the one hand, and the American supporters of free enterprise on the other. Truman's administration, like most American governments, had close links with industry and finance, and such men as Robert Lovett and Dean Acheson clearly believed in using American influence to promote the revival of capitalism rather than socialism in Germany, partly because a threat to capitalism anywhere might threaten it in America. Both Adenauer and his American supporters pointed to the weak economic position of Britain under its Labour government as an argument against the socialistic measures the SPD was advocating, with London's agreement, for the British zone: in fact, after 1947, when the British and American zones were merged, America's influence was strengthened by the economic dependence on her of the whole Bizone, and socialization in Germany was no longer practical politics. There was henceforth little doubt that the spirt of free enterprise—represented on the German side by Ludwig Erhard, who was to emerge from running the Bizone Economic Council in 1949 to preside with Adenauer over the 'economic miracle'—was to dominate German public policy, with wholehearted American approval.[13]

Bilateral Relations: from JCS 1067 to the Occupation Statute

This survey of the attitudes of American and West German political leaders has indicated that those who held power on both sides were disposed to co-operate increasingly closely between 1945 and 1949. The substance of American-German bilateral transactions during these four years can be summarized as the modification of the policy of Document JCS 1067—the harsh Joint Chiefs of Staff directive of April 1945—and its replacement by the Occupation Statute, which gave West

Germany a very large measure of internal autonomy, exactly four years later.

The Joint Chiefs of Staff Document 1067, laying down guidelines for United States policy in Germany, legally controlled all American activities there until July 1947, subject only to minor modifications brought about by the Potsdam Agreement of August 1945. The document itself, a most detailed directive twelve pages in length, has been summarized by one authority as follows:

In general, it was a harsh and stern set of instructions largely negative in character. It forbade fraternization on the part of American personnel with the German people, ordered a very strict program of de-nazification extending to both public life and business, emphasized agricultural reconstruction, and prohibited American aid in the re-building of German industry. Under this directive the German people were definitely considered a menace to humanity and guilty of crimes against other people; as such they were to be dealt with very firmly though properly. Punishment was to be meted out to them by reducing their standard of living drastically and by preventing them from regaining economic strength. Along with its negative and punitive provisions, JCS 1067 stipulated the preparation of the German people for democratic political institutions, but it may be fair to conclude that such preparation was of the sort which penal institutions are supposed to furnish in the making of good citizens. This directive showed the United States as a short-sighted country, motivated largely by revenge, and with little appreciation of the fundamental problems of an occupation. It constituted what may be called without undue exaggeration a heavy millstone around the neck of the American military government.[14]

The American authorities in Germany, almost as soon as they found themselves responsible for applying these prescriptions, began to make steady progress with reducing the size of the millstone, before freeing themselves from it altogether. This development entailed changes over the entire range of policies laid down in JCS 1067, from non-fraternization to de-nazification, which cannot be dealt with here.[15]

The two issues of greatest political salience, however, were those of Germany's economic reconstruction and the shape of her political institutions. On economic policy, the terms of directive JCS 1067 were quite categorical: the American

Commander-in-Chief was instructed that apart from measures of reorganization needed to prevent ' starvation ' or ' such disease and unrest ' as would endanger the occupying forces, ' no steps will be taken (a) leading toward the economic rehabilitation of Germany or (b) designed to maintain or strengthen the German economy.'[16]

The process by which American decisions none the less helped a very considerable ' rehabilitation ' of Germany began with the exploitation of what one of the officials concerned described as this ' loophole '[17] in the JCS 1067—the authorization to give aid to prevent ' disease and unrest '—as a means to modify the document's injunction not to ' maintain or strengthen the German economy '.

The first series of measures, in which the needs and wishes of the Germans found willing acceptance by responsible Americans (both on the spot and increasingly in Washington too), entailed the distribution of large quantities of foodstuffs to overcome the post-war threat of famine. In the early months after the war, and even as late as the severe winter of 1946–7, this threat was very real, and the use of the ' loophole ' in JCS 1067 was thoroughly legitimate. By 1949 American expenditure on food for Germany and on fertilizers and seed for German agriculture had amounted to $1.52 billion.[18]

Germany's further economic recovery, beyond the immediate relief operations, demanded two main changes in the policies of the occupying powers: a relaxation of the limits they had placed in 1945 on her industrial production, and a reform of her grotesquely inflated currency. On both of these issues the United States, among the four occupying powers, adopted an attitude closest to that of the Germans and their emerging public authorities.

The question of the appropriate level for Germany's economic output was first discussed in the United States in the wartime debates on the Morgenthau Plan.[19] This plan, though never adopted by Roosevelt as official policy, exercised considerable influence, and left distinct traces in some of the more punitive provisions of JCS 1067. Morgenthau's project for a ' pastoralized ' Germany, territorially amputated and permanently dismembered, implied a level of economic activity barely sufficient to keep the Germans at subsistence level. As early as the Yalta Conference in February 1945, Roosevelt was envisaging the much more realistic concept—realistic both in political and in humanitarian terms—of a German standard of living ' not higher than that of other countries such as the Soviet Union ', and a similar economic level for Germany was indicated by JCS 1067 three months later. During and after the Potsdam Conference, American views of the permissible level became perceptibly more favourable to Germany, and when the inter-allied Level of Industry Committee established at Potsdam began its work later in 1945, the view of the American representative was patently the most lenient. As a State Department policy document of 12 December 1945 put it, after denying any intention ' to impose permanent limitations on the German economy ': ' The United States intends . . . to permit the German people . . . to develop their own resources and to work toward a higher standard of living subject only to such restrictions designed to prevent production of armaments as may be laid down in the peace settlement.' [20]

By March 1946, when the Level of Industry Committee produced its report, the fairly generous American proposals had been tightened in the interests of a compromise with the Russians, but within two months the previous position of positive American support for German reconstruction was reinstated: after repeated failure to achieve allied (especially French and Soviet) consent to the administration of Germany as an economic entity (as provided for in the Potsdam Agreement), General Clay called a halt to industrial dismantling in the American zone, proposed its economic merger with the British zone, and gave serious attention to the idea of a currency reform.[21]

These changes, taken together, effectively spelt the end of the Level of Industry Plan of March 1946, and the ' Revised Plan for Level of Industry in the US/UK Zones of Germany ', published in August 1947 (the merger of the two zones having taken place in January), confirmed the American policy of promoting German economic growth: the permitted level of steel production was almost doubled, production ceilings in general were raised to 75 per cent of the pre-war levels, and many restrictions on German export industries were removed completely.[22]

At about the same time (July 1947), the restrictive document JCS 1067 was replaced, as the central guideline for American policy in Germany, by the new directive JCS 1779, which had a totally different emphasis, much more favourable to German interests. After reaffirming the doctrine evolved during 1945–6, that the United States had no intention of permanently limiting Germany's economic capacity, JCS 1779 stated that a just and lasting peace, a basic American interest, required 'the economic contributions of a stable and productive Germany', and that the US proposed to ensure for Germany 'a form of political organisation and a manner of political life which, resting on a substantial basis of economic welfare, will lead to tranquillity within Germany and will contribute to the spirit of peace among nations.'[23]

This new directive for American policy in Germany, issued in the summer of 1947, coincided with the Marshall Plan for European recovery, in which West Germany was fully incorporated. By 1948 the decision-makers in Washington no longer regarded it as a reasonable aim of policy to limit German output even to the generous figures established in the Second Level of Industry Plan of the previous August, and by 1949 the programme for the dismantling of industrial plant was restricted to a few hundred factories.[24]

This outcome, reached by the time the Federal Republic was established in 1949, reflected the growing awareness of the United States that the American interest in building up a stable and prosperous West Germany coincided closely with the natural wish of the Germans themselves for economic recovery. The same coincidence of American and German interests could be observed on the issue of the reform of the West German currency—an issue in some ways simpler, but with widespread implications for Germany's revival.

American efforts to overcome the catastrophic situation of 1945, when the inflated Reichsmark had totally lost both its international and its domestic value, were originally undertaken on the assumption that collective four-power control of Germany would remain a reality. The American financial experts who studied the problem and reported to General Clay in the spring of 1946 suggested a three-year time-table for the replacement of the Reichsmark by a new Deutsche Mark, the whole operation to be supervised by the four occupying powers according to the procedures laid down in the Potsdam Agreement.

As early as August 1946 the United States and Britain had approved the plan, but France and the Soviet Union opposed it, and German industrial and commercial activity continued to stagnate, despite the formal relaxation of limits on industrial output in the Western zones. It was only in March 1948, after the breakdown of the Allied Control Council, that the three Western powers agreed to carry out the currency reform, which went into effect on 20 June 1948. The whole development of this issue—the planning and execution of a policy which vastly improved Germany's prospects of economic revival—was marked by a very clear convergence of German and American interests.[25]

The same convergence was apparent in political as in economic affairs. The story of how the Federal Republic was established cannot be recounted here in any detail;[26] one of its most important themes, however, is the clear agreement from beginning to end between the Americans, from Clay downwards, and the politicians from the southern and western parts of Germany, that the constitutional basis of the new state should be a strongly decentralized federalism. Throughout the successive phases of Germany's political evolution, from the first local elections of 1946 to the creation of the Federal Republic in 1949, the American authorities defended this point of view: they thus found themselves in opposition to the original British view that the new German state should have a powerful central government (a view which they quickly overcame) and in a large measure of agreement with the views of France. In the words of one authority,

> if the attempt of 1947 to force the British to accept the federalist views of America had failed, agreement with France in 1948 and 1949 would have entailed much greater difficulties. The federalists of South Germany could go ahead with strength and self-confidence in the internal German arguments about the definitive structure of the West German state, because Clay had defended their strongholds during the years 1946 to 1948.[27]

Alliance Politics: the Beginnings of Western Union

The alliance now in process of formation between Washington and the embryonic regime of Bonn developed within the broader pattern of an emerging structure of Western unity—the agreements which foreshadowed the establishment of NATO. The earliest of these agreements, the Anglo-French Dunkirk Treaty of March 1947 and the Brussels Pact of March 1948, were in form directed against Germany, being undertakings by her war-time West European enemies to continue their co-operation against any revival of her power. Even before the Brussels Pact, however, it was clear that the emerging West German state was to play a prominent and ultimately equal role in the framework of Western unity. Before the Federal Republic was established, the Western zones of Germany were to be represented in the Organisation for European Economic Co-operation set up in June 1948 to administer Marshall Aid (as indeed they had been included in Marshall's original offer a year earlier). The newly created Federal Republic was also to become a member of the Council of Europe set up a year later; and by the end of 1949, when the Republic had been in existence for only a few months, there were clear indications that it would before long become a member of NATO, with the full support of the United States.

Within the developing structure of the Western alliance, then, as on the central economic and political issues within Germany itself, American and German decision-makers found themselves in a large measure of agreement.

Marshall's proposal for American economic aid to Europe, put forward in his Harvard speech of June 1947, in fact grew in considerable part out of the problems of Germany. The need to accelerate Germany's economic revival—pressed on Washington, as we have seen, by the administrators of the American zone—was also a prominent argument in the policy planning documents of the spring of 1947, which led to the elaboration of the Marshall Plan.[28]

The problem of fitting an economically reviving Germany into the structure of Western Europe as a whole, which by 1947 assumed the form of defining her status as a beneficiary of the Marshall Plan, had as its background the original hostility of France to any substantial rehabilitation of German power. From 1945 onwards the French governments, first of General de Gaulle and then of his successors, tenaciously pursued a policy of limiting Germany's economic revival, obstructing any moves towards the creation of central political authorities in Germany, and detaching portions of German territory which were under French control, notably the Saar.[29]

As German resentment at these policies became manifest, the Germans developed a natural tendency to seek American support against France, a pattern which was to become familiar in later years. The potential conflicts between the Western powers—notably between the United States and France—did not, however, become critically serious in the immediate post-war years, largely because their common interests were forcibly brought into overwhelming prominence by the hostile behaviour of the Soviet Union. Soviet pressure on Iran, Greece, and Turkey had already imparted serious strain into Soviet-American relations by the time the Truman Doctrine was announced in March 1947;[30] simultaneously, at the Moscow Conference of Foreign Ministers, the Soviet Union, by flatly refusing to back France's claim to the Saar, alienated this potential ally in Western Europe and left France no choice but to join the Western bloc in the developing Cold War. This meant that French opposition to American policies in Germany—the relaxation of economic controls, the proposed currency reform, and the move towards a political merger of the occupation zones—was perforce attenuated.

The American administration, for its part, was well aware that American policy in Europe had to avoid being limited to the development of a ' special relationship ' with the defeated enemy. European fears that the United States authorities in Germany would absorb an excessive share of Marshall Aid funds were met by giving the Marshall Plan's European Representative in Paris, Averell Harriman, special responsibility for holding the balance between German and other European claims.[31] In any case, the broader political motive of the United States for granting economic aid—to help the development of a federated Western Europe—was usually expressed in terms which assuaged French fears that special favouritism was being shown to Germany: the Select Committee of Congress under Congressman Herter, which examined the foreign aid programme in the summer of 1948, reported its view ' that the solution to the problem of preventing the resurgence of aggressive German nationalism is to be found within the pattern of European federation, of which a democratic Germany will be an integral but not a dominating part.'[32]

Germany's position was, quite naturally, the central preoccupation of American thinking about Europe, and the construction of a framework adequate to contain Germany's power necessarily implied the attempt to collaborate as closely as possible with her neighbours, particularly with France. After 1947, at least, it was possible for American policy to encourage the growth of a system of organizations which included Germany—OEEC, the Council of Europe, and potentially a closer form of European integration—without causing any serious tension between Washington and the emergent German authorities, and with relatively little between Washington and any of the other allies. The attainment of this high degree of unity between the Allied capitals was in large measure due to the mounting pressures which they all felt from the direction of the Soviet Union.

Relations with the Adversary: the Cold War and its Impact

The primary reason for the dramatic rapprochement between American and German leaders in the four years from 1945 to 1949 was the equally drastic erosion—indeed, the virtual disappearance—of America's war-time alliance with the Soviet Union. As we have seen, the breakdown of this alliance, marked by failure to agree on policy towards Germany, by conflicts in the Balkans and eastern Mediterranean, and by such open crises as the Czech coup and the Berlin blockade, impelled American policy-makers step by step along the path of building up the economic and political strength of West Germany. They would probably have taken this path anyway, given the heavy economic burden of the United States in Germany, even without the decline in American-Soviet relations: but the speed of the new policy's adoption and the intimacy of the ensuing American-German relationship were profoundly conditioned by the American-Soviet conflict.

The American offer of a twenty-five-year pact with the Soviet Union including an agreement to keep Germany totally disarmed, remained official policy from July 1945 until the spring of 1947. There was, however, no adequate basis of mutual confidence for such proposals to have any real meaning; and before the year 1945 ended, it was clear that both super-powers preferred to try to achieve the secure incorporation of their ' own ' part of Germany in their own sphere of influence.

The failure of the Moscow Conference of Foreign Ministers in March-April 1947 to agree on any of the main East-West problems gave the cue for the intensive American programme of aid for the economic and political recovery of Western Europe, including as a central feature the recovery of West Germany.

The Czech coup of February 1948, and still more the Berlin blockade of June 1948 to May 1949, brought German and American political leaders into ever closer agreement. The Berlin crisis, coinciding with the meetings of the Parliamentary Council determining the future political structure of West Germany, did a great deal to accelerate the creation of a Federal Republic incorporated in the Western grouping.

There were still, of course, certain influential advisers in Washington who believed that although the *economic* rehabilitation of the Western zones of Germany was imperative, any attempt to take the *political* step of establishing a West German state would damage a dwindling but still extant prospect of continued collaboration with the Soviet Union. George Kennan, for instance, who, as Director of the State Department's newly established Policy Planning Staff, played a leading role in developing the policy which was to become the Marshall Plan, argued that ' it is imperatively urgent today that the improvement of economic conditions and the revival of productive capacity in the west of Germany can be made the primary object of our policy in that area.' [33] He believed, however, that strict limits should be set to the political and military constructions to be attempted in Western Europe, lest Soviet hostility be needlessly provoked. A year after the Truman Doctrine had been proclaimed, Kennan argued that Soviet actions in March 1948—the Communist take-over in Czechoslovakia, and the beginnings of pressure to force the Western Allies out of Berlin—were ' defensive reactions on the Soviet side to the initial success of the Marshall Plan initiative *and to the preparations now being undertaken on the Western side to set up a separate German government in West Germany*.' [34]

Kennan's main argument against letting the American-German rapprochement go to the lengths of bringing a West German state into being—that it would provoke a defensive consolidation of the Soviet bloc—applied also to the plans for a North Atlantic Treaty which developed during 1948. When the Russians imposed the Berlin blockade in June 1948, as a response to the currency reform in West Germany, and when the blockade had the predictable consequence of hastening both the creation of a West German state and the commitment of American power to a North Atlantic Treaty, Kennan toiled hard and passionately to secure approval in Washington for a final Western initiative in favour of the reunification and neutralization of Germany. The essence of the so-called 'Plan A', which he and his colleagues urged the American government at least to put to the Russians, was the withdrawal of all Allied occupation garrisons to the perimeter of a German state which would be reunified under a provisional all-German government.[35]

By now, however, the breach in trust between the Soviet Union and the Western powers had gone much too far for any scheme of this kind—which would depend on the abstention of all the occupying powers from any attempt to exploit Germany's neutrality—to be workable.

The majority of Western policy-makers, including Truman and Dean Acheson (Secretary of State since January 1949, in succession to Marshall) regarded the development of Soviet policy since 1945 as evidence of implacable hostility: hostility, at all events, to any co-ordinated four-power policy in Germany. In late May 1949, despite the ending of the Berlin blockade, the situation looked very unpromising when the Council of Foreign Ministers assembled in Paris for a further attempt to bridge the growing gap between East and West: it was during the American preparations for this conference than Kennan and his colleagues had urged the consideration of their 'Plan A' for Germany's reunification and neutralization.

Foi Acheson, as for Bevin and Schuman, the Paris conference finally confirmed the clear impossibility of agreeing with the Russians: after hearing Vyshinsky's condemnation of Western intentions in Germany, Acheson cabled to Truman 'Today's session was completely sterile',[36] and the rest of the conference —which lasted from 23 May to 20 June—only confirmed this impression.

After the deadlock of the Paris conference—which, as the

Cold War deepened, was to be the last East-West meeting at Foreign Minister level for nearly five years—the way was clear for the full implementation of the Western powers' 'London Programme' for West Germany. This programme, agreed in principle by Acheson, Bevin, and Schuman early in April when they signed the North Atlantic Treaty, provided for the establishment of a West German Federal Republic under the control of an Allied High Commission, and for the retention of only relatively limited powers by the Allies under a new Occupation Statute.[37]

The granting of a large measure of internal autonomy to a German government was naturally in accordance with the wishes of Germany's political leaders: as we have seen, the views of Adenauer and the newly founded CDU were particularly close to American views on a number of critical points, and this concordance was to become even more pronounced when Adenauer took office as Chancellor in September.[38]

There is no doubt that the high degree of German-American collaboration indicated by the setting-up of the Federal Republic, while partly due to the proclivity of the two political systems to co-operate for other reasons, owed a great deal to the external factor of Soviet pressure, which brought Germans and Americans together in a solidarity based on increasingly evident common interest.

NOTES

1 For a fuller assessment of Soviet policies in this period, see Roger Morgan *West European Politics since 1945* (1972), ch. 1.

2 See below, pp. 27–8.

3 Schumacher to Alexander Schifrin, 23 Jan. 1946, quoted by H.-P. Schwarz, *Vom Reich zur Bundesrepublik* (1966), p. 592.

4 See *The Private Papers of Senator Vandenberg* (1952), *passim*; Dean Acheson, *Present at the Creation* (paperback edn, 1970), esp. ch. 25. Congressional attitudes to foreign policy are analysed in detail by E.-O. Czempiel, *Das amerikanische Sicherheitssystem 1945–1949* (1966).

5 Henry Morgenthau, Jr, *Germany is our Problem* (1945).

6 Acheson, *Present at the Creation*, pp. 258–60.

7 Ibid. p. 258.

8 Schwarz, esp. pp. 141–6.

9 Acheson, *Present at the Creation*, p. 447.

10 See Louis J. Edinger, *Kurt Schumacher* (1965); Schwarz, pp. 483–564; Morgan, *West European Politics since 1945*, pp. 107–11.

[11] On Kaiser, see Schwarz, pp. 299–344 and W. Conze, *Jakob Kaiser, Politiker zwischen Ost und West. 1945–1949* (1967).

[12] Schwarz, p. 125.

[13] Ibid. pp. 123–5.

[14] Harold Zink, *The United States in Germany, 1944–1955* (1957), p. 94, where an account of the origins and effects of JCS 1067 is given. See also Paul Y. Hammond, 'Directives for the Occupation of Germany: the Washington Controversy', in Harold Stein, ed., *American Civil-Military Decisions: a Book of Case Studies* (1963), pp. 311–464, and John H. Backer, *Priming the German Economy, American Occupational Policies 1945–1948* (1971) pp. 21–30, 58–9. The text of JCS 1067 is given in B. Ruhm von Oppen, ed., *Documents on Germany under Occupation, 1945–1954* (1955), pp. 13–27.

[15] For details see Zink; E. J. Gimbel, *The American Occupation of Germany: Politics and the Military, 1945–1949* (1968); and Conrad F. Latour and Thilo Vogelsang, *Okkupation und Wiederaufbau* (1973).

[16] Quoted by Backer, p. 23. The State Department's representative in Germany, Robert Murphy, has recorded the reaction of Gen. Clay's economic adviser, Lewis Douglas, to JCS 1067: 'This thing was assembled by economic idiots!' (*Diplomat among Warriors*, paperback edn, 1965, p. 281).

[17] Backer, p. 59, quoting private confirmation by John J. McCloy.

[18] Official sources, quoted ibid., p. 58, at the end of a useful 25-page account of the relief programme.

[19] The related question of reparations policy, which influenced American policy in a similar direction, is analysed in detail in Bruce Kuklick, *American Policy and the Division of Germany: the Clash with Russia over Reparations* (1972).

[20] Quoted, with other similar statements, by Backer, p. 77.

[21] Ibid. pp. 80, 91–4.

[22] Ibid. p. 81. See N. Balabkins, *Germany under Direct Control* (1964), esp. chs 1 and 4.

[23] *DOSB*, 27 July 1947, as quoted by Backer, p. 83.

[24] Backer, p. 87.

[25] Ibid. pp. 90–96.

[26] See Schwarz; F. Golay, *The Founding of the Federal Republic of Germany* (1958); Peter Merkl, *The Origin of the West German Republic* (1963).

[27] Schwarz, pp. 125–6.

[28] See, e.g., Will Clayton's memorandum quoted by Acheson, *Present at the Creation*, p. 308, and the memorandum by Kindleberger, Cleveland, and Moore quoted by Max Beloff, *The United States and the Unity of Europe* (1963), pp. 14–18.

[29] See Schwarz, esp. pp. 179–99; Morgan, *West European Politics since 1945*, pp. 39–48; F. R. Willis, *France, Germany and the New Europe*, 2nd edn (1968).

[30] See above, p. 10.

[31] Beloff, p. 30.

[32] Quoted ibid. p. 30. See E. van der Beugel, *From Marshall Aid to Atlantic Partnership* (1966), esp. ch. 2.

[33] Lecture at National War College, 6 May 1947, in G. Kennan, *Memoirs: 1925–1950* (1968), p. 334.

[34] Ibid. p. 401 (my italics). Cf. ibid. p. 419.

[35] Ibid. pp. 418–26.

[36] Acheson, *Present at the Creation*, p. 390; on the conference as a whole, pp. 382–96.

[37] These developments are summarized by A. Grosser, *Germany in our Time* (1971), ch. 4. The draft Occupation Statute, dated 8 Apr. 1949, is printed in Ruhm von Oppen, pp. 375–7.

[38] Adenauer's own account of the pre-history of the Federal Republic, including the work of the Parliamentary Council in 1948–9 (*Erinnerungen 1945–1953* (1967) pp. 125–233 *passim*) indicates the importance of his collaboration with the US representatives during this process. See also T. Prittie, *Adenauer: a Study in Fortitude* (1972).

CHAPTER THREE

The Alliance Consolidated 1949–1955

Background: the Cold War

THE onset of the phase of acute cold war between Soviet Russia and the West was marked by the breakdown of even the formalities of direct contact between governments: after a series of roughly six-monthly wrangles had culminated in deadlock in Paris in May-June 1949, the Council of Foreign Ministers met no more for almost five years, until Molotov and the Western Foreign Ministers came together in Berlin in 1954 to discuss—without success—a settlement in Germany. The Berlin meeting of 1954 was in turn followed by the Geneva summit conference of 1955, and the semblance of direct East-West dialogue at governmental level was thus resumed. From 1949 to 1954, however, the Foreign Ministers of East and West had no direct contact with each other, and the one serious attempt at agreeing even on an agenda for a possible meeting—when their deputies met in Paris in 1951—was a fiasco.

The rupture in communications between East and West was accompanied by fairly drastic shifts in the balance of power in the world. The Soviet Union exploded its first atomic bomb in September 1949, inaugurating the age of nuclear bipolarity. Another change, which occurred almost simultaneously, was the proclamation of the People's Republic of China in October 1949, after the Communist victory in the Civil War. As well as apparently providing a powerful new ally for the Soviet Union, this Communist victory proved to be a source of strain in the relations between the United States and at least one European ally. Although France did not consider recognizing the new Chinese regime because of her conflict in Indochina, and Germany was not yet free to conduct any foreign policy of her own, the British Labour government took an independent line and extended recognition to the new People's Republic—as did India and some other members of the Commonwealth.

The establishment of the Communist regime's authority throughout China was before long to make itself felt in two areas of dispute in Asia, whose conflicts were to preoccupy the United States and to exercise a marked influence on events in Europe. The fighting in Indochina, which had hitherto been a relatively localized colonial war between France and the nationalist movement led by the Communists under Ho Chi Minh, took a new turn with the extension of Chinese Communist power to Indochina's northern frontier: the new capacity of the Chinese Communists to deliver arms and other supplies directly to the Vietminh turned a colonial conflict into something much more like a trial of strength between the forces of Communism and anti-Communism, and allowed France to obtain ever-increasing military aid from the United States. Even with this help, the cost to France herself, in terms both of men and of money, continued to rise. The tying-up of a large part of her army in Indochina contributed substantially to her unwillingness to accept West Germany's rearmament inside a European Defence Community in which the German component would inevitably have predominated. Even the collapse of France's position in Indochina after she lost the battle of Dien Bien Phu in May 1954 did not allow her to concentrate fully on European affairs (though she did accept the principle of German rearmament at the end of the year), since she was by now embroiled in the further problem of decolonization in North Africa.

At the other extremity of China's coastline—in Korea—the Cold War was to take the form of a bloody military encounter between Communist and anti-Communist forces following the North Korean attack on 25 June 1950. The subsequent intervention of China, induced by the crossing into North Korea of the United Nations counter-attack commanded by General MacArthur, brought Americans and Chinese into direct conflict by 1951, and at one stage appeared likely to entail a risk of all-out war between the two powers. In the meantime, the very fact of aggression from the Communist side in a country divided by the Cold War had caused fears of a similar attack on West Germany, and led—as we shall see—to the hurried and determined American decision to bring about West Germany's rearmament.

The final breakdown of communication between the Communist and non-Communist powers, and the onset of open fighting in Indochina and Korea created a worse environment than ever for the development of East-West relations in Europe. The division of the continent into two hostile blocs became ever more marked; each of them contained one of the two nascent German states, held firmly under the control of its respective patron or patrons. The institutions that now developed in Europe reflected this division: with the break-up of the Council of Foreign Ministers and the four-power Control Commission for Germany, the only organization which bridged the East-West gap was the United Nations Economic Commission for Europe in Geneva, which continued to play a valuable but fundamentally apolitical role in compiling objective statistics and preparing factual economic reports. The organizational development of Europe now proceeded within the two blocs, not between them: in the Cominform and later Comecon on the Eastern side, and in the West in OEEC, the Brussels Pact, the Council of Europe, and NATO. By the early 1950s West Germany had become a member of the two non-military organizations of these four, OEEC and the Council of Europe, and by the spring of 1950 she was offered the possibility of even closer integration with her European neighbours. On 9 May 1950 the French Foreign Minister, Robert Schuman, disappointed by the Council of Europe's very slow progress towards integration, put forward a proposal devised by Jean Monnet for the placing of Western Europe's coal and steel industries under a common authority. The Schuman Plan, which offered West Germany a chance of equality with France —Germany regaining a further degree of control from the Allied occupying powers, while France gave up control to the new Coal and Steel Community—was eagerly accepted by Chancellor Adenauer, who combined a strong 'European' faith with a belief in promoting West Germany's national interests.[1]

The Korean War, with its immediate effect of making many Western policy-makers expect a similar conflict in Europe, provided another opportunity for Adenauer to contribute both to European unification and to Germany's recovery of status. When the United States demanded a West German contribution to Europe's defence, and France reluctantly responded by proposing an integrated European Defence Community (the Pleven Plan forming a military counterpart to the Schuman Plan), Adenauer's answer to both of them was that Germany would participate in a European army only on a basis of full equality with the other members. Britain refused to join the European Defence Community, as she had already refused to join the European Coal and Steel Community; and, with France fearful of domination by Germany, the fate of the Pleven Plan remained undecided for several years, despite American pressure for the plan's rapid adoption. In August 1954, after the EDC treaty had been ratified by five of the six national parliaments concerned, the sixth—the French National Assembly—rejected the whole project. Thus it was that West Germany came to embark on her rearmament the following year, as a member of NATO with only marginal limitations on her national sovereignty.

Even though the pressing fear of war had lifted by the time of Germany's entry into NATO in May 1955 (Stalin's death in March 1953 had led Churchill to envisage the prospect of a 'new Locarno' in East-West relations, and the agreement to evacuate and neutralize Austria seemed to bear out his hopes) the habits of German-American co-operation formed during the Cold War years had by now become very strong.

Internal Politics: Affinity Confirmed

With President Truman's assumption in January 1949 of his full term of office, and with his nomination of Dean Acheson as Secretary of State, power in America was in the hands of men who had very clear ideas of what they wanted to do with it. The modified conservatism of Truman's 'Square Deal' in economic and social policy, combined with the enlightened *Realpolitik* of Acheson's approach to foreign affairs, indicated an administration with a fairly precise sense of the ends in view, coupled with a flexible pragmatism about the means to be employed.

In foreign policy, Acheson's appointment to the State Department confirmed the triumph of the 'realist' school of thought, already apparent when General Marshall succeeded James Byrnes at the beginning of 1947. The two other schools which had been influential at the end of the war—the leftist and the neo-isolationist [2]—were now finally defeated, and this reduced the fears of many West Europeans, including the Germans, that America's growing commitment to Western Europe might be attenuated by super-power collusion or by a retreat into isolationism. The Germans, as they brought their new Republic into being in close collaboration with the occupying powers, had little reason to fear any weakening of support from the sectors of the American executive responsible for foreign policy; the same firm support was also assured from the Pentagon, particularly after General Marshall moved from the State Department to replace Louis Johnson as Secretary of Defense in September 1950. In the legislative branch the neo-isolationists who had exercised considerable sway in Congress from 1946 to 1948 retained some influence, though it was now curtailed by the Democrats' success in winning control of both Houses at the time of Truman's election to the presidency. Some of the domestic pressures on legislators are reflected in a letter written by Senator Vandenberg, a recent and powerful convert from isolationism, in July 1949:

> We always seem to be wrestling with some sort of a paradox. On the one hand it is clearly of indispensible interest to the United States to stabilize Western Europe (and particularly Western Germany) as the 'holding line' against Soviet aggression (which of course is ultimately aimed at us). On the other hand the effective economic stabilization of Western Europe (and particularly of Western Germany) pours a flood of new competitive commodities into the world's markets and our American producers find themselves menaced in much of our essential export trade.[3]

The conclusion Vandenberg drew in this letter was the same as that being put forward by Paul Hoffman, the administrator of Marshall Aid: that the recovery of Europe's economy would bring not only political stability but also a rise in consumer demand on both sides of the Atlantic.

The threat he tried to answer—that a revived Germany and a revived Europe would be competitors bringing damage to American interests—was later to be a constant source of friction in American-German relations, though on the whole one which successive administrations were able to manage.

There were also other sources of pressure within the United States for the administration to take a tougher line with Germany on certain issues: for instance, the fact that 1950 was a Congressional election year caused Truman to come under unusual pressure to induce the Europeans, including the Germans, to make a bigger effort for their own military defence.[4] Such demands within the American political system might have caused some German-American friction if both governments had not tacitly accepted the principle of German rearmament by the late summer of 1950,[5] but as things were, demands of this kind did little more than bring a degree of superficial controversy to an increasingly harmonious relationship. Truman and Acheson were on close and confident terms with Adenauer: his relations with the Washington of Eisenhower and Dulles, after the change of administration in January 1953, were if anything even closer. This was particularly true of the relationship between Adenauer and Dulles, to whom Eisenhower left a very free hand in foreign affairs. One of Adenauer's advisers, Felix von Eckhardt, has described the rapid growth of the Chancellor's feeling of trust in the new Secretary of State:

> John Foster Dulles was naturally quite new to us, but I observed how the Chancellor . . . very quickly developed a very close relationship . . . and their conversations very soon had a great degree of intimacy . . . which later developed into a certain friendship . . . I very soon got the feeling that the relationship between these two men was very quickly established, and that they soon achieved a relationship of confidence. One could see this from the way they spoke very freely with one another . . . They really expressed their views with great freedom, not like diplomats usually do, very cautiously, but in fact with almost complete frankness . . .[6]

In view of the way in which Adenauer's Germany, within a year or two, appeared to become the central pillar of Dulles' policy towards Western Europe, it is worth noting the testimony of John J. McCloy, High Commissioner in Germany and a friend and adviser of Dulles, that the latter, though he had known Germany between the wars, had not followed German affairs with any particular attention in the period before his appointment as Secretary of State (this confirms von Eckhardt's statement that in 1953 Dulles ' was naturally quite new to us '). As McCloy put it, Dulles was not ' unduly slanted towards Germany,' but slowly came to the firm conclusion that Germany's economic and political strength made her a major factor in Europe: '. . . this was only realism, and I don't think he took a position in regard to Germany that was invidious at all, in respect of other countries. . . .' [7] The rapport between Dulles and Adenauer was thus, from Dulles's side, due to a powerful mixture of personal sympathy and political calculation.

All in all, the American political system, at every level from the leadership to mass opinion, showed a remarkable degree of willingness to support a people who had so very recently been America's enemy. There was of course a good deal of residual anti-German feeling—particularly among Jewish and left-wing groups—but the majority of the American people were clearly willing to support a policy of rapprochement with Germany. In part this was due to the favourable experiences of many American servicemen in the occupation of the American zone, but there were also deep-rooted similarities of approach to economic, political, and other issues.[8]

As to the German side of the partnership, there were very few elements likely to disrupt the process of rapprochement with the United States. Adenauer and his leading colleagues all saw very clearly the advantages for Germany of collaboration with America—advantages extending from the basic prospect of protection against the Soviet Union to the chances of economic recovery and political rehabilitation—and the views of Dr Erhard on economic policy (inevitably one of Germany's main priorities) were particularly close to American attitudes.[9]

There were some political leaders—apart from the Social Democratic official Opposition—who criticized certain aspects of Adenauer's pro-Western policies, but they remained without great influence. Jacob Kaiser, who had earlier supported a neutralist position between East and West, was now safely ' tamed ' by Adenauer in the post of Minister for All-German Affairs. Gustav Heinemann, a dissenter of more recent date, whose resignation as Minister of the Interior in September 1950 was provoked by Adenauer's decision to seek rearmament, departed into a political wilderness from which he only emerged —and then into great eminence—when he joined the SPD in the 1960s.

The SPD under Kurt Schumacher, in the early years of Adenauer's regime, was the major potential German source of tension in German-American relations. Acheson's opinion of Schumacher has already been quoted,[10] and the SPD's foreign policy of these years would, if implemented, have caused considerable difficulties with Washington. This policy consisted of vehement opposition to many aspects of Adenauer's pro-Western policies, starting with Schumacher's denunciation of him in the Bundestag in November 1949 as a 'Chancellor of the Allies,' [11] and continuing through to the last-ditch opposition to rearmament of the 'St Paul's Church movement' of 1955.[12]

Since the SPD was *not* in power, but in a situation of opposition which was reinforced when Adenauer won his increased majority in 1953,[13] the Party's opposition to rearmament and West European integration did not in fact cause any serious trouble between Germany and the United States. What it did was to increase the leverage Adenauer could exert in favour of German national interests. He could take the SPD's complaints against some of the plans for German rearmament, for example, Carlo Schmid's accusation that the Pleven Plan would make the German contingent 'only a Foreign Legion,' [14] and use them to demand more favourable terms from Germany's partners in order to win German acceptance for the proposed arrangements.

In general, however, the German political system—particularly as all its major forces were deeply committed to liberal democracy—provided no more serious impediments to German-American entente than did the American.[15]

Bilateral Relations: from the Occupation Statute to Sovereignty

The main theme of German-American bilateral relations from 1949 to 1955 was the progressive restoration of authority in economic, political, and ultimately military matters from the occupying powers to the German government. This course was to proceed from the Petersberg Agreement of 24 November

1949 (which further relaxed Allied controls on the German economy) to the Allied agreement to allow West Germany to establish a Foriegn Ministry in 1951, and thence to the Bonn and Paris Agreements on German sovereignty and rearmament in 1952, the projected European Defence Community which was abandoned in 1954, and the acceptance of the Federal Republic into Western European Union and NATO in 1955.

Most of these decisions to restore authority to Germany required the agreement of all three of the Western occupying powers. Other aspects of the process, notably the interaction between German rearmament and the recovery of sovereignty, entailed very complex alliance politics which require analysis elsewhere.[16] Throughout the whole development, however, there ran a clear thread of growing collaboration between Washington and Bonn. Every stage of the economic and political rehabilitation of West Germany from 1949 to 1955, like the previous stage from 1945 to 1949, showed evident traces of an American wish to build up Germany's prosperity and authority, which coincided with the German wish to recover them.

Almost as soon as the Federal Republic was established, with Adenauer's new Cabinet operating under the control of a High Commission composed of John J. McCloy, André François-Poncet, and General Brian Robertson (the last-named to be replaced in 1950 by Sir Ivone Kirkpatrick), the issue arose of America's readiness to stop even the limited dismantling of German industry which survived the agreement made earlier in the year. Early in October 1949 McCloy, expressing his government's view, said that further dismantling would be 'pointless' (American opinion was by now a little restive under the cost of supporting the Bizone), and that a general supervision of German industry by the Allied Military Security Board would be sufficient.[17]

These pressures for a change of policy led to a new agreement between Germany and the occupying powers. The Petersberg Agreement of 24 November 1949 included a number of significant concessions to Germany, in large part due to American (as well as British) pressure on France: the dismantling programme was drastically reduced; Germany was to be allowed to build ocean-going ships both for her own use and for export; the permitted level of steel production was raised to eleven million tons; and the way was open for the Federal Republic to join the Council of Europe, the International Monetary Fund, and the World Bank.[18]

It was no coincidence that, as we shall see, Adenauer's first public indication of West Germany's readiness to make a military contribution to Western defence—for a suitable political price—came within a few days of the successful conclusion of the Petersberg Agreement. The whole course of the negotiations leading to Germany's entry into NATO in May 1955 was to reflect the determination of the United States to bring about German rearmament. However, it is important to note that this determination was only part of a general American willingness to rehabilitate Germany which was very clear, as the Petersberg Agreement showed, even before the question of German rearmament was raised in public.

The next important landmark in the Federal Republic's recovery of sovereignty was reached on 19 September 1950, after the question of German rearmament *had* been raised, when the Foreign Ministers of the United States, the United Kingdom, and France concluded a meeting in New York by issuing a communique listing a number of new proposals: the state of war with Germany was to be ended; the Occupation Statute would be amended to give the Federal government greater powers; Bonn was to be allowed to establish a Ministry of Foreign Affairs and to open diplomatic relations with foreign states 'in all suitable cases' (though not yet with the occupying powers themselves); Allied controls over legislation and economic policies would be relaxed; limits on ship-building capacity and steel production would be removed where this would facilitate the Western defence effort; in security matters, any attack on the Federal Republic or Berlin would be considered by the Western powers as an attack on themselves; and finally—this was clearly considered as a first step towards Germany's own rearmament—West German 'mobile police formations' were to be established for the protection of the country's security.[19]

Many of these provisions were put into effect, again thanks to American pressure on France, in March 1951. The amendment of the Occupation Statute and of the Charter of the Allied High Commission was then announced; a Ministry of Foreign Affairs (with the Chancellor as his own Foreign Minister) was set up in Bonn; various Allied rights under the Occupation

Statute—including the High Commission's right of prior approval of German legislation—were relinquished or attenuated; and a commitment was made to start a process of further revision.[20]

Two months later, on 10 May 1951, intensive negotiations began between Adenauer and the High Commissioners to seek agreement on the terms on which the Occupation Statute would be totally replaced by contractual agreements between Bonn and the Allies, and a rearmed Federal Republic would join the European Defence Community. Many months of negotiations finally produced the agreements signed in Bonn and Paris on 26 and 27 May 1952, providing for the Occupation Statute to be replaced by five Conventions regulating West Germany's new relationship with her allies. The essential point of this new relationship, which in fact became clear during the negotiations themselves, was that West Germany was now clearly established as an independent power, bargaining on something like equal terms with her interlocutors. She derived this position from the wish of the United States to promote her strength and her rearmament—aims which coincided with those of Adenauer, but which were now presented to him in a context which gave him the maximum bargaining strength. By skilfully alluding to the strong objections to rearmament and a pro-Western diplomatic alignment of the Social Democratic Opposition and even of his Free Democratic coalition partners, Adenauer was able to extract better terms from the Allies. The American government was happier to accept these than either Britain or France (particularly the latter), and the German-Allied negotiations often took the form of a bilateral German-American 'coalition' against hesitations expressed in Paris or London.[21]

The intimacy of the developing partnership between Washington and Bonn was confirmed in the summer of 1953 by the readiness of Dulles to come openly to Adenauer's help in the campaign for the election of the second Bundestag. Dulles made it quite clear that he would prefer Adenauer's re-election to a victory of the SPD under Erich Ollenhauer (leader of the Opposition since Schumacher's death the previous August), which might have produced a neutralist Germany and nullified the still unconsummated European Defence Community. Adenauer's twelve-day visit to the United States in April 1953—a well-publicized demonstration of Germany's new status—

has to be seen in part as an American contribution to Adenauer's election campaign. As one of his closest advisers put it, 'the resonance which came from America to Germany was one of Adenauer's greatest aces in the campaign, because the Germans realized that the United States were putting their money, were so to speak betting, on Konrad Adenauer.' [22]

In June Dulles helped Adenauer further by allowing him to publish an extract from their correspondence suggesting that they were actively considering a conference to re-start East-West negotiations in Europe; in July President Eisenhower joined in with an open letter to Adenauer declaring that the EDC would help towards German reunification; and early in September Dulles himself made a further statement that an electoral defeat for Adenauer would have disastrous consequences.[23] These statements played their part in helping Adenauer to return to power with a greatly increased majority. Dulles certainly expressed a very close and durable affinity with Adenauer when he said, on arriving in Bonn in the midst of the EDC crisis a year later, 'The post-war Federal Government has consistently followed such enlightened policies that its views must now command great respect.' [24]

Alliance Politics: the Issue of Rearmament

From the outbreak of the Korean War in June 1950 until West Germany's final admission into NATO nearly five years later, the politics of Western Europe and the development of Europe's institutions were dominated by the problem of German rearmament. A recent analyst of Washington's difficulties in pressing for a German military contribution, after noting that this had to be accomplished without provoking unacceptable reactions either from the Germans themselves, or from France and the other European Allies, or from the Russians, summarizes the situation thus: 'These circumstances produced in late 1950 a three-cornered relationship between the United States, France and Germany in which the containment of the Soviet Union was to be achieved through the co-operation of a state which itself had to be contained.' [25] Of the various parties to the protracted 'Querelle de la CED ',[26] the two whose views were most consistently in harmony throughout were the United States and Germany.

In the European background to the Korean crisis of June 1950, and its sequel in Washington's demand for German rearmament and the French response of the Pleven Plan in October, two factors stand out: the potential existence of the European Coal and Steel Community proposed by Robert Schuman in May, and the role already played by the idea of German rearmament in the transatlantic political dialogue.

The Schuman Plan for a Coal and Steel Community, grouping the industries of a number of countries under a supranational authority, was under active discussion in the summer of 1950 when the Korean War precipitated the demand for West German rearmament. It provided a model for what was called 'functional' integration—the placing under a common authority of a specific sector of national life—and it also provided a precedent for bringing West Germany into an integrated structure of this kind on a basis of equality with her partners. It thus formed a natural (though ultimately an unhelpful) model which the French government of 1950 used in proposing the European Defence Community later in the year.

The other important part of the EDC's background was the idea of German rearmament which was already in the air, even before Korea: it was both an idea which impressed the leaders of the American armed forces as militarily desirable and an offer that Adenauer was prepared to make in order to enhance Germany's status. The military argument was voiced quite openly in the American armed forces, up to the Chiefs of Staff level, particularly after the Berlin blockade increased the sense of a Soviet threat to Western Europe. The awareness of American commanders in Europe that they faced a possibly overwhelming army, and that Britain, France, and America's smaller European allies could not compensate for America's numerical inferiority without further help, led the US Chiefs of Staff, as early as autumn 1949, to order studies to be made of the possible means of raising West German troops.[27] The idea was being fairly widely discussed in the American press and in Congress by November—the month in which the Petersberg Agreement returned a considerable measure of power to the new German government—and Adenauer now saw his chance to give a public indication of the terms of a possible bargain. In an interview published in the *Cleveland Plain Dealer* on 4 December 1949, and in several subsequent clarifications, he declared that although he opposed the idea of German rearmament in principle, he would be prepared to consider it, provided German forces were brought into the Western alliance as fully equal partners, and not with any sort of 'Foreign Legion' status.[28] Although the first Allied reaction, including that of McCloy, was that Adenauer's remarks were ill-judged and not to be taken seriously, the bargain he proposed was in fact to form the basis for a German-American partnership to bring about German rearmament.

Even in the circumstances of the official American demand for German rearmament—the atmosphere of near-panic that pervaded Washington in the weeks following the invasion of South Korea—the principle of equality for Germany was clearly present in the requirement that the Western forces should be 'integrated'.[29]

There were of course moments during the rearmament debate when the United States had to concentrate on negotiations with other partners, notably Britain and France, and at one stage Adenauer complained that he was reduced to following the argument as reported in the press,[30] but in general the process was marked by a considerable degree of German-American understanding.

The initial American reaction to the Pleven Plan of October 1950 was cool and even hostile—the Secretaries of State and Defense, Acheson and Marshall, appear to have believed it was unworkable—and the declarations of American policy continued to emphasize German rearmament as the end in view, without any reference to the EDC as the means.[31] It was only in the course of long negotiations in 1950–1 that a compromise emerged between France's wish to have German military units integrated into a European army, integration going down to a low level of command, and Germany's wish—supported by the United States—for equality of political rights with her future NATO partners. America's desire for German troops thus formed the lever used by Adenauer to win the political concessions outlined earlier, culminating in the Bonn and Paris Agreements of May 1952.

The implementation of these agreements was delayed by France's reluctance to follow the example of her partners in ratifying the treaties, and by their final rejection when the Mendès-France government put them to the vote on 30 August

1954. The long delay of two years, while successive French governments failed to take action, naturally cemented the rapprochement between Bonn and Washington, particularly after the American hesitations about the EDC were abandoned when Dulles replaced Acheson at the beginning of 1953. The Democratic administration had in fact overcome most of its original distaste for the EDC by 1952, but Dulles embraced the project with a fervour that made him forbid American diplomats even to mention the possibility that it might fail.[32]

When the EDC *did* fail, the signal was given for a dramatic burst of diplomatic activity, not only by Eden, who brought about the substitute solution of admitting Germany to NATO by means of WEU, but also by Dulles, who was deeply concerned by the fear that Germany might be dangerously demoralized by the setback. When Dulles arrived in Bonn on 16 September—deliberately avoiding Paris, so as to emphasize that France had brought isolation upon herself—he and Adenauer quickly reached agreement on the need to restore sovereignty to Germany and to admit her as an equal member of NATO.[33] The American and German governments worked steadily together at this task in the months that followed, until West Germany was duly welcomed into NATO in May 1955. Both the circumstances in which Germany's NATO membership was agreed, and the form it took, brought about a much closer American-German alignment than would have occurred if the EDC had actually come into existence.[34]

There had of course been moments of disagreement between Washington and Bonn on how the organizational arrangements of the Western alliance should be handled, but in general the two capitals worked in close agreement, and were driven together, rather than apart, by the pressures originating in other parts of the alliance, notably in Paris. The integration of West Germany's heavy industries into the Coal and Steel Community created no problems for the United States, and the much more sensitive problem of her rearmament also found a solution, characterized by substantial German-American agreement, five years after the Korean crisis had raised it.

Relations with the Adversary: no Risk of Discord

The period from 1949 to 1955 was, of all those covered in this book, the one when the fear of dealings by either Washington or Bonn with the Soviet Union or her allies was least likely to cause German-American discord. The anti-Axis coalition of the Second World War, which had tenuously survived for a few years after 1945, had now been shattered by the Cold War, and the intimations of East-West détente which were to trouble the German-American relationship in later years were still far off. Even though, in 1954 and 1955, there were East-West conferences which appeared to suggest that agreement on the future of Germany was possible, this proved to be an illusion. The predominant pattern of diplomatic behaviour during the whole period was that of allies negotiating intensively with each other —particularly such close allies as Washington and Bonn— without serious communication between the hardening blocs of the Cold War.

On the Western side—and again particularly in Washington and in Bonn—the view prevailed that ‘ negotiation from strength ’ offered the only hope of obtaining concessions from the Soviet Union, and that since the West was manifestly lacking in strength, no negotiations should be envisaged until it had acquired some.[35]

George Kennan, a constant Western partisan of negotiations with the East, has stated that he was never given a clear reason why his disengagement plan of 1949 was not even submitted to the Soviet Union for consideration.[36] The explanation is probably that Acheson, and the Western leadership as a whole, had decided that any idea of evacuating and neutralizing Germany entailed unacceptable risks. The same view was taken in March 1952 when the Soviet Union proposed the reunification of Germany, to be followed by its neutralization and evacuation by the occupying powers.

Stalin's motive in making this proposal was no doubt to prevent or delay the signature of the Bonn and Paris Agreements, but both Adenauer and the other Western governments were seriously criticized for not exploring the possibility of an agreement. However, Bonn, Washington, and the other Western capitals agreed that a neutralized Germany would be a factor of dangerous instability in Europe, and preferred to press ahead with the incorporation of the Federal Republic into the Western alliance ‘ as if the Soviet note did not exist ’.[37]

With the advent of Dulles as Secretary of State early the following year there appeared to be a decisive shift in the emphasis of American policy. An important theme of the Republican Party's election campaign had been that the Democratic policy of 'containing' Communism had been sterile, and that a more active policy of the 'liberation' of peoples subjugated by Communism was more appropriate. This doctrine of the 'roll-back' of Communism had a natural appeal to Germany, since it appeared to promise support not only for the defensive aim of protecting West Germany from aggression, but also for the more ambitious one of reunifying the two German states, and possibly even of recovering the territories east of the Oder-Neisse Line. German-American agreement on a policy of defence appeared likely to give way to agreement on a policy of territorial change. The limitations of the new administration's actual policy, however, were quickly revealed by the outcome of the East German rising of June 1953, when the United States made no attempt to exploit the situation to liberate East Germany. Despite some disappointment among the West German public, the Bonn leadership was not surprised: they realized that American intervention in East Germany would have meant war.[38] The situation thus remained as before: the Western powers tacitly accepted the territorial status quo in Europe, and also rejected any idea of negotiations with the Soviet side with a view to making the status quo less tense.

It was at this stage that the notion began to spread, among liberal circles in the United States as in Britain and France, that West Germany was being placed by American policy in the situation of exercising a 'veto' over any conceivable Western diplomatic approaches to the Soviet bloc: East-West negotiations, it was claimed, might well succeed in bringing about a European settlement, if only the West Germans were not allowed to insist on the principle of reunification through free elections, and of the right of the resulting unified German state to join NATO if it chose—obviously an unacceptable demand for the East. The West German government's frequent reiteration of the case for free elections did a little to counteract this kind of accusation, but it remained the view of a substantial minority in Western countries.[39] The Eisenhower administration made it plain that, for its part, it did not regard West Germany as 'vetoing' any kind of agreement with the Soviet Union that Washington might actually wish to conclude. When the Foreign

Ministers of East and West met in Berlin early in 1954 to discuss the problem of Germany, the Western position remained identical with the West German one—that reunification through free elections was the only acceptable alternative to the status quo.

Soviet rejection of this demand put a stop for a time to discussion of Germany, and the next phase of East-West negotiations—in Geneva in the summer of 1954—was concerned with Indochina. When the affairs of Europe were again discussed with the Russians at the Geneva summit conference of 1955, the harmony between American and German views was more pronounced than ever.[40] The close understanding between the two governments, sustained by the forces operating at a number of levels, was cemented by the persistence of the Soviet hostility which had contributed so much to its creation.

NOTES

1 For a fuller discussion, see Morgan, *West European Politics since 1945*, ch. 5.

2 See above, pp. 12–14.

3 Vandenberg, p. 481.

4 Laurence W. Martin, 'The American Decision to Rearm Germany,' in H. Stein, ed., *American Civil-Military Decisions* (1963), pp. 654–6.

5 See below, pp. 42 ff.

6 DOHP, F. von Eckhardt interview transcript (Princeton Univ. Library), pp. 5–6.

7 Ibid. John J. McCloy interview, supplemented by direct information from Mr. McCloy.

8 Kennan, *Memoirs: 1925–1950*, esp. p. 433.

9 A detailed analysis of Adenauer's method of conducting foreign policy is given by Arnulf Baring, *Aussenpolitik in Adenauers Kanzlerdemokratie* (1969). A shorter account by the same author will be found in K. Kaiser and R. Morgan, eds, *Britain and West Germany: Changing Societies and the Future of Foreign Policy* (1971).

10 See above, p. 15.

11 Prittie, pp. 154–6.

12 On the 'Paulskirche-Bewegung,' in which large sectors of intellectual opinion opposed rearmament, see Theo Pirker, *Die SPD nach Hitler* (1965), pp. 205 ff.

13 The CDU/CSU vote went up from 31 per cent to 45.2 per cent of the total, and their parliamentary strength from 139 to 243.

14 See *Int. Aff.* July 1951, quoted by R. McGeehan, *The German Rearmament Question* (1971), p. 74.

15 For fuller analyses, see the valuable studies by Wolfram Hanrieder, esp. *West German Foreign Policy 1949–1963* (1967), ch. 4, and *The Stable Crisis: Two Decades of German Foreign Poiicy* (1970), pp. 129–46.

16 The issue of rearmament—which involved strong pressures from other allies, particularly France—is analysed in the section on multilateral alliance problems, pp. 42–5 below. The present section deals, by way of prelude, mainly with the related issues which entailed essentially bilateral German-American transactions.

17 *Manchester Guardian*, 10 Oct. 1949, quoted by Prittie, p. 153. The Chatham House Press Library contains copious evidence (classified under the heading 'Germany: Allied Occupation—Economic Policy—Dismantling') of American congressional, trade union, and business pressures against continued dismantling.

18 Prittie, p. 155. Text of the agreement in Ruhm von Oppen, pp. 439–42.

19 *DOSB*, 2 Oct. 1950, cited by McGeehan, pp. 57–8.

20 Ibid. 19 March 1951, and other sources quoted by McGeehan, pp. 117–18.

21 On the negotiations of 1951–2, see Prittie, pp. 165–9; Acheson, chs 57, 61, 64, 67. The close German-American alignment was frequently noted by press commentators, e.g. *Le Monde*, 27 Feb. 1951; *NYT*, 11 Sept. 1951; *NZZ*, 10 Aug. 1952.

22 DOHP, F. von Eckhardt interview transcript, p. 8.

23 G. Freund, *Germany Between Two Worlds* (1961), pp. 13, 86.

24 Statement to the press, Bonn, 16 Sept. 1954, Dulles Papers (Princeton Univ. Library), Cat. IC.

25 McGeehan, p. 39.

26 See the work of this title, R. Aron and D. Lerner, eds (1956).

27 G. Wettig, *Entmilitarisierung und Wiederbewaffnung in Deutschland 1943–1955* (1967), p. 274, which draws on Martin, in Stein, ed.

28 Summary of Adenauer's statements, Wettig, pp. 284–8; the earlier American public debate, ibid. pp. 276–8, and Martin, pp. 646–9.

29 The 'package' of American proposals, including this one, is summarized by McGeehan, p. 27. This work, and those of Wettig, Martin, and Baring give comprehensive accounts of the German rearmament debate, which is not recounted in detail here.

30 McGeehan, p. 72.

31 Ibid. pp. 76–80.

32 Wettig, p. 551; DOHP, testimony of Livingston Merchant (Dulles's Assistant Secretary for European Affairs).

33 Wettig, pp. 598–9.

34 See Martin Saeter, *Okkupation, Integration, Gleichberechtigung* (1967), pp. 25–6.

35 Coral Bell, *Negotiation from Strength: a Study in the Politics of Power* (1962), is a critical analysis of this concept.

36 Private conversation with the author: on the background to the plan, see above, pp. 26–7.

37 Adenauer, quoted by Prittie, p. 239; on the German reactions to the Soviet note, see ibid. pp. 239–41.

38 F. von Eckhardt's interview, DOHP, confirms this.

39 For a perceptive discussion of the 'veto' problem, see Herbert von Borch, 'Für die Amerikaner,' *Der Monat*, May 1965, pp. 49–56.

40 See ch. 4 below.

CHAPTER FOUR

From German Sovereignty to Apparent Détente 1955–1958

Background: the Spirit of Geneva

Before the NATO ministerial meeting in Paris of 6–13 May 1955 Secretary of State Dulles took the draft of the official statement welcoming West Germany as a new member, and added in his own handwriting: 'We now welcome to our company the Federal Republic of Germany. We recognize that the area of freedom is thus enlarged and strengthened.' [1] The period of history running from Germany's recovery of sovereignty in May 1955 to Khrushchev's ultimatum of November 1958 on Berlin was thus to be one in which Germany played the role of an independent and increasingly powerful actor on the world scene. As the Secretary of State's sister was to recall, Dulles—who repeatedly met Chancellor Adenauer during these years—was also particularly glad to see Vice-Chancellor Erhard when the latter visited Washington in March 1958, since 'Germany was beginning to look beyond its borders as its influence in the world continued to grow.' [2]

The world in which Germany was to exert this growing influence was in many ways more complex than that of the early 1950s, as the Cold War, by general consent, began to give way to a more relaxed phase of East-West relations. Khrushchev's denunciation of Stalin at the 20th Congress of the CPSU in February 1956 set the tone for widespread optimism about the prospective liberalization of the Soviet system, which was presumed to imply the relaxation both of the Soviet hold on its satellites and of tension between the Warsaw Pact and NATO. An unprecedented outbreak of journeys by leaders of both blocs appeared to confirm this trend: Khrushchev and Bulganin visited some Asian countries in late 1955 and London in early 1956; both Adenauer and Mollet went to Moscow in the same period; and Mikoyan visited Bonn in April 1958.

By the end of 1956 hopes of a dramatic improvement in East-West relations had been dashed by the brutal Soviet suppression of the Hungarian rising—which came in the wake of stirrings of independence not only in Hungary but also in Poland; however, these hopes were resuscitated during 1957. Several prominent Western citizens, Hugh Gaitskell and George Kennan among them, revived and elaborated the ideas of a mutual military 'thinning-out' by both European alliances, which had been aired by Eden and others at the Geneva 'summit' conference in the summer of 1955.[3]

These Western ideas echoed the plans put forward late in 1957 by the Polish Foreign Minister Adam Rapacki for a nuclear-free zone covering territory on both sides of the Iron Curtain. Such plans—and the whole issue of how European security might be improved by agreements to limit the military strength of both alliances—were discussed in the disarmament negotiations conducted by the Soviet Union and the Western powers throughout this period, both before and after the Geneva 'summit' of 1955.

Despite these intimations of détente, the governments of Washington and Bonn proceeded actively with the policy of integrating the Federal Republic into the West, the main lines of which had been laid down during the early fifties. The Messina Conference of the Foreign Ministers of the Six, held a month after Germany regained her sovereignty, began the negotiations for a European Economic Community which were to lead to the signature of the Treaty of Rome in March 1957 and to its implementation by January 1958 (in the meantime, in January 1957, the Saar had rejoined the Federal Republic). In May 1958 the Fourth French Republic fell, and General de Gaulle returned to power. In the field of Western defence the new member of NATO set about levying the troops Bonn had promised in exchange for regaining her sovereignty: the original target, the raising of 500,000 men within two years, proved quite impracticable, but by 1958 Adenauer's new Minister of Defence (from October 1956, Franz Josef Strauss), had attained the more realistic goal of 172,000 men.[4] The government in Bonn had by this time encountered difficulties with Washington on a number of issues of which more was to be heard later: Germany's access to the control of nuclear weapons, the level of American conventional forces in Europe, and the size of Germany's contribution to the cost of keeping them there.

Both Washington and Bonn, particularly the former, were also concerned with developments outside Europe. Although the earlier fighting in Korea and Indochina had no counterpart in this period, unfinished conflict in China continued to lead to sporadic firing across the straits separating the two Chinese regimes: the shelling of the islands of Quemoy and Matsu reached a peak in September 1958—as it happened, shortly before new Soviet pressure was put on Berlin. (A despatch from the United States mission in Berlin on 7 October 1958 indicated how the two areas were linked in German minds: the American diplomat reported to the Secretary of State that Berliners, including their Mayor, Willy Brandt, welcomed the Secretary's firm declaration that the American guarantee both of Quemoy and of West Berlin was to be taken seriously: there had been, he said, 'the fear that a neutralization of Quemoy might be taken by some to mean withdrawal from Berlin.')[5]

Washington—and to some extent Bonn, too—were also forced to give close attention to events in the eastern Mediterranean and Middle East. As well as the conflict over Cyprus, which brought Greece and Turkey to the brink of war and threatened the stability of NATO's southern flank, there was a series of grave crises in the Middle East. Egypt's nationalization of the Suez Canal in July 1956 set off a train of events leading to her invasion in October by the forces of Israel, France, and the United States, an episode which had profound repercussions on the relations of these states with Washington, and also on European-American relations more generally. The 'Eisenhower Doctrine' of January 1957 represented a commitment of American power to preserving the stability of the Arab/Israeli balance—as it was already committed to the 'Northern Tier' by the Baghdad Pact concluded in 1954—and this had to be honoured in July 1958. A revolution in Iraq appeared to imperil the stability of the governments of Jordan and the Lebanon: British troops defended the former, and American the latter—at the cost of some discord between Washington and Bonn, since the American troops employed in the operation were flown from air bases in Bavaria, and Adenauer was fearful that Germany's relations with the Arab world might be endangered.

As will be seen, this was only one example—although an unusually dramatic one—of the way in which relations between Washington and Bonn in this period ran the risk of disturbance from problems arising in remote areas. In the years 1955–8 the general trend appeared to be towards East-West détente, but the Soviet invasion of Hungary and Soviet threats during the Suez crisis are instances of its liability to sudden disruption, and by mid-1958 Adenauer felt once more that 'a cold wind was rising in the East.' [6]

As Soviet and East German pressure on West Berlin mounted, heralding Khrushchev's new assault on the problem in November 1958, it seemed that the Soviet Union might be trying to exploit its new prowess in missile technology, demonstrated by the success of the *Sputnik* satellite in October 1957, to win diplomatic advantages.

In this period of uncertain international détente, both Eisenhower and Adenauer had to pay special attention to affairs within their own countries. Both of them had to fight elections—the former in November 1956, the latter in September 1957—in which they both won conclusive victories.

Internal Politics: Harmony with a Query

Christian Pineau, the Socialist Foreign Minister of France from early 1956 to mid-1957, has recalled a remark made by Dulles when they first met, at a ministerial meeting of SEATO in Karachi in March 1956. According to Pineau's report, Dulles said, 'Pour nous il y a deux sortes de gens dans le monde: il y a ceux qui sont chrétiens et partisans de la libre entreprise, et il y a les autres.' [7]

Judged by these criteria, Adenauer, eminently Christian and a strong believer in private enterprise, was a thoroughly acceptable partner for Dulles. The Christian Democratic government in Bonn aroused in the latter none of the apprehensions he felt in dealing with Paris, where he found Socialists like Mollet and Pineau in office, and repeatedly asked to be reassured (as Pineau tells us) that there were significant differences between Socialists and Communists.[8]

The temperamental affinity between the Roman Catholic Chancellor and the Presbyterian Secretary of State was very close—an American Ambassador who worked closely with them has confirmed this, adding that 'they used to go and pray together '[9]—and they judged the issues confronting their two countries from points of view remarkably alike. There were, however, pressures both within and outside their national political systems that tended to create divergences even between two statesmen with such similar views. Dulles seems to have been aware of this when he wrote to Adenauer ('My dear friend ') on 30 June 1958, after a first encounter with de Gaulle newly returned to power, that he regretted not being able to see the Chancellor, as 'I really feel there is a need for us to have a good talk together to keep our thinking in harmony. Written communications are no adequate substitute.'[10]

One of Dulles's problems was that his own position in Washington was somewhat weaker in Eisenhower's second term than in his first. Although all accounts agree in confirming that Eisenhower had very great confidence in Dulles's ability to conduct foreign policy, and left him a great deal of leeway,[11] the President acted a little more independently of Dulles, and was subject to a slightly wider range of other influences, after his re-election in 1956.

As early as the end of 1954 the influence of Senators Knowland and McCarthy, who had redoubled the strongly 'Cold War' line of Dulles and rendered deviations from it difficult, had been removed. The Senate was now rather more inclined to seek East-West détente and limit American spending on armaments; and this view, which naturally appeared highly dangerous to Adenauer, appealed to Eisenhower much more than it did to Dulles.

The President, after all, had owed his election in 1952 to his promise to end the Korean War (for which he successfully placed the blame on the Democrats) and in 1956 a corresponding promise to seek an end to the Cold War in Europe was a natural line for a Republican President to take. The desire to go down in history as a peace-maker, together with the traditional Republican precept that the budget should be balanced, led Eisenhower—especially after he was re-elected in 1956 and entered what must perforce be his last term—to limit military spending and to try to find ways of reaching East-West agreements on disarmament or at least on arms control. Eisenhower's farewell address warning his compatriots of the perils of the 'military-industrial complex' [12] in American life, was no isolated outburst. It was an expression of the concern that made the President suggest the idea of a disarmed area in Central Europe as early as May 1955,[13] and the 'open skies' plan for aerial inspection of military forces slightly later.[14]

The Soviet development of a hydrogen bomb in 1953 had inevitably led to a situation in which the United States was more vulnerable than during her period of nuclear monopoly; and the President's response to this, the search for disarmament negotiations with the Soviet Union, was quite natural. It did, however, raise difficulties both with the West German government, which was alarmed at the prospect of arms control agreements that would in effect freeze Europe's political status quo (including Germany's division), and also with Dulles, who believed the idea of disarmament to be illusory. So it probably was, in the sense of *general and complete disarmament*—this was the somewhat old-fashioned sense in which Dulles, remembering the Disarmament Conference of 1932, conceived the problem [15] —but the search for more limited arms control agreements did not appear to the President to be necessarily so hopeless, and he pursued it.

In March 1957 Eisenhower made another pronouncement in favour of disarmament, this time suggesting the establishment of trial areas for inspection to check if nuclear weapons were being stocked, and German concern was rearoused. The source of many of Eisenhower's disarmament proposals at this time was Harold Stassen, the President's Special Assistant for Disarmament from 1955 to 1958. Stassen, a powerful figure in the Republican Party, was a strong believer in negotiations on arms control with the Soviet Union, and held the view that such agreements, which, according to his thinking, could greatly increase international security, should not be made dependent on the solution of outstanding political differences. This approach gave rise to deep suspicion in Bonn, where the belief naturally prevailed that a first step towards a true East-West détente in Europe must be the removal of one of the main political sources of East-West tension, the division of Germany. In Adenauer's view any agreement about force-limitations, if it came before an agreement on German reunification, could only render the latter more difficult by making the status quo more acceptable to Germany's allies. It was thus a constant preoccupation of Bonn, during the period of Stassen's activity, to establish between arms control and reunification such a firm linkage (or, as German lawyers called it, *Junktim*) that agreement on one would always remain dependent upon agreement on the other. By October 1957 Adenauer was convinced that Stassen's influence on the President was having a baneful effect on American policy towards the Soviet Union. Stassen, he feared, was succeeding in separating the issues of arms control and German reunification in the President's mind, and he took the unusual step of complaining about Stassen to the leading American journalist James Reston.[16]

If the peace-directed activities of Harold Stassen constituted one source of danger for German-American relations, another source—located in a quite different part of the Washington machinery—was Admiral Radford. Consternation was created in Bonn when the *New York Times* reported on 13 July 1956 that the Admiral, Chairman of the Joint Chiefs of Staff, was considering a plan for the reduction of American ground forces by 800,000 men, and that he proposed to replace them by increased reliance on nuclear weapons. The substance of this notion, and its effect in Bonn, will be considered in more detail later:[17] it is enough here to note that the relatively independent position of the Chairman of the Joint Chiefs of Staff gave him the authority to make statements which, while not in fact administration policy, appeared to Bonn to have the sanction of the White House and therefore caused a degree of harm to German-American relations.[18]

If the American body politic thus contained many elements of a kind to disturb the Germans—the Senate, Mr Stassen, Admiral Radford, and the apparent hesitancy of the President—the German political system had fewer components likely to cause disquiet in Washington. Dr Adenauer himself, and such of his leading colleagues as Erhard and von Brentano, were eminently reassuring to those responsible for American policy.

There were only three potential sources of concern: Franz Josef Strauss, the Social-Democratic opposition, and Adenauer's coalition partner, the FDP. Strauss, who was Minister for Atomic Energy from 1955 and became Minister of Defence in October 1956 in succession to the somewhat ineffectual Theodor Blank, was a man determined to stand up for German national interests, even against the protective United States. According to one observer there was a phase during which Strauss, a former supporter of German demilitarization and neutrality, felt drawn towards the Americans: 'Once he was Defence Minister, he took visible delight in his contacts with the Pentagon, and increasingly assumed the habits of thinking fitting for the military super-power of our age.' [19] As will be seen, however, there came a point when Strauss's tough support of German interests, and in particular his claim for a share in the control of nuclear weapons, created some displeasure in Washington.

The Social-Democratic opposition constituted a much less immediate challenge to Washington than Herr Strauss. Led by Erich Ollenhauer, the party in 1955–6 was still licking its wounds after its defeat in the 1953 election, and appeared scarcely likely to do any better in 1957. Its attempt in 1955 to broaden its appeal by taking the lead in a vast anti-rearmament movement (the '*Paulskirche-Bewegung*' named after its establishment at a mass meeting in St Paul's Church, Frankfurt) failed to win the support of more than limited groups of intellectuals, trade unionists, and young left-wingers; and to experts it never looked a serious threat to Adenauer and the CDU.

To less expert eyes, however—for instance, those of Dulles—it could be argued (and Adenauer very effectively *did* argue) that if Germany were not given equal treatment by the West, the 'neutralist' tendencies represented by the SPD would spread in new forms to broader sections of the population, and Germany would slip into a position of dangerous neutrality between East and West. This skilful playing on a scarcely real menace of 'neutralism' was a powerful card in the hands of Adenauer and Strauss.

Although the Free Democratic Party might have been useful in the same way, it was in fact something of an embarrassment to Adenauer, since the FDP was a member of the governing coalition. Many of its leading Ministers—Franz Blücher,

Hermann Schäfer, and others—saw virtually eye-to-eye with Adenauer on matters of foreign policy, but this was not the case with Dr Thomas Dehler, the party's chairman. Dehler represented the so-called 'National Liberal' tradition in the FDP: although there were times when he supported Adenauer's policy of West European integration, he more often denounced it as a betrayal of German national interests, along lines similar to those of Kurt Schumacher. Adenauer was deeply worried when the FDP went beyond its insistence on taking up diplomatic relations with Yugoslavia—one of their spokesmen, Karl-Heinz Pfleiderer, was Ambassador in Belgrade from 1955 to 1957—and also argued that a neutral, 'Yugoslav' position would suit Germany's interests too. As the Chancellor later wrote, 'I am convinced that if this FDP-supported policy for Germany had been adopted, the Americans would have radically changed their European policy and made a deal with the Russians'.[20]

The embarrassment of FDP 'neutralism' in the cabinet was ended only after the election of 1957, when the CDU was strong enough to rule alone, and the coalition was brought to an end.

Bilateral Relations: Force Levels and Stationing Costs

Felix von Eckhardt, Adenauer's chief press spokesman for almost the whole period from 1952 to 1962, later recalled American disappointment over Germany's slowness in building up her armed forces to the high levels which the first Defence Minister Theodor Blank and his colleagues had optimistically promised in the early 1950s:

> . . . but to enlist, arm and train 500,000 men here in Germany, from nothing, was a promise that could not be kept. I believe it was a great achievement of the next Defence Minister, Strauss, that he immediately destroyed this illusion. In fact he went with his own special clear and cool way to America and said 'This is impossible. Here are the figures that can be attained, in men, money and buildings.' The barracks were not there. We had no military training grounds. Everything was missing. Now Strauss made a realistic proposal, which meant a slowing-down in contrast to Blank's plans, but represented a realistic plan . . .[Strauss] convinced the military leadership in the United States, and in this way John Foster Dulles must have been convinced too. This does not mean that he was not

always pressing. He was pressing us to go forwards, to go forwards energetically, and laid great importance on seeing something of our army, at the end of a certain period of time. He did all this.[21]

Adenauer himself has confirmed the continued importance attached by Dulles to West Germany's fulfilling her military obligations to NATO. In a conversation in Washington in June 1956, Adenauer reports, Dulles took the unusual step of interrupting his interlocutor to impress upon him the need for Germany to make her contribution to Western defence. Dulles used an argument calculated to appeal to Adenauer's own conception of the interest of rearmament for Germany:

A nation that does not possess adequate military forces of its own cannot count as fully sovereign, but at best as a protectorate, which cannot speak with a full voice in matters of foreign policy. The size of the contribution it makes to the forces needed to uphold peace and order is a measure of the maturity and sovereignty of a people.[22]

This was only one example of many expressions of American disquiet at the slow progress of German rearmament.

The 'realistic plans' drawn up by Strauss provided Germany with an agreed strength of 67,000 men at the end of 1956, which rose to 120,000 in 1957, 172,000 in 1958, and 230,000 in 1959.[23]

Although this rate of growth was satisfactory to the majority of interested members of the Senate in Washington—even though a minority of Senators felt that massive West German rearmament might be an obstacle to the prospects for détente and disarmament—in the eyes of the Pentagon and Dulles it was quite inadequate.

There was no doubt that Adenauer and Strauss had to overcome considerable opposition to rearmament inside Germany, stimulated by the SPD's campaign of 1955 and by the wave of public alarm when NATO manoeuvres the same year indicated that war would mean very large numbers of deaths in Germany. The evolution of America's own defence policy added a further difficulty: when Admiral Radford, Chairman of the Joint Chiefs of Staff, spoke out in July 1956 for a reduction of America's conventional forces, it was hard for America's allies to press the view that their own forces should be increased. By the autumn of 1956 Adenauer and Strauss were thus arguing that conscription in West Germany should be limited to twelve months, that the pace of her conventional armament should be slowed down, that the emphasis on different types of weapons should be changed, and in particular that the Bundeswehr should receive nuclear weapons.[24] These German demands were not well received in Washington: as will be seen in connection with NATO's strategic discussions,[25] the question of Germany's access to nuclear weapons raised very difficult issues, and her reluctance to produce troops as fast as expected was a disappointment.

From the very beginning of Germany's rearmament in 1955 there was also a further question which potentially troubled her relations with Washington, and which was to do so acutely in the 1960s: the question of who was to pay the financial cost both of Germany's own troops and of American troops in Germany. In January 1956 it was reported that the previous month's North Atlantic Council meeting had been the occasion for a warning to the Germans not to expect the United States to cover the budgetary deficit on their three-year defence plan. This warning was described as ' a corrective to a view widely held in West Germany that Washington was prepared to underwrite any deficit the Bonn Government might incur in building up its armed forces.' [26]

By the time Adenauer visited Washington the following June a bilateral agreement had been reached on the subject of stationing costs,[27] but the first sounds had now been heard of a conflict that was to assume much larger proportions in later years. The American feeling that Germany's prosperity would allow her to contribute more to the general costs of the Western alliance—whether in men, money, or overseas aid—also found expression in the demand that Germany's increasingly affluent market should be opened more widely to American imports. Fortunately, by the time Adenauer left Washington, the communique on his talks with Dulles recorded ' the satisfaction of the United States Government with the action just taken by the Federal Republic of Germany to remove quota restrictions on imports from the dollar area, in accordance with the provisions of the GATT.' [28]

A demand from the German side—for the return of German assets seized in the United States during the war—was not agreed to by the American administration. On a subsequent visit to Washington, Adenauer again raised the question, but without success.[29] By July 1957 German pressure on this issue had become so strong that President Eisenhower undertook to grant what Germany asked, but a year later the administration was still unwilling to put the request to Congress. It was reported from Bonn in July 1958 that the administration's failure to act had 'aroused bitter disappointment here. Members of the Government and an overwhelming majority in Parliament feel that the policy represents a repudiation of a pledge made by the Eisenhower Administration last year (July 1). The *Bundestag*, the Lower House, rushes through a protest resolution a few hours before adjournment for the summer last night.'[30]

By the autumn of 1958, the problem was still unresolved, and the German government's protests were taking a sharper form:

Foreign Minister von Brentano announced in the Bundestag on Friday further efforts by the Federal Government for the recovery of the property confiscated in the United States during the war. He said that this last remaining burden on German-American relations must disappear as soon as possible. . . . Brentano expressed his regret that the hopes aroused on this question after his and the Chancellor's conversations in America had not yet been fulfilled. Nothing would be neglected, however, to put an end to this 'very unsatisfactory situation'. Brentano added, however, that he was not in a position to foresee the date of a satisfactory solution.[31]

The issue of confiscated German property was thus not resolved before the Berlin crisis started in 1958, opening a new phase in German-American relations.

Despite these elements of strain, the bilateral relationship between Bonn and Washington remained very close, as was shown by the active American intervention on the side of Chancellor Adenauer during the election campaign of 1957. The American administration scarcely hid its view that a new Adenauer government would be more welcome to Washington than a change[32] and there was real cordiality in Dulles's message of congratulations sent to the Chancellor after his victory via the American Ambassador David Bruce: 'I rejoice greatly at the verdict of the German people. All the free world should pay heartfelt tribute to the dynamic and statesmanlike leadership you have given.'[33]

Alliance Politics: the Radford Plan and Control of Nuclear Weapons

Those German-American transactions of 1955–8, whether harmonious or otherwise, arising out of the two states' membership of NATO are hard to separate from the bilateral issues, already discussed, of German troop levels and American stationing costs. However, the questions of NATO strategy and the European share in controlling nuclear weapons in fact have a multilateral dimension which places them in a distinct category.

Germany had been a member of NATO for about a year, and was beginning to develop her armed forces (as Adenauer reaffirmed when he visited Dulles in June 1956), when German public opinion was shaken by a press report that Admiral Radford, the Chairman of the US Joint Chiefs of Staff, was considering a plan for the reduction of America's conventional forces by 800,000 men (i.e. from 2,800,000 to 2 million) and, in consequence, for greater reliance on nuclear deterrence.[34] The newspaper report was correct in saying that the plan did not represent American official policy—Radford had merely been trying out some ideas in an appearance before the Senate Sub-Committee on the Air Force—but there appeared to be enough official approval behind the proposed reduction to justify German concern that it might rapidly *become* official policy. A few days later, Dulles was asked at a press conference whether he thought NATO would be weakened by a 'substantial reduction' in its ground forces, and replied evasively: 'I certainly do not think that there would be any destruction of NATO if, in accordance with competent military advice, there was a reforming of the defense pattern of NATO.'[35] A little later again, 'Mr Dulles, privately relaxing among reporters, let it be known that the administration approved the idea in principle.'[36]

The notion of reducing American ground forces and placing more reliance on nuclear weapons was not new in itself; it underlay the Dulles declaration of January 1954 about 'massive retaliation', which in turn went back to President Eisenhower's instructions that American defence policy should be thoroughly re-thought when he took office in 1953.[37] Together with the idea of an overall reduction of American ground forces and reliance on tactical nuclear weapons (in which Radford placed particularly strong faith) went the notion of reducing America's strength in the outposts of her alliance system, and building up a mobile reserve force for use when and where she chose.

The German government had some reason to be alarmed at this prospect (the fact that Britain and France also spoke of reducing their conventional, at the expense of their nuclear, forces made the situation only marginally worse, but worse all the same): the logic of American defence policy appeared to be moving in an opposite direction from the line Germany's strategic planners had been taking since they began their work in 1950. German defence policy was still based on the commitment to create all-conventional forces of 500,000 men (Strauss had not yet replaced Blank and revised the latter's target downwards), and Adenauer had had a hard fight in the Bundestag, as recently as a week before the Radford Plan leaked out, in winning approval for this programme. Adenauer now felt that the Radford Plan implied that German rearmament to the proposed level was unnecessary, and that 'my arguments, that we would cause the Americans to withdraw from Europe if we failed to fulfil the hopes they placed in us, seemed to have been falsified.' [38]

Adenauer was well aware of the reasons for Washington's interest in the new strategy: 1956 was an election year, and the return to civilian life of 800,000 soldiers was clearly a vote-winner,[39] but the consequences for Germany could still be grave. As the *Neue Zürcher Zeitung* put the matter on 19 July, the presence of substantial American ground forces in Germany was a guarantee that Congress would in fact agree to go to war in the event of a Soviet attack: this line of argument was to become a familiar one in the 1960s and still more in the 1970s.

The Chancellor immediately summoned to Bonn his Ambassadors in Washington, London, and Paris and instructed them to seek reassurances that Germany would not be denuded of Allied forces and that the basic lines of NATO strategy were unchanged.

Washington's reply came in the form of an official denial, on 31 July 1956, that any reduction in America's commitment to NATO was being contemplated, and further in a long and reassuring letter from John Foster Dulles and a visit from his brother, Allen Welsh Dulles, now head of the Central Intelligence Agency. In the course of a criticism of the Radford Plan, Adenauer complained to his visitor that American policy seemed divided and hesitant, and that this was already having a negative effect on his standing with the German electorate, as measured in recent polls: he told Dulles 'that my policy was based on firm confidence in the United States, and that if this was disappointed, it would have grave internal political effects for my government.' [40]

At the same time as hinting in this way that American policy could have unwelcome effects in Germany, by strengthening the opposition Social-Democratic party, Adenauer did not hesitate to undertake a modest intervention in American domestic politics, which took the form of an approach to the opposition Democratic Party. The Democrats were making the need for effective conventional forces a central plank of their election campaign, and it was therefore logical for Adenauer, as part of his own campaign against the Republican Party's Radford Plan, to send a prominent emissary, his press spokesman Felix von Eckhardt, to make contact with Democratic Party spokesmen, including Harriman, Finletter, Stevenson, and Kennan.[41]

As von Eckhardt later recalled,

> I spoke with John Foster Dulles and with Radford, and with many people, including Lyndon B. Johnson, who played a leading role in the Senate, and a number of other people. Of course it was not this mission of mine which brought down the Radford Plan—it was only a small stone in the whole campaign against the plan—but in the end, thank God, it did not go through. I had the feeling, if I remember rightly, that John Foster Dulles and his colleagues in the State Department, to whom I explained the Chancellor's views on this matter, were very impressed: in fact, that they were saying to themselves, if the Federal German Government rejects such a military development as strongly as this, it really cannot be carried out . . . John Foster Dulles certainly took up the side of the German argument.[42]

In fact no more was heard of the Radford Plan, as the resistance both in Washington and in the alliance was too strong, but its basic concept of a reduction of American conventional strength in Europe was to cause renewed strain in German-American relations in the future.

In the meantime the growth of Germany's own armed forces proceeded—though, as we have seen, its tempo was disappointing to the Americans. At the same time Adenauer and his new Defence Minister Franz Josef Strauss clearly felt by late 1956 that Germany was contributing enough to the alliance to be able to claim equality in access to the most modern weapons with her allies: ever since 1950, in fact, Adenauer had seen German rearmament as being, among other things, a way for Germany to win equality of status, and this, he argued,should now mean a share in controlling the nuclear capacity of the alliance. By the end of 1956, as we have noted, Germany was demanding a say in this issue, and in April 1957 Adenauer declared at a press conference in Bonn that 'of course' Germany, like France and Britain, should share in the control of tactical nuclear weapons, which he professed to see as 'nothing more than a development of artillery.'[43]

By this time the United States had formally declared, through a statement by Secretary of Defense Wilson at the NATO Council Meeting in December 1956, that American legislation would prohibit any passing-on of nuclear weapons to Germany.[44]

Adenauer, however, continued to regret that American policy favoured the development of independent nuclear forces by Britain and France, particularly the former, while Germany was discriminated against.[45] Strauss had to accept, in describing the situation to the Bundestag in March 1958, that with the system of control now being developed by NATO, 'warheads remain American property under American control, as we wish it', while the missiles might be in German or other European hands.[46] Although it gave Germany at least some degree of equality with her allies, this system of control was still far from satisfying the full scope of the demands she had put to Washington. It was only in 1959 that a further step was to be taken in meeting German requests for a share in the control of nuclear weapons.[47]

In this situation, where neither Washington nor Bonn was fully content with the other's contribution to the alliance, there appeared a third party whose rising influence in 1957–8 foreshadowed a more decisive impact later: Paris. Relations between Paris and Washington had been relatively tense throughout the 1950s, largely because of France's hesitation about

German rearmament, and had reached a state of serious crisis over Suez in late 1956. The failure of the United States to support her European allies during this episode provoked even Adenauer to a public utterance to the effect that Europe would henceforth have to do more to protect her own interests.[48]

The basis was hereby laid for Franco-German solidarity against the United States, of a kind which had been inconceivable in the early 1950s and was only to reach fruition—short-lived, even then—in the 1960s. In France's post-Suez disillusionment with American leadership, she sought German support for a reorganization of NATO in which the European members would claim a larger share in decisions. A French Minister—Maurice Faure, Under-Secretary of State for Foreign Affairs in Félix Gaillard's government—came to Bonn in November 1957 to discuss the project with Adenauer. The Chancellor, who was in any case a lifelong francophil, agreed with his visitor that the development of intercontinental missiles by both super-powers was making them start to feel their way towards a mutual understanding, and that there was a case for European co-operation in military research and production.

France's concern, stimulated by the action of the United States and Britain in selling weapons to Tunisia at a critical phase of the Algerian war, was to build up a Continental front against Anglo-American domination of NATO. Adenauer expressed his agreement with this view in his conversations both with Faure and with Gaillard the following month. It is striking that one of his reasons for agreeing with the idea of a nuclear EDC (France to provide the nuclear warheads, Germany at the most to do research on rocket developments) was the feeling that United States leadership was liable to go through periods of serious unreliability every four years, the next presidential election being due in 1960.[49]

The projected Franco-German collaboration on atomic research came to nothing as a result of Gaillard's fall in April 1958 and that of the Fourth Republic a month later; but it is instructive to note that, as an attraction for Adenauer, the ' French factor '—France not just as the partner in European integration of the early 1950s, but as an explicit alternative to Washington—was clearly present even in the last years of the ' Dulles era '.

Relations with the Adversary: from Geneva to Berlin

The late 1950s were a period when the perspectives of the United States and Germany markedly diverged—in contrast to the Cold War period earlier in the decade—because the United States was a world power and Germany was not. This meant, essentially, that the United States began to seek global détente with its fellow super-power, the Soviet Union, at a time when the latter was still stoutly resisting interests which Germany saw as vital: reunification and rearmament. East-West negotiations were thus essentially something that interested Washington rather than Bonn. Adenauer did indeed visit the Soviet Union in September 1955, although somewhat reluctantly, and established diplomatic relations with Yugoslavia the same year. However, these relations were broken off in 1957 after Yugoslavia had recognized the German Democratic Republic, and this led to the enunciation of the Hallstein Doctrine—that no state recognizing the GDR (with the one sensible exception of the Soviet Union) should be permitted to have diplomatic relations with West Germany. This underlined the fact that East-West negotiations were above all something for the United States, not West Germany. The best-publicized moment was the summit conference held in Geneva in July 1955, between Eisenhower, Bulganin, Eden, and Edgar Faure. This provided essentially for an exchange of views on East-West relations, after which the four leaders instructed their Foreign Ministers to meet for a further conference in October-November to explore the precise questions of Germany and European security, disarmament, and the development of East-West contacts. The main issue in these East-West conferences, as far as German-American relations were concerned was whether the German view would prevail that reunification was an essential pre-condition for European peace, and that Europe must not be allowed to get used to the division of Germany as a permanent fact,[50] or whether the Soviet Union would persuade America and the other Western powers that negotiations on disarmament and/or European security could perfectly well proceed without waiting for agreement on Germany: the latter course would naturally have been most unwelcome to Germany, and would have opened a serious breach between Bonn and her allies.[51]

By the end of the summit conference, when it was evident that no substantial rapprochement was in sight on any other issue, a serious dispute arose about the drafting of the final communique. For the sake of good relations with Germany, Dulles was determined that the communique should reaffirm the responsibility of the four powers for German reunification, as well as mentioning their intention to negotiate on other matters. Molotov, who took the place of Bulganin, obdurately refused to agree to this during the penultimate day's talks—the session lasted until 2.30 the following morning—and it was only at 5.30 on the last afternoon that the Soviet Union acquiesced. The two collaborators of Dulles who have recounted this episode—Robert Bowie, then head of the State Department's Policy Planning Staff, and Livingston Merchant, then Assistant Secretary of State for European Affairs—emphasize Dulles's strong commitment to German-American solidarity in the face of Soviet pressure.[52]

Although he supported Dulles in Geneva, President Eisenhower was, as we have seen,[53] more hopeful of the prospects of disarmament negotiations conducted in isolation from the question of Germany; and in the period 1955–8 he allowed his disarmament adviser, Harold Stassen, to undertake intensive negotiations with the Russians. It was impossible for the German government to oppose the idea of disarmament talks altogether, but it made a sharp distinction between plans for general and complete (including nuclear) disarmament, which would in fact reduce the other powers to Germany's current level, and schemes for thinning-out or limiting forces in Europe on a geographical basis; in every case schemes of the latter sort would have increased German insecurity (this was Germany's objection to the Eden Plan of 1955 and the Rapacki Plan of 1957) and had the disadvantage of leaving Germany divided. Some of Stassen's activities thus won the approval of Adenauer—for instance, his proposal of April 1957 at the United Nations London disarmament conference, to provide for the inspection of all stocks of fissile materials[54]—but his subsequent enthusiasm for more limited disarmament schemes aroused suspicions in Adenauer's mind that German interests were being neglected.

Although Stassen worked hard and devotedly in the attempt to bring about a disarmament agreement—to the point where

Adenauer felt that dangerous influences on Eisenhower were counteracting the wholesome work of Dulles [55]—the Secretary of State always had the last word. This is shown by the fact that although Eisenhower allowed Stassen to defend some of his ideas at the NATO Council—for instance, the ' open skies ' proposal of 1955—Stassen's repeated requests for permission to discuss proposals with Adenauer were always vetoed by Dulles. The latter was concerned that the Chancellor would take fright at Stassen's ideas, and afraid of the consequent damage to German-American relations.[56] In the field of disarmament, therefore, although Eisenhower had some sympathy for ideas and individuals who were alarming to Adenauer, their effect was always mitigated—at least until 1958—by the firm hand of Dulles.[57]

This was particularly noticeable in the debate that arose in 1957–8 on the possibility of disengagement from Germany by the major powers. The idea of Germany being neutralized as a means to reunification (that is, before the integration of the two German states respectively into NATO and the Warsaw Pact became irrevocable) was put forward, as we have seen, by the British Opposition leader Hugh Gaitskell, by the Polish Foreign Minister Adam Rapacki—in the limited form of a nuclear-free zone—and with notable eloquence by George Kennan in his BBC Reith Lectures in the autumn of 1957.[58]

The idea of a neutralized Germany had some support in the United States, for instance among Democratic Senators such as Mansfield, Fulbright, and Kennedy; and it also had a considerable appeal in Germany: there was a group of ' heretics ' in the Bonn Foreign Office who regretted West Germany's ties with the West, and Kennan's lectures were even cited with open approval by Theodor Heuss, the Federal President, in his broadcast on New Year's Day 1958.[59]

Adenauer's government naturally reacted with horror against any suggestion of neutralization, and Kennan was also strongly criticized by Americans who had taken the lead in building up the Federal Republic as an ally of the West.[60] In response to the views propounded in Kennan's Reith Lectures, his former master Dean Acheson decided to deliver a further rebuke to the man whom he described to friends as ' poor George ',[61] and wrote a stinging rebuttal.[62]

Dulles joined in the discussion with a comment to the Senate Foreign Relations Committee on 6 June 1958:

I think it is very important . . . that a reunited Germany be integrated into the West . . . I believe that a Germany which was left in a position of neutrality, or some people call it disengagement, in the center of Europe, would be under an almost irresistible temptation to play one side or the other, and that this would be a very dangerous situation, dangerous for the West, dangerous for the Soviet Union and dangerous for the Germans themselves.[63]

This revealed the intrinsic ambiguity of Dulles's policy towards Germany: the West German state must be regarded as a close ally, or else a very different Germany might once again be a threat to peace.

There was one area of the world where a crisis in 1958 quite unexpectedly led to a degree of German-American tension: the Middle East. As a rule, in the view of the American Ambassador to Bonn at this time, relations with the Germans were easier than with some of America's other allies: 'they [the Germans] had no colonial possessions. Nor at that period did they take any particular interest in overseas problems of any sort.'[64] However, when the Iraqi revolution of July 1958 led to American military aircraft taking off from bases in Germany, carrying troops to protect the Lebanese government, Adenauer was deeply offended. The reasons for his protest to Washington were twofold: firstly, the use of bases in Germany might bring retaliation on that country, and its government should at least have been informed; secondly, Bonn's carefully cultivated relations with the Arab world could be compromised by the American action.

Adenauer was outwardly appeased within a few days by a reassuring message from Dulles, and the government even defended the American action, but a current of suspicion remained. As the *New York Times* reported from Bonn:

The Government's ambivalent attitude is one of the poorest-kept secrets in Bonn. Echoes of this attitude may be found in an almost unbridled press campaign against the United States and British Governments. Even newspapers that normally support United States policy are participating in this attack. . . . Except for its effort to justify the use of West German air bases for United States air-lift operations to the Middle East, the Bonn Government has done little to counter the press criticism. . . . The demands on all sides for a NATO discussion of United States and British policy in the Middle East lead to a second conclusion: that in the German view, American power should not be employed outside of the continent of Europe without the previous consent of the European allies.[65]

This demand sounds strikingly close to those which were to be formulated within a couple of months by the new President of France. The potential basis for Franco-German co-operation was becoming stronger, and the more general point was underlined that, as Germany's interests were developed and diversified, German-American discord might arise from issues outside as well as within the central balance of power.

NOTES

1 Dulles Papers, Cat. IX, 'Conference dossiers and files on special subjects.'

2 Eleanor Lansing Dulles, *John Foster Dulles, the Last Year* (1963), pp. 103–4.

3 See Hugh Gaitskell, *The Challenge of Co-existence* (1957), Godkin Lectures, Harvard Univ.; and George Kennan, *Russia, The Atom and the West* (1958), Reith Lectures, BBC. On the controversy aroused by the Reith Lectures, see Kennan, *Memoirs: 1950–1963* (1972), pp. 234–61.

4 B. Bandulet, *Adenauer zwischen West und Ost* (1970), p. 60.

5 Dulles Papers, Cat. II, Correspondence.

6 Adenauer, *Erinnerungen 1955–1959* (1969).

7 DOHP, Pineau interview.

8 Ibid. Dulles asked Pineau this 'une dizaine de fois'.

9 Private information.

10 Dulles to Adenauer, 30 June 1958 ('Secret'), Dulles Papers, Cat. III.

11 See R. Goold-Adams, *The Time of Power* (1962); Dwight D. Eisenhower, *The White House Years*, ii: *Waging Peace 1956–1961* (1963): and DOHP, testimony of von Eckhardt and others.

12 Eisenhower, p. 616.

13 Bandulet, pp. 36, 257; and on Dulles's action to counteract German alarm, Goold-Adams, p. 256.

14 G. Barraclough and R. Wall, *Survey of International Affairs, 1955–1956* (1960), pp. 153–8.

15 DOHP, Bowie interview.

16 Private information, Washington. Adenauer, *1955–1959*, pp. 322–5, records this conversation, but without referring to Stassen.

17 See below, pp. 63–5.

18 Bandulet, p. 251, and sources there given.

19 P. Merkl, *Germany: Yesterday and Tomorrow* (1965), p. 152.
20 Adenauer, *1955–1959*, p. 77.
21 DOHP, von Eckhardt interview transcript, pp. 24–5.
22 Adenauer, *1955–1959*, p. 164.
23 Official figures quoted by Bandulet, p. 60. See J. L. Richardson, *Germany and the Atlantic Alliance* (1966), ch. 3.
24 Bandulet, pp. 61, 186, and sources there given.
25 See below, pp. 66–7.
26 *NYT*, 18 Jan. 1956.
27 Adenauer, *1955–1959*, p. 161.
28 *NYT*, 14 June 1956.
29 Ibid. 30 May 1957.
30 Ibid. 7 July 1958.
31 *FAZ*, 18 Oct. 1956.
32 Freund, *Germany between Two Worlds*, p. 86.
33 Telegram of 17 Sept. 1957, in Dulles-Adenauer Correspondence, Dulles Additional Papers (Princeton Univ. Library), AM 17034.
34 *NYT*, 13 July 1956.
35 Ibid. 19 July 1956.
36 *The Observer*, 22 July 1956.
37 Private information. See Dulles's article in *For. Aff.*, Apr. 1954, and the discussion of his statement of Jan. 1954 in C. Bell, *Survey of International Affairs, 1954* (1957), pp. 98–102; J. L. Richardson, pp. 39–40.
38 Adenauer, *1955–1959*, pp. 200–1.
39 Ibid. p. 198.
40 Ibid. pp. 206–13.
41 F. von Eckhardt, *Ein unordentliches Leben* (1967), pp. 451–60.
42 DOHP, von Eckhardt interview, pp. 21–2.
43 Adenauer, *1955–1959*, p. 298.
44 H. Speier, *German Rearmament and Atomic War* (1957), p. 220, cited by Bandulet, p. 258.
45 See, e.g., Adenauer, *1955–1959*, pp. 296–7.
46 Bundestag, *Verhandlungen* . . . , cited by Bandulet, p. 253.
47 On the arrangements made in 1959, see Bandulet, p. 62.
48 See J. L. Richardson, p. 67.
49 Adenauer, *1955–1959*, p. 331. The Franco-German negotiations of this period are fully described, ibid. pp. 325–35, 341–5, and assessed by Bandulet, pp. 128–31, 273–5.
50 Adenauer, *1955–1959*, p. 30.
51 This is made clear by Adenauer, ibid. pp. 29–60.
52 Testimony in DOHP.
53 See above, p. 55.
54 Adenauer, *1955–1959*, p. 300.
55 See above, p. 56.
56 DOHP, Stassen testimony.
57 For an example, see *NYT*, 28 May 1957.
58 See above, p. 58. George Kennan had of course put forward similar pleas since 1949, when they had led to his breach with Acheson: see their memoirs.

59 Freund, *Germany between Two Worlds*, p. 66.

60 e.g., James Conant's remarks reported in the *New York Times*, 10 Jan. 1958.

61 Private information. Acheson's public criticism of Kennan as a man who 'never grasped the realities of power relationships' is quoted in the latter's *Memoirs: 1950–1963*, p. 250.

62 Acheson, 'The Illusion of Disengagement,' *For. Aff.*, 36/3 (1958), pp. 371–82.

63 Cited by Freund, *Germany between Two Worlds*, p. 126: see ibid. p. 125 for a critical German reaction to Dulles's remarks.

64 DOHP, David Bruce interview.

65 *NYT*, 21 July 1958.

CHAPTER FIVE

Berlin Crisis and Eisenhower's Departure 1958–1960

Background: the End of the Fifties

In November 1958 Khrushchev's ultimatum on Berlin started a new and protracted crisis. In November 1960 John F. Kennedy was elected President of the United States. The intervening two years—the last two of the Eisenhower administration—were characterized by a blend of tension and détente somewhat similar to that of the mid-1950s. On the one hand West Berlin was the subject of threats which appeared at times likely to lead to an acute conflict, but on the other hand diplomatic visits between the two camps reached a new level of intensity, with Khrushchev going to the United States in September 1959 and Vice President Nixon to Moscow in July 1960. The culmination of this mixture of dialogue and confrontation was reached when a general summit conference convened in Paris in May 1960, only to disperse before its sessions actually began because an American espionage aircraft had been shot down over the Soviet Union.

The essence of the demands made by Khrushchev in November 1958 was that four-power control of Berlin (officially provided for in the Potsdam Agreement) must now be regarded as ended; that the Western allies must henceforth deal with the German Democratic Republic and not with the Soviet Union in matters concerning access to West Berlin; and that, if they did not accept the new arrangements within six months, these would be unilaterally established in a direct treaty between the Soviet Union and the GDR.

These demands clearly arose from a variety of motives: Khrushchev may have wished to strengthen the position of the GDR, and hence the Soviet Union's western flank, in order to be able to deal more effectively with a threat from the rising power of China; he may have hoped to create disarray and confusion among the three Western allies, and between some of them and Bonn, in which he certainly succeeded; and he may simply have wished to see how far Russia's growing military strength could be exploited to gain some concrete or symbolic diplomatic advantage. As it transpired, the Soviet demands were almost entirely withdrawn at the end of 1962, but not before immensely laborious diplomatic activity had been undertaken—in all the capitals involved, in the Geneva Foreign Ministers' Conference of 1959, in the summit preparations of 1960, and also subsequently—as a result of the Soviet démarche of November 1958.

The impact of this démarche on German-American relations will be analysed later: for the moment it is enough to note that this Soviet pressure over Berlin, unlike that of 1948–9 which had greatly strengthened Western solidarity, had the contrary effect of opening up serious divergences between the United States, Britain, and the continental allies France and West Germany.

In addition to Berlin, the other main theme of East-West negotiations was disarmament. The talks on this subject had gone on throughout the 1950s without achieving any success, but in the West some sections of public opinion were still pressing their governments to pursue the attempt, and some Western statesmen at least—notably Eisenhower—remained optimistic. There were differences of opinion about whether the emphasis should be on nuclear or conventional disarmament, and whether, in the case of nuclear disarmament, delivery systems or nuclear stockpiles should be reduced first. There was also disagreement about whether an inspection system was necessary (and if so, of what kind) and whether certain regions, for example, Central Europe, could be singled out for special treatment. These differences of view provided material for considerable debate in 1958–60, both between and within the two military alliances.

At the same time, notable changes were taking place within the structure of the Western camp. The European Economic Community, established in January 1958, had made good enough progress in the first stages of integration for its members to decide in May 1960 to proceed with the accelerated second phase the following January. The principal members of OEEC who had decided not to join EEC—Britain, Denmark, Norway, Austria, Portugal, Sweden, and Switzerland—agreed in July 1959 to establish the European Free Trade Association, whose rules were agreed by November and which came into force in June 1960. (This followed France's refusal in November 1958 to allow a broader free trade area, proposed by Britain, to be grafted on to the EEC.)

In March 1959 de Gaulle removed the French Mediterranean fleet from NATO command, after the failure of his attempt in September 1958 to persuade Eisenhower to give France a larger say in the policy of the alliance.

The OEEC itself underwent a transformation in 1960: it was agreed in January that the organization should enlarge its functions from European co-operation to world economic development, and its membership from European states to include the United States and Canada. These changes took effect in December, and the OEEC changed its name to Organisation for Economic Co-operation and Development.

The same concern with problems of the non-European world was reflected in the discussions between the West's political leaders. The Far East and the Arab world were relatively calm during these two years (except for the continuing war in Algeria) but the granting of independence to most of France's African colonies in 1958, and to Britain's shortly afterwards, appeared to make Africa a potential source of some international tension, especially if Soviet or Chinese influence there increased. At a conference of the four Western leaders in December 1959 de Gaulle deeply impressed Adenauer by observing that the United Nations Organization would shortly comprise '30 black states, 20 Moslem states, 18 Asiatic, 10 Soviet, 18 Central or South American states, 1 or 2 other states, and only 15 Western states.' According to Adenauer, this prospect of a proliferating General Assembly led Eisenhower and Macmillan to remark that the Security Council would have to 'help,' and the subject was then dropped,[1] but the need for Western capitals to take account of non-European developments was clear: they became increasingly preoccupied by the prospect of a competition between the Western and Communist systems for influence in the Third World—to be won by economic aid and technical assistance.

In the event, the only two under-developed countries to become centres of conflict (again, apart from Algeria) were the (Belgian) Congo and Laos, and in both the situation did not become critical until 1960, as the Eisenhower presidency was nearing its end.

Internal Politics: Beginnings of Divergence

The most important change in the American political scene in this period, in so far as foreign policy was affected, was certainly the death of John Foster Dulles on 24 May 1959. The Secretary of State, suffering from cancer, had resigned in April after making a final trip to Europe in February. For Adenauer, who had come to regard co-operation with Dulles as 'our firmest anchor and our firmest support,' his death

> opened up a gap which could not be filled. For all our respect for President Eisenhower's person and his achievements, for all the firmness with which he stood up and would continue to stand up for the interests of the free world, Dulles was irreplaceable both in the necessary day-to-day routine and as a spokesman for the interests of the West in all the forthcoming East-West conferences.

Dulles's successor, his Under-Secretary, Christian Herter, although 'a clear head and a clever man', seemed to Adenauer to lack the experience and toughness which the confrontation with the Russians would need.[2]

Another disturbing feature of the Washington scene, from the German point of view, was the Republicans' loss of control of the Senate in the mid-term election of 1958: many of the leading Democrats were less than fully committed to support of Bonn. The new Chairman of the Senate Foreign Relations Committee, William Fulbright, was an apostle of East-West détente; Senators Humphrey and Mansfield were known to be optimistic about Soviet intentions and sceptical of the need to keep up American troop-levels in Europe; and in 1957 another rising star, Senator John F. Kennedy, had criticized the 'unnecessarily forced speed of German rearmament' and commented that 'Adenauer's time is now over. The main question . . . must now be the name of Adenauer's successor.' [3]

The Chancellor, naturally worried at the election results of November 1958, wrote to Dulles: 'I can imagine that . . . you will not always have an easy time. But it seems to me that Senator Humphrey has heard and seen a good deal in Moscow that was new to him.' [4] Despite Adenauer's hopeful last note, the risk of an American swing against Bonn never seemed very far away. The Eisenhower administration—already in its 'lame duck' phase as the presidential election of 1960 approached—was doubly weakened by the death of Dulles and the changes in Congress, and Adenauer continued to feel unsafe. As he told de Gaulle in December 1959, his 'thoughtful and careful' Ambassador in Washington, Wilhelm Grewe, was reporting 'a clearly visible change in the foreign policy attitude of the United States.' [5]

In fact, in the East-West discussions of 1959 and 1960, Eisenhower and Herter remained close to the lines of policy laid down by Dulles, but their style was much less firm than his, and there were many moments of great anxiety for Bonn.

The German political system, too, was going through a phase of uncertainty which demanded careful attention by Washington. The Federal President, Theodor Heuss, was due to reach the end of his second term in the summer of 1959 and from mid-April until mid-June it appeared likely that Adenauer would take over the presidency. His last letter to Dulles, written on 30 April from his Italian retreat at Cadenabbia, dealt with this subject:

> As you know, I may accept nomination for election as Federal President. I shall do this for reasons of state [*Staatsnotwendigkeiten*], to ensure the continuity of our policy. I should then put all my strength into carrying on the policy we have so successfully pursued in the last years, under the leadership of the United States.[6]

By the time this letter was written Adenauer was developing serious doubts about the wisdom of exchanging the chancellorship for the presidency, since he judged his Economics Minister

Ludwig Erhard, who appeared to be the strongest contender for the former post, as quite unsuitable. His main reason was Erhard's weakness in dealing with foreign affairs, an area vital to Adenauer and one to which, as Chancellor, he himself gave his main attention.[7] He felt he had plentiful evidence for this view. Erhard, according to Adenauer, had made a very bad impression on the American Secretary of the Treasury, Robert Anderson, by subjecting him to a two-hour lecture on how to overcome the problems of the American economy.[8] More serious, Erhard's lukewarm attitude towards European integration—as expressed, for instance, in speeches in Oslo in May 1958 and in Rome in March 1959—threatened not only to perturb Germany's partners in the Six but also to weaken America's commitment to Western Europe. Adenauer explained his position in a letter to Heinrich Krone, Chairman of the CDU parliamentary group, on 19 May 1959:

> The basis of our whole existence in foreign policy is and remains the process of European integration. Only European integration causes the United States to remain in Europe. The decisive interest that the United States takes in European integration has been expressed to me by American politicians and journalists, and also by Secretary of State Herter, in the very last few weeks. Unfortunately Herr Erhard has so far taken a somewhat unfriendly, if not directly negative attitude towards the integration of Europe. . . .[9]

When it became clear that if Adenauer moved to the presidency Erhard still stood a good chance of succeeding him, despite all his efforts, Adenauer decided that the best way of ensuring the continuity of German policy was to remain Chancellor. He went to Washington for the funeral of Dulles at the end of May, and the late Secretary's sister Eleanor Lansing Dulles, who was carefully watching the Chancellor's expression during the service in Washington Cathedral, formed the opinion that this was the moment when Adenauer made his final decision to remain in the chancellorship.[10] It has also been affirmed that a re-reading of the German constitution gave him a salutary reminder that the powers of the Federal President were substantially more limited than those of his new-found friend President de Gaulle, whose conduct of French affairs he increasingly admired.[11]

Adenauer thus stayed at his post as Chancellor, but his

failure to bar Erhard's promotion weakened his position—Erhard was strongly supported by many CDU parliamentarians [12]—and his authority never fully recovered.

It was not only on the government side that American policy-makers, looking at Bonn, had to take note of changes: the Social-Democratic Party, which had now spent ten years in opposition, after being beaten in all three federal elections, was at last equipping itself with a more appealing programme and new leadership. In November 1959 the Party conference in Bad Godesberg adopted a programme which abandoned the traditional Marxist phraseology and pledged the party to a programme of moderate reform, economic free enterprise, and support for Christian beliefs; in June 1960 the SPD's spokesman on foreign policy, Herbert Wehner, announced in a speech in the Bundestag, that the party recognized its error in opposing German rearmament, membership of NATO, and European integration, and would henceforth align it policy more closely with that of the CDU; and in October of the same year, the worthy but uninspiring party official Erich Ollenhauer was replaced as SPD ' Shadow Chancellor ' by the dynamic and popular Mayor of West Berlin, Willy Brandt.

These changes did not necessarily portend difficulties in German-American relations. Brandt, for instance, was greatly respected in Washington, and it happened that he had been the last foreign visitor to call on the dying Dulles,[13] but they did mean that the SPD stood a better chance of gaining power and that the old era of the 1950s, when right-wing governments in both Washington and Bonn sustained each other, might soon be over. In the event, Kennedy was to win power in Washington—and greatly alarm Adenauer—several years before Brandt was to become Chancellor in Bonn—and somewhat alarm Nixon.

The more immediately disturbing element on the German political scene, in the sense that it disturbed American opinion, was a strange outbreak of anti-semitic sign-painting in Germany early in 1960. The appearance of swastikas and anti-Jewish slogans on synagogues and walls all over Germany naturally aroused widespread comment in the liberal press in the United States: even though it transpired that the perpetrators were bored youngsters rather than serious neo-Nazis, the episode lingered in American memories for some time, influencing

Congressional attitudes towards Germany and making the pro-German policy of the Washington administration slightly harder to sustain.[14]

Bilateral Relations: First Strains in the 'Economic Substructure'

We have noted how the burdens of military spending had begun to cause strains in German-American relations even in 1955–8. Before 1955 Germany had paid occupation costs to the United States, as to the other occupying powers, but this arrangement had ended with the recovery of sovereignty in 1955, and the expectation had even been entertained in Bonn, though quickly disappointed by Washington, that American funds would be available to cover part of the deficit in Germany's budget caused by rearmament. Although the United States was unwilling to pay Germany's own defence expenditure, it had not been a great hardship to pay the costs of stationing troops in Germany, since it appeared to be in the interests of American policy to mitigate the shortage of dollars in Western Europe by large-scale expenditure there in dollars. It was not until some time after the renewed convertibility of European currencies in 1958 had led to a striking increase in the American balance of payments deficit in 1958–60 (in these three years it reached 11.2 (US) billion dollars, compared with only 6.5 billion in the seven years from 1951 to 1957) that the Eisenhower administration felt that any action was called for. At the end of November 1960—in fact, after Kennedy's election victory—a high-level mission led by Robert Anderson (Secretary of the Treasury) and C. Douglas Dillon (Under Secretary of State for Economic Affairs) visited Bonn to request Germany to pay an annual contribution of $600 million towards off-setting the balance of payments drain caused by the stationing of troops in Germany.

The Americans were careful to make the distinction, psychologically vital vis-à-vis German public opinion, between this kind of help with the balance of payments problem and any suggestion that this amounted to a reintroduction of the occupation costs paid before 1955: none the less, the request was rejected by the German government (which had an eye to the Bundestag elections now less than a year ahead), and counter-proposals were made. When Anderson and Dillon returned to Washington it was reported that although their talks had been 'conducted in a most friendly atmosphere' they must be 'generally regarded as fruitless'.[15] In fact a wide gap separated the two national positions.

As Heinrich von Brentano, the German Foreign Minister, told the CDU parliamentary group, West Germany would not resume the direct payment of troop costs for 'political and psychological' reasons. 'The Federal Government does not regard the question as one of prestige,' he said. 'We are, however, an equal partner of the Atlantic Alliance and the Alliance is an indivisible whole. . . . For us the support of the dollar is as important as our own security,' and for this reason West Germany was ready to accept a recent American request to other recipients of American aid not to spend these funds in such hard-currency countries as West Germany. At the same time it was announced that German-American talks would soon start on Germany's counter-proposals to Anderson and Dillon: that the dollar deficit should be mitigated by advance repayment of West Germany's $600 million post-war debt to the United States, and that Germany should pay a larger share of the costs of NATO's infrastructure in Europe.[16] The agreement that was to be reached in 1961 in fact provided for large-scale purchases by the Bundeswehr of American military equipment and weapons.[17] Both psychologically and militarily satisfactory to Germany, as well as corresponding economically to American interests, this agreement was to provide a temporary solution for a potentially acute and difficult problem.[18]

Another issue which disturbed Washington's relations with Bonn during this period was to prove of shorter duration, but created some tension while it lasted. By 1959 the Western world was suffering from surplus coal production: this was affecting the functioning of the European Coal and Steel Community established at the start of the 1950s, and it also created difficulties for coal producers in the United States. American exports of coal to Europe—especially to West Germany—had been fairly substantial, but the situation of over-production in Europe led the German government to impose a 10 per cent tariff to reduce these imports. Strong protests were made by Washington, but the German government persisted in its action.[19]

This problem was to be overcome within a few years, as coal production both in Germany and in America was reduced to the lower levels of demand. It provided, however, a further reminder that the prevailing harmony of interests between the two governments was liable to be exposed to new varieties of strain, and that West Germany would no longer obediently execute any wish expressed by Washington.[20]

Alliance Politics: Franco-German Rapprochement

As soon as General de Gaulle returned to power in France in June 1958 both Dulles and Adenauer realized that they confronted a force to be reckoned with. Dulles visited de Gaulle early in July and immediately sent a message to Adenauer, apologizing that the shortness of his stay in Europe had made it impossible for him to pay his usual visit to Bonn as well. After reporting that de Gaulle seemed confident of evolving a compromise solution for Algeria, and even for the British Free Trade Area proposal, Dulles continued:

> Undoubtedly problems will develop from the General's strong desire that France play a greater role in NATO and in the world and from his hope that France can develop her own nuclear weapons. I can see that we both may need to be conciliatory and helpful, but I have also in mind that no such developments should operate to the detriment of our own close relationships with other Western powers, including your own, or to the Western interests in other areas such as the Middle East.

Dulles expressed concern about de Gaulle's views on the custody of NATO nuclear weapons in France—that is, the claim for French control—but remained hopeful of a compromise. Adenauer, in thanking Dulles for the information on his talk with de Gaulle, contained both in letters and in a message transmitted by the American Ambassador David Bruce, gave the clear impression that the two statesmen, who had now worked together for more than five years, would closely watch the important new force represented by de Gaulle, and co-ordinate their reactions to his activities.[21]

Within a few months developments were to occur which would seriously test the German-American entente confronting the newcomer and would revive the prospect of a Franco-German front, already adumbrated in the period of Gaillard's prime ministership,[22] against presumed American neglect of

West European interests. When Khrushchev launched his demands on Berlin in November 1958, and the American response turned out to include a remarkably conciliatory statement to the effect that the West might allow East German officials to control traffic going to West Berlin as 'agents' of the Soviet Union,[23] de Gaulle happened to be conferring with Adenauer at the small German spa of Bad Kreuznach (chosen for the meeting because it was almost equidistant from Colombey-les-deux-Eglises and Adenauer's home at Rhöndorf). In the course of an earlier meeting at Colombey-les-deux-Eglises in September, Adenauer had impressed on de Gaulle the need for close Franco-German collaboration, saying that 'we could not count on the help of the United States for ever,' and that America herself might withdraw from NATO (as the treaty allowed after 1969), in the event of an unfavourable American presidential election result in 1968; he had expressed concern at the way in which the United States had 'neglected NATO for a long time', and agreed with de Gaulle's view that Western Europe should not become 'an instrument of the Americans'. He told de Gaulle that he 'had had differences of opinion with Dulles over American policy towards Russia', though he added that unity with America was essential, and that the necessary reorganization of NATO must be carried out in consultation with the Americans.[24]

At Bad Kreuznach, when Adenauer received the news of Dulles's surprising readiness to recognize East German officials as 'agents'—the American statement had not been cleared in advance with Adenauer—the Chancellor and his *entourage* were aghast at Washington's weakness, and Bonn's rapprochement with Paris was considerably expedited: the way was now open for de Gaulle to obtain German support on a number of issues, including the rejection of Britain's proposal for a European Free Trade Area to be grafted on to the EEC.[25]

Adenauer had described Britain in his earlier conversation with de Gaulle as 'a problem of the second rank, and an island',[26] and this negative view of the United Kingdom was strengthened by what he regarded as Britain's very passive response to Soviet pressure on Berlin.

At the beginning of February 1959 Adenauer was informed by the British Ambassador that the Prime Minister, Harold Macmillan, and the Foreign Secretary, Selwyn Lloyd, would

MOR—4

visit Moscow later in the month to explore the possibilities of East-West agreement. Adenauer gloomily criticized this plan as a blatant piece of electioneering, designed to appease the British public before the General Election due in May, and claimed that ' the visit by Macmillan and Lloyd would be seen throughout Russia as a triumph for Khrushchev. Its results in Asia could also be easily imagined: the West was allowing the Soviet Union to break its treaty obligations, and then falling back in the face of its threats.' [27] He was to be concerned by what he regarded as further evidence of British weakness during the Geneva Conference in the summer of 1959,[28] and his fear that the American attitude was also softening was confirmed by a message from the White House in July that he should ' stop quarrelling with Britain and close Western ranks in the face of Soviet threats '.[29]

By December 1959, when the four Western leaders met to discuss the prospects for the projected summit conference with the Russians, Adenauer was more than ever disillusioned with what he saw as the weak attitude of the United States and Britain. Eisenhower showed himself, from the Chancellor's point of view, lamentably ready to allow the Russians to change the legal status of West Berlin, and unwilling to consider the use of force to defend it, whereas de Gaulle delighted Adenauer by declaring his agreement with him ' on every point ', and forcing Eisenhower to change his views.[30]

Even though it continued to be clear that substantial differences persisted between Britain and America on the one hand and West Germany on the other,[31] Adenauer's rapprochement with de Gaulle blossomed during a series of meetings in the early part of 1960. In a conversation in Paris on 14 May, the eve of the summit conference that was not to take place, de Gaulle assured Adenauer of his support against potential concessions by Macmillan and perhaps Eisenhower on the question of an interim solution for Berlin. Adenauer again expressed concern about the state of opinion in America,[32] and—after conversations with Macmillan and Eisenhower—felt that both of them were ' very vague ' compared with de Gaulle, with whom he resolved to strengthen Germany's ties.[33]

When Adenauer visited Rambouillet for further talks on 29–30 July, after the failure of the summit conference, the same themes of Anglo-Saxon unreliability and the need for

Franco-German solidarity recurred. De Gaulle adumbrated his plans for continuous political consultations between the Six—the nucleus of the later 'Fouchet Plan'[34]—and told Adenauer that France's membership of NATO 'in its present form' could not continue for long after the American election.[35]

Adenauer, who had been somewhat perturbed to hear from the French ex-Minister Antoine Pinay earlier in the year about the extent of de Gaulle's anti-Americanism, attempted to impress both on de Gaulle and later on his Prime Minister Michel Debré the need for the closest possible links with America to be maintained.[36] However, Germany's readiness to back France's demands for a reorganization of NATO, giving its continental members a greater say in decisions of all kinds (including those concerning nuclear strategy) emerged clearly from these Franco-German meetings of 1960. The new United States administration would clearly have to face a more demanding group of European allies, among whom West Germany could no longer be automatically counted on to adopt the American point of view.

In the meantime, the Eisenhower administration—or some of its officials—were beginning to take steps to satisfy Germany's demands for a greater share in the control of the nuclear forces of the alliance. As we have seen, Franz Josef Strauss had been demanding tactical nuclear weapons for the German army since the end of 1956,[37] and by 1960 arrangements had been made for the transfer of tactical delivery vehicles to the *Bundeswehr*, the warheads to remain under a dual German and American veto. The NATO Supreme Commander in Europe, General Norstad, in fact wished to go further than this, and to give the European member governments of NATO direct control of a section of the nuclear deterrent, and the right *in extremis*, to use it without American permission.[38] However, Adenauer and Strauss clearly felt that these proposals, particularly as they did not win approval in Washington, were inadequate to meet the Franco-German wish for a restructuring of NATO. There was indeed a good deal of discussion in 1960 in NATO circles, and also in Washington, of Norstad's idea of turning NATO itself into a 'fourth nuclear power' (alongside America, Britain, and France), but everything was still in a very tentative and unsatisfactory state when the Eisenhower administration left office.

In March 1960, according to one of the best-informed journalists in Washington, Eisenhower wrote to reassure Khrushchev that there was no intention of establishing a NATO nuclear force. (In fact, added the commentator, Norstad's proposal was being systematically played down by the administration.)[39]

There was one curious episode in alliance relations early in 1960, when an ill-considered action by Germany led to considerable misgivings in America. The German military authorities, including the Defence Minister Straus, argued that West Germany lacked adequate space for large-scale manoeuvres at home, and decided to hold them in Spain. Although an ally of the United States, Spain had been excluded from NATO on the grounds that her political institutions hardly qualified her as a member of the 'free world', and Germany's action revived disagreeable memories of German military collaboration with Franco during the Civil War more than twenty years earlier. The misgivings aroused in American opinion by this episode were not long-lived, but—like the almost simultaneous outbreak of anti-semitism in West Germany[40]—it did something to make the relationship less smooth than it might have been.[41]

Relations with the Adversary: Flexibility even from Dulles

It will have become clear that a principal cause of anxiety in German-American relations from 1958 onwards, whether in the bilateral dimension or that of repercussions in the alliance, was the obvious hesitancy of Dulles's response to Khrushchev's demands concerning Berlin. Pressure from the Soviet leader began with a speech on 10 November 1958 in which he announced that the Soviet Union no longer wished to abide by the Potsdam Agreement—already violated, he claimed, by the Western powers—but proposed to hand over its responsibilities for Berlin to the German Democratic Republic.[42]

The first Western responses to this threat were firm and clear: the German Federal government declared on 12 November that a unilateral Soviet disengagement from its responsibilities in Berlin would be a breach of an international agreement, and that any attempt to change the four-power status of Berlin would threaten world peace. On the following day a

White House spokesman, without using quite such strong language, affirmed that the responsibilities of the four powers in Berlin had been freely confirmed by the Soviet Union in 1949 and formed part of internationally accepted usages.[43]

The tension grew, and it seemed that there might even be an escalation into a world war: this risk was very clearly present in the minds of decision-makers in the main capitals concerned, and it should not be forgotten in any consideration of the reasons why 'compromise' or 'interim' solutions were put forward. According to a verbal report made to the British Prime Minister in January 1959 by Sir Christopher Steel, the Ambassador in Bonn, even Adenauer was very concerned about the risks of catastrophe: 'he stands (officially) for absolute rigidity and a solid front against Soviet Russia. Behind the scenes, he wrings his hands and says that Russia and the West are like two express trains rushing to a head-on collision.'[44]

Against this background, Dulles's readiness to consider a minor compromise becomes easier to understand. Asked at a press conference on 26 November 1958 whether the United States could accept the control of traffic to West Berlin by East Germans instead of Russians, he replied that if the former were recognized to be acting as 'agents' of the latter, the suggestion might be considered.[45]

Several explanations have been given of this apparent readiness to grant a degree of recognition to the GDR, which, as we have seen, gave Adenauer such an unpleasant shock when the news reached Bad Kreuznach. It has been argued that the Secretary of State was acutely conscious that he had been accused of undue rigidity in the crises in Lebanon and Quemoy, and was now determined to show more flexibility over Berlin, especially as the stakes were much higher and the partisans of peace more vocal, both in the United States and in the German opposition.[46] Dulles's sister, who was the official in charge of German affairs in the State Department at the time, has argued that he was not giving up any fundamental Western position—the 'agent-theory' was legally acceptable—and was merely speculating in his press conference about possibilities that *might* be considered.[47]

An alternative theory is that Dulles was absolutely determined not to go to war over the right of East Germany to control traffic on the *Autobahn*, and that his readiness to entertain the idea of East German agents marked a serious shift in United States policy—the first step towards de facto recognition of the GDR and hence of Germany's division: Dulles is said to have made it absolutely clear to Adenauer, when he visited him in Bonn in February 1959, that vital interests of the United States —notably peace—were not to be compromised by rigid adherence to the principle of non-recognition of the GDR.[48]

A third view—expressed after the event by a senior German official who was closely concerned with the matter, and certainly not so relaxed about it at the time—is that Dulles was in fact carrying out a brilliant legalistic trick in proposing to admit the East Germans as ' agents ' of the USSR, since this seriously down-graded them from the position of full sovereignty officially claimed for them by the Soviet Union since 1955.[49]

Willy Brandt, Mayor of Berlin at the time, later recalled that Dulles's remarks had made the Berliners ' not very happy ' —though Dulles made a special point of saying to Brandt, when the latter reported on Berlin to the NATO Foreign Ministers in Paris the following month, ' you shouldn't worry ', and when Dulles received him in Washington in February 1959 he gave a firm assurance that there was no change in the American government's refusal to recognize East Germany.[50]

The risk of Washington's departing from the agreed American-German position on East German control over Berlin (even though Dulles was thus to minimize the importance of his declaration of 26 November 1958) was one that remained in the minds of German policy-makers. In the short run, however, this problem was overshadowed by Khrushchev's next declaration: a threat issued on 27 November that if West Berlin were not turned into a demilitarized ' free city ' within six months by international agreement, the Soviet Union would transfer her occupation rights to the GDR by a separate treaty.[51]

The Western powers again responded with firm refusals to negotiate under the threat of such an ultimatum, but again some of them—particularly the United States and Britain— began to evolve notions about possible ' compromise ' or ' interim ' solutions that might be put to the Soviet side as a basis for discussion of how to render the situation less dangerous.

Dulles once more speculated, at his press conference on 13 January, in a manner which appeared to the West Germans to amount to the abandonment of an agreed Western viewpoint. Asked whether he still believed that free elections throughout Germany were a necessary preliminary step towards reunification, which had always been the Western view, Dulles replied: 'It seems to us to be a natural method. But I wouldn't say that it is the only method by which reunification could be accomplished.' [52] He went on to suggest among other possibilities a confederation between the two German states as an alternative first step towards reunification. The project of reunification via confederation was also included in an American working-paper for the allied Foreign Ministers' Conference of 31 March–1 April in Washington, but was withdrawn after a West German complaint.[53] Although this rather long-term speculation naturally aroused less alarm in Germany than the recognition of the GDR implicit in the Secretary's statement of November,[54] it helped to contribute to German impressions of a weakening in Washington.

When Dulles visited Europe in early February—he was in fact dying and was making what Adenauer and others realized must be his last journey [55]—he reassured Adenauer that no change in America's basic position had occurred,[56] but he gave a slightly different impression in London. Macmillan was surprised to find that Dulles (and Eisenhower) had rejected an earlier Pentagon plan to respond to a new Berlin blockade by sending armed forces along the *Autobahn*, and were now envisaging more diplomatic counter-measures. More surprising still, when Macmillan put to Dulles various ideas for measures of détente in Europe—the mutual 'thinning-out' of troops, among others—the latter 'was not unduly shocked. He seemed to be ready to discuss new ideas. This may be partly the result of having lost control of Congress. . . .' [57] Another explanation of Dulles' new-found flexibility, apart from his realization of the danger of war, may have been that he was ill and tired. In any case, his hesitation on points which had hitherto been firmly agreed was a source of serious concern in Bonn.

The concern mounted after Dulles had died and as the Western negotiators at the Geneva Foreign Ministers' Conference (May–June and July–August 1959) appeared at times to be putting forward compromise proposals that could only weaken the Western position in Berlin. For instance, by 28 July the Western powers had offered the Russians, as part of an 'interim solution' leading to German reunification through free elections, an undertaking not to increase Western forces in West Berlin, not to instal atomic weapons there, and to allow the United Nations to supervise propaganda activities in both parts of Berlin. In exchange, the Russians were asked to recognize the continuing rights of the Western powers and to guarantee the access to West Berlin of their armed forces.[58] The compromise was rejected by the Russians, but while negotiations on such proposals were going on, the nervousness of the West German government inevitably persisted.

President Eisenhower gave the Chancellor further cause for alarm at the end of August, when he came to Bonn and pressed Adenauer to try a new approach to reunification by arranging exchanges of individuals on a professional basis between East and West Germany. The East German system, the President felt, would be demoralized by the patent superiority of West German factory foremen, lawyers, and others, and a first step towards reunification would have been taken. The horrified Adenauer rejected the proposal completely: not only would it be difficult to spare the foremen from their factories in West Germany, but—worse—the East Germans would send only spies or reliable Communists, and the whole scheme, far from contributing to reunification, would amount to nothing less than de facto recognition of the GDR.[59]

Eisenhower did nothing to alarm Bonn during Khrushchev's visit to the United States in September 1959, but in the Paris discussions of the four Western leaders in December he again worried Adenauer. On Berlin, Eisenhower

> . . . took the floor and made long statements which were in direct contradiction to the demand that the legal basis of the present status of Berlin should not under any circumstances be altered. He said among other things that the expressly agreed rights of the Western powers in Berlin were not important enough for public opinion outside Germany to see a breach of them as sufficient grounds for the use of force. . . . The Western powers could hardly stand up against the idea of a peace treaty between the Soviet Union and the 'DDR,' because the Western powers themselves had signed a peace treaty with the Federal Republic.[60]

This represented a false interpretation of the situation—the Western agreements of 1954 had by no means constituted a peace treaty—and Adenauer was at pains to point out the dangers of negotiating with the Russians on such a basis: as we have seen, he was strongly supported by de Gaulle in his point of view.

The year 1960 did not in fact bring any effective East-West negotiations on Berlin or on anything else. In May the summit conference was prevented from taking place by the U2 episode, and the disarmament talks held later in the year failed to register any significant progress.

There was thus relatively little risk of Eisenhower and Herter giving away any vital German interest to the Russians, but the feeling persisted in Bonn that the eyes of Washington were now turned more firmly towards détente with the Soviet Union, and that the price of the new American flexibility might be some interest deemed essential by West Germany, whether on Berlin or on reunification.

These apprehensions were to be markedly increased after the election of Senator John F. Kennedy to the presidency.

NOTES

1 Adenauer, *1959–1963* (1968), p. 26.
2 Adenauer, *1955–1959*, pp. 544–5.
3 'A Democrat Looks at Foreign Policy,' *For. Aff.*, 36/1 (1957), pp. 44–59.
4 Adenauer to Dulles, 23 Dec. 1958, Dulles Additional Papers, AM, 17034.
5 Adenauer, *1959–1963*, p. 17.
6 Adenauer to Dulles, 15 Apr. 1959, Dulles Papers, Cat. II (Correspondence).
7 It also occupies about nine-tenths of the space in his memoirs.
8 Adenauer, *1955–1959*, p. 546. Such behaviour by Erhard in America is confirmed by a report in the *New York Times*, 30 Mar. 1957.
9 Adenauer, *1955–1959*, p. 536. Adenauer's story of the whole presidential issue is given at length, ibid. pp. 489–557. See also Wolfgang Wagner, *Die Bundesprasidentenwahl 1959* (Adenauer-Studien II, 1972).
10 Private information from Eleanor L. Dulles, Washington. For the Chancellor's impression of the funeral service, see Adenauer, *1955–1959*, pp. 546–7.
11 Grosser, *Germany in Our Time*, p. 106.
12 Adenauer, *1955–1959*, p. 557. See also Arnulf Baring, 'Seine Sorge hiess Europa' (a review of Terence Prittie's biography of Adenauer), *Die Zeit*, 12 Nov. 1971.
13 See below, p. 90.

14 Newspaper reports and private information, New York and Washington.

15 *NYT*, 27 Nov. 1960. For Eisenhower's statement of 28 Nov. see *DOSB*, 43/1121 (1960).

16 *NYT*, 7 Dec. 1960.

17 H. Mendershausen, *Troop Stationing in Germany: Value and Cost* (Dec. 1968), pp. 65 ff., quoted by Elke Thiel, ' Truppenstationierung und Devisenausgleich,' *Europa-Archiv* 24/7 (1969), p. 222, footnote.

18 The situation at the time of the Anderson-Dillon mission is described in G. Barraclough, *Survey of International Affairs 1959–1960* (1964), pp. 126–9 and 565–6.

19 *NYT*, 24, 30, 31 Jan. 1959, quoted by Freund, *Germany between Two Worlds*, p. 113.

20 See Karl W. Deutsch and Louis J. Edinger, *Germany Rejoins the Powers* (1959), p. 201, for an assessment of the coal-tariff issue as an illustration of Germany's growing independence.

21 Dulles to Bruce (for transmission to Adenauer) 7 July 1958; Adenauer to Dulles, 10 July 1958; Bruce to Dulles, 11 July 1958. Dulles Papers, Cat. II (Correspondence).

22 See above, p. 67.

23 See below, p. 88.

24 Adenauer, *1955–1959*, pp. 429–35. See also C. de Gaulle, *Mémoires d'Espoir*, i: *Le Renouveau 1958–1962* (1970), pp. 184–90.

25 Private information on Adenauer's reactions. On the European Free Trade Area proposal, see Miriam Camps, *Britain and the European Community, 1955–1963* (1964), pp. 93 ff. Adenauer's memoirs make no mention of the Bad Kreuznach meeting, but its main contents are summarized in de Gaulle, pp. 190–1.

26 Adenauer, *1955–1959*, p. 432; cf. de Gaulle, p. 188.

27 Adenauer, *1955–1959*, pp. 473–5.

28 See below, p. 92.

29 *NYT*, 19 July 1959. The message was reported to have been transmitted to Adenauer by McCloy. In *Waging Peace*, p. 351, Eisenhower describes American attempts to bring Britain and Germany together.

30 Adenauer, *1959–1963* (1968), pp. 24–6. See also *New York Herald Tribune* (European edn), 22 Dec. 1959.

31 *New York Herald Tribune*, 13 Jan. 1960, cited by Adenauer, *1959–1963*, p. 29.

32 Adenauer, *1959–1963*, pp. 43–5.

33 Ibid. pp. 50–1.

34 Ibid. pp. 65–7: for a detailed account, see A. Silj, *Europe's Political Puzzle: a Study of the Fouchet Negotiations and the 1963 Veto* (1967).

35 Adenauer, *1959–1963*, p. 67. De Gaulle, p. 189, confirms that he told Adenauer as early as Sept. 1958 that France would leave the NATO system ' un jour ou l'autre '.

36 Adenauer, *1959–1963*, pp. 54–76, *passim*: Debré visited Bonn on 7 Oct. 1960.

37 See above, p. 66.

38 Norstad's views as reported by Adenauer to Debré, 7 Oct. 1960, Adenauer, *1959–1963*, p. 71. See also Norstad's television interview of Feb. 1958, in J. L. Richardson, pp. 50–1, and also D. Mahncke, *Nukleare Mitwirkung* (1972), pp. 77–80.

39 H. von Borch, ' Gezahlt wird später ', *Die Welt*, 2 Apr. 1960. The proposal made in Dec. 1960 by Herter, and later withdrawn by Kennedy, is discussed below, pp. 106–7.

40 See above, pp. 81–2.

41 Freund, *Germany between Two Worlds*, pp. 141–2, gives details.

42 For extract of his speech, see Gillian King, ed., *Documents on International Affairs 1958* (1962), p. 146, n. 4.

43 For texts, see Adenauer, *1955–1959*, pp. 451–2.

44 Harold Macmillan, *Memoirs*, iv: *Riding the Storm 1956–1959* (1971), p. 581.

45 *DOSB*, 39/1016 (1958), pp. 947–9.

46 Goold-Adams, p. 290; and private information from colleagues of Dulles.

47 She did, however, feel it necessary to go to the Secretary of State's office to warn him of the bad reception his words would have in Germany: E. L. Dulles, *John Foster Dulles, the Last Year*, pp. 211–12, supplemented by private information.

48 Private information, Washington.

49 DOHP, F. von Eckhardt interview, pp. 31–2. In his *Ein unordentliches Leben*, pp. 542–50, von Eckhardt, gives further details.

50 DOHP, Brandt interview; E. L. Dulles, as n. 47 above, p. 227. Brandt was Dulles's last visitor on his last day in the State Department, 9 Feb. 1959.

51 Jean Edward Smith, *The Defense of Berlin* (1963), pp. 166–78.

52 *DOSB*, 40/1023 (1959), p. 161.

53 H. von Siegler, *Dokumentation zur Deutschlandfrage*, II (1961), p. 181, cited by Bandulet, p. 280.

54 Adenauer does not mention the January statement in his memoirs, where he says Dulles's November remarks ' disturbed ' him: *1955–1959*, p. 466.

55 Ibid. p. 475; DOHP, von Eckhardt interview, p. 36.

56 Adenauer, *1955–1959*, pp. 476–81.

57 Macmillan, pp. 587–8.

58 *Die Welt*, 16 Apr. 1960.

59 Private information, Washington. The existence of an American tendency to press the Bonn government towards détente is confirmed by Adenauer's note to Washington recording the general situation in late January, which says that if the Berlin problem were solved, ' one could consider taking up diplomatic relations . . . with Poland and Czechoslovakia, on the suggestion of the US ': Adenauer, *1955–1959*, p. 471.

60 Adenauer, *1959–1963*, pp. 24–5.

CHAPTER SIX

Kennedy's Thousand Days: Phase I 1961–1962

Background: the Start of the Sixties

THE Kennedy administration took office in January 1961 proclaiming high hopes of creating a new world order, but it was immediately confronted with a number of pressing and intractible problems: the conflict in the Congo simmered on, and was to erupt in a new crisis with the assassination of Lumumba in February; in Laos, fighting between the rival factions continued, and a compromise solution was to be patched up only after long negotiations in Geneva; the new administration inherited a plan for military intervention against the Castro regime in Cuba, which President Kennedy was to apply in a drastically modified form (and with a total lack of success) in April; and in the issues affecting the central power balance, America's European allies and the Soviet Union were expecting new moves on the problems both of Berlin and of armaments.

Developments in all these matters were to occur during 1961, and many of them were to reach some kind of turning-point by the middle of the following year. In particular, the months of May and June 1962 saw the end of one phase of the Berlin crisis, with the public denunciation by Chancellor Adenauer of the latest series of compromise proposals under discussion between Washington and Moscow. (These talks were then practically broken off.) This period also marked a turning-point in the critical question of NATO strategy, when the Athens ministerial meeting of May 1962, followed a month later by Secretary McNamara's speech at Ann Arbor, made it clear that NATO's nuclear ' hardware ' was to be kept closely under the control of Washington, and that the European allies could expect no more than an increased degree of consultation.

The first serious test of the Kennedy administration's ability to handle foreign affairs came with the Bay of Pigs incident in April 1961. Although he abandoned any idea of using American forces to overthrow the Castro regime (in power since 1959), the new President none the less gave his support to an attempted invasion of the island by a group of Cuban émigrés hostile to Castro, who were transported to Cuba with American help. Kennedy seems to have been gravely misled by CIA assessments of the degree of support the invaders could expect from the Cuban population—wrongly reported to be seriously disaffected to Castro—and this, combined with their military incompetence, allowed them to be easily rounded up and executed by the Cuban government.

This set-back for American policy weakened Kennedy's position when he met Khrushchev (after preliminary exchanges of views with Macmillan, Adenauer, and de Gaulle) early in June in Vienna. The Soviet leader seems to have taken a strong line to the effect that Communist movements were destined to win the world-wide struggle against capitalism—Khrushchev himself was under strong pressure from the militant government of Peking, which was beginning to accuse him of collusion with Western imperialism—and he showed little readiness to make concessions to the young new President.

On Berlin, notably, Khrushchev brutally reminded Kennedy that his predecessor Eisenhower had himself conceded that the situation was ' abnormal ', and presented him with an *aide-mémoire* urging the American government to negotiate about ' improvements '.[1] Two months later, as the stream of refugees from East to West Berlin reached record proportions, Khrushchev followed words with action. On 13 August 1961 the East Germans erected barbed-wire barricades separating the Eastern and Western sectors of Berlin; these were replaced a few days later by the more solid barrier of the Berlin Wall. The Western allies protested at this further breach of the legally-ordained unity of Berlin, but it took them four days to do so, and there was clearly no serious chance that they would resist the East German action by military force.

America and her allies made it clear, by reinforcing their garrisons in West Berlin, that they would not give up their position in the city, but a more important element in their reaction, particularly the British and American reaction, was to embark on discussions with the Soviet Union about a whole range of possible measures which might de-fuse the potentially explosive situation. As will be seen, these ideas, which all implied some degree of recognition of the East German government, caused dismay in Bonn and contributed to a state of great confusion in the Western alliance.

By the early part of 1962, when France appeared to be near to disentangling herself from Algeria (the Evian Agreement providing for this was concluded in March, approved in a French referendum in April, and implemented in July), de Gaulle was able to come forward more boldly with his challenge to American leadership in NATO, and to offer the disgruntled Adenauer an alternative to the frustrations of dealing with Washington.

In other parts of Western Europe things were also on the move: in Italy the leftward evolution of the ruling Christian Democratic Party was preparing the way for the 'opening to the left' which would lead to a coalition with the Socialist Party by 1963; the British Prime Minister at last announced, at the end of July 1961, that Britain would seek entry to the European Economic Community; and the six existing members of the Community were negotiating actively, throughout 1961 and 1962, on the project for political union suggested by de Gaulle in 1960, now known as the 'Fouchet Plan'.

Despite all this activity in Europe, the Kennedy administration was also forced to direct its attention to the likelihood of conflicts—including those in Laos, the Congo, and Cuba—arising in other parts of the world, and to the prospects of removing their causes. The activities of Adlai Stevenson at the United Nations, the nominations of Chester Bowles as Under-Secretary of State, J. K. Galbraith as Ambassador to India and G. Mennen Williams as Assistant Secretary of State for African Affairs, and Kennedy's announcement of an 'Alliance for Progress' in Latin America were all evidence of this concern.

Kennedy, preoccupied by the fearful arsenals of atomic weapons now possessed by the Soviet Union as well as the United States, also paid particular heed to the views of his Scientific Adviser Jerome D. Wiesner (a promoter of the 'Pugwash' conferences with Soviet scientists) on the need to seek a constructive dialogue about arms control with the Soviet Union.

In this global perspective, which characterized Kennedy's Washington even more than the closing years of Eisenhower's, such problems as that of access to West Berlin—still obsessively prominent in the minds of Adenauer and his advisers—tended to assume the proportions of minor irritants, surely capable of solution by a rational compromise.

Internal Politics: Divergence becomes Blatant

Enough has been said to show that Washington under Kennedy was very different from Washington under Eisenhower, or under the previous Democratic administration at the start of the Fifties. As Kennedy's inaugural address put it, 'the torch has been passed to a new generation'[2] and even though several members of older generations were prominent as advisers, some of them—to German eyes at least—were less reassuring than others. On the one hand, Adenauer was delighted to see Dean Acheson appointed as an adviser on European affairs and Paul Nitze as Assistant Secretary of Defense for International Security Affairs; on the other hand, however, the return to office of Averell Harriman as Ambassador-at-large, George Kennan as Ambassador to Yugoslavia, and Walt Rostow as a White House adviser (later Head of the State Department's Planning Staff) brought men back to Washington who either had last had official dealings with Germany in the Roosevelt and immediate post-war periods (as in the case of Harriman and Rostow), or else (like Kennan) had openly disapproved of the entire policy of building up West Germany carried out by Acheson and Dulles.

Despite all the thinking the Democratic Party had given to future policy during its eight years in opposition,[3] Kennedy's early months in office were inevitably a time of improvisation and uncertainty. As a leading authority on the presidency has remarked, 'The first twelve to eighteen months become a learning time for the new President who has to learn—or unlearn—many things about his job.'[4] Even when the span of eighteen months came to an end, the American foreign policy apparatus struck one experienced observer as still being far from 'a unified, coherent, purposeful instrument. It appears, rather, as a whole congeries of groups, and sub-groups, and committees, and personages all relentlessly traveling in their own directions.'[5]

It is not surprising that Adenauer, when he went to Washington to meet the new President in April 1961 (he had indicated a wish to go earlier, but had been told that 'jumping the queue' would be unwelcome[6]) formed the opinion that Kennedy was surrounded by 'too many "cooks"': his impression, as he told de Gaulle a month later, was that Kennedy's most influential advisers in European affairs would be Vice President Johnson, Dean Acheson, and Henry Kissinger.[7]

The new administration was of course preoccupied with an enormous spectrum of issues, from global security to domestic reform, and the part of this that concerned Germany naturally represented only a small section of the whole. In so far as the President's attention was directed towards this section of the range of foreign-policy issues, he was subject to two main currents of influence. There was the traditional State Department view that laid great weight on consulting with Germany, and not deviating from agreed positions, since this was likely to cause alarm in Bonn: this view was represented, in the President's entourage, by Dean Acheson, General Lucius Clay, Paul Nitze (a Kennedy speech-writer in the 1950s, and now in a key position in the Defense Department), and of course the State Department, particularly the Office of German Affairs and, higher up, the Assistant Secretary of State for European Affairs, Foy D. Kohler and his Deputy (and in 1962 successor) William R. Tyler.[8]

Several variants of the opposite viewpoint—that the vital priority was for a global dialogue with the Soviet Union and that relations with the West European allies might have to take second place—were well represented among the galaxy of innovators brought into the White House and elsewhere by the new President with the aim of generating alternative options to those put up by the Department of State. (It should be added that the President usually waited for State Department suggestions before turning elsewhere.) They included Averell Harriman (Ambassador-at-large, later Under-Secretary of State), Chester Bowles (Under-Secretary, later Ambassador to India), George Kennan, Jerome D. Wiesner (Scientific Adviser), McGeorge Bundy (Special Assistant for International Security Affairs) and Bundy's assistant Carl Kaysen, Arthur Schlesinger, Theodore Sorensen, to some extent Henry Kissinger, and others. The spokesmen for this second viewpoint, who, it should be emphasized, represented a wide range of opinions on the issues concerned, were strongly backed from Congress by influential men including Senators Fulbright, Mansfield, and Humphrey.

As will be seen, the tension between the two alternative policies for America, ' bipolarity or alliance cohesion ',[9] was still undecided by 1962: nothing critical had been given away with regard to the Western presence in West Berlin, but on the broader issues of whether and how to negotiate with the Russians about Berlin's future and the strategic balance, the innovators had brought about a marked change from the days of Dulles.

Washington was not the only capital to go through a phase of unsettlement in 1961–2. In Bonn, too, Adenauer's standing had still not recovered from the setback of 1959 [10] (it never did) and his position in 1961 was very weak. He appears to have assumed that he would win the Bundestag elections of 17 September 1961 without difficulty—election posters of the wise old Chancellor and his Economics Minister Erhard standing closely shoulder-to-shoulder were designed for effect, though they hardly corresponded with the reality—and it was therefore a surprise when the CDU lost 28 seats, while the SPD gained 21.[11] The CDU thus lost its absolute majority in the Bundestag, and Adenauer was forced to resume the coalition with the Free Democrats which he had dropped with relief in 1957. The negotiations on the new coalition lasted until November, and during these critical weeks the cohesion and standing of Adenauer's government were naturally undermined. The FDP Ministers who entered the new Cabinet, including the new Vice-Chancellor Erich Mende, had views on foreign policy somewhat different from Adenauer's. So did the new Foreign Minister Gerhard Schröder, who represented the more ' Atlanticist ' Protestant wing of the CDU, whereas his predecessor Heinrich von Brentano was a Catholic ' European ' and a faithful disciple of Adenauer. This change strengthened the view in German foreign policy that it was vital to keep in step with the United States. Adenauer himself had responsively begun speaking of the need for more flexibility in East-West relations as soon as Kennedy was elected President, and Strauss was also emphasizing the need for close Atlantic unity.[12] But there were divisions underlying this apparent harmony.

Thus, if the Bonn government regarded the Kennedy administration as divided and unreliable, the government of Adenauer was regarded in Washington as ' deeply neurotic '.[13] According to one of his advisers, Kennedy ' found Adenauer hard to please and hard to budge, and his government hard put to keep a secret.' [14] It was a standard Washington complaint at this time that the Bonn government was in the habit—especially on any issue affecting East-West negotiations—of leaking American draft proposals to the press, so as to be able to disparage them publicly.[15]

One of the obstacles to close consultation between the American and West German governments during the Kennedy period was that the German Ambassador in Washington, Wilhelm Grewe, was not successful in establishing good relations with the new administration. Like most German officials, he was perturbed at the prospect of American-Soviet relations' improving at the expense of America's allies, but his over-insistent way of drawing attention to the problem did nothing to contribute to its solution. During the anxious weeks of waiting early in 1961, while the new administration was thinking out its position on Germany (as events showed, not very thoroughly) Grewe made a speech in Boston in which he said that Germany, without expecting her relations with America to be a ' love-affair ', really wanted to know whether she was regarded as an ally or a trouble-maker in America's foreign policy.[16]

In the difficult period from September to November 1961, while Adenauer was struggling to form his new government, and the Berlin Wall had sharpened the need for East-West discussions, Grewe in Washington was repeatedly pressed to state the German view. He did so—naturally, given the lack of precise instructions from Bonn—in terms which struck his interlocutors as inflexible and legalistic, and helped to weaken his standing with the administration.[17] At this time, for instance, during a television interview with Robert Ellsworth, a Republican

Congressman and future Ambassador to NATO, he reminded his American audience that Germany had been ' pressed ' to join NATO in 1954, and had done so only despite ' considerable obstacles ' in ' getting German opinion used to the idea of rearmament '.[18]

In general, Grewe appears to have been much less successful in adapting to the style of the Kennedy administration than his French and British colleagues Hervé Alphand and David Ormsby-Gore—the latter a personal friend of the President. This situation is said to have made Grewe nervous in his dealings with Kennedy, and to have reduced his effectiveness in representing German interests at a difficult and critical time.[19] As we shall see, relations between Washington and Bonn worsened by the summer of 1962 to the point where Grewe, though not responsible for the deterioration, was recalled to Bonn at Washington's request.[20]

Bilateral Relations: Common Interests and Common Problems

In the words of one of Kennedy's advisers: ' Kennedy altered the Dulles policy of regarding the Chancellor as our principal European advisor and Adenauer knew it.'[21]

It has been claimed that during the same period another of Kennedy's advisers, Acheson, ' repeatedly ' offered ' a bilateral treaty between the Federal Republic and the USA ' to a member of Adenauer's Cabinet.[22] Such a move needless to say, would not have corresponded with the Kennedy administration's prevailing view, and no word of the projected treaty was ever heard in public. The relationship between Bonn and Washington was in fact characterized by increasingly hard bargaining between two somewhat distant partners, in contrast to the pronounced harmony of the Dulles era.

The main subject for negotiation was the cost of maintaining American troops in Germany. As we have seen, the American balance of payments deficit had led at the end of the Eisenhower administration to urgent efforts to secure larger German financial contributions, and the German government, while resistant to any form of direct subsidy, had agreed to consider large military purchases from the United States.[23]

The ensuing German-American negotiations, which produced an agreement by the autumn of 1961, started on the basis of a series of actually or potentially convergent interests on the part of the two governments and of those of their agencies directly concerned. The equipment of the *Bundeswehr*, whose strength had now reached 380,000, was largely American and had been supplied under military grant aid or under military assistance programmes. The American balance of payments deficit and Germany's surplus made any further grants undesirable, but on the other hand continued procurement from America was desirable both for re-equipment and for the *Bundeswehr*'s continuing growth. American suppliers were keen and well prepared to continue exporting to Germany, whereas German industry was neither prepared nor eager, in view of flourishing domestic and foreign markets for other products. The Defense Department in Washington favoured the sale of arms to a NATO ally, who would thus be further committed to service and replace them from American rather than other sources.

Among various groups on the German side the interest in American weapons was strong for at least four reasons: they would ensure that the *Bundeswehr* was equipped with similar weapons to those of its main partner, the American army; they would facilitate a common handling of supply, maintenance, and other logistics tasks within NATO, which had been strongly supported by Franz Josef Strauss as Defence Minister; they seemed a small price for Germany to pay to ensure a sustained, or even increased, American military presence, regarded as essential in view of the continuing Berlin crisis; and they were technically the 'best buy' available, in terms of delivery dates, quality, and often price.

The agreement concluded in the autumn of 1961 by Strauss and the American Deputy Secretary of Defense, Roswell L. Gilpatric, reflected these convergent interests. It provided for German procurement of new equipment from the United States, American supply and maintenance support for the existing equipment of the *Bundeswehr*, the use by the *Bundeswehr* of American training facilities, and a number of research and development projects with shared costs. It was calculated that German payments for these supplies and services would be large enough to offset the entire German-currency payments of the US forces in Germany. From 1962 onwards, when the agreement came into effect, a solution appeared to have been found to the most acute problem of German-American bilateral relations.[24] In the course of time, however, the limitations of the 1961 agreement were to come plainly to light.

Alliance Politics: the Calm before the Storm

In strategy as well as in foreign policy, the Kennedy administration undertook a thorough reappraisal of existing American policies. Of necessity, the first stage of the reassessment carried out by Secretary of Defense McNamara and his colleagues concerned America's own needs and capabilities. One commentator, remarking favourably on the strategic reassessment made by the Kennedy administration in its first eight months—inevitably concentrated on America's own defence policy—observes: 'Exactly what it [i.e. the reassessment] would mean for NATO would become apparent only when America's long-term military programme had gained sufficient scope and momentum to permit a range of new decisions and initiatives concerning allied strategy and capabilities.' [25]

This meant that an important proposal submitted to the NATO Council in December 1960 by Herter, on behalf of the Eisenhower administration, was shelved until further notice. This was the notion of making NATO itself a 'fourth atomic power' by establishing a force of 5 submarines with a total of 80 Polaris missiles, as well as 100 further land-based missiles.[26] This suggestion, which corresponded with the wishes of the Supreme Allied Commander in Europe, General Norstad, was very welcome to the German government: as we have seen, Strauss had been pressing for a greater say in nuclear defence since 1957,[27] and he now proposed a NATO summit conference for spring 1961, to work out the details.[28] It must have been with this aim in mind that Strauss made an unexpected visit to Washington in January 1961, but the capital appears to have been preoccupied with Kennedy's inauguration and its consequences, and Strauss made no contact with the new administration.[29]

The German Defence Minister made further references to the Norstad/Herter proposal during 1961.[30] His repeated suggestions during this and the following year, that NATO should develp into a full 'Atlantic Union' must also be understood as an attempt to keep the idea alive: for instance, his speech at Georgetown University in November 1961 in which he insisted that there were no fundamental conflicts of interest between Europe and the United States, and argued in favour of political institutions for an Atlantic union to replace the illusory powers of 'sovereign' national governments.[31] A month later, in a broadcast talk in Germany, he insisted that the question of making NATO into a fourth atomic power 'absolutely must' be decided in the course of the coming year, 1962.[32]

However, the Norstad/Herter plan had come under increasing opposition since its official presentation in December 1960 and the Kennedy administration's hesitation about it the following month. The idea of creating a new centre of nuclear decision-making in NATO ran counter to the doctrine of 'flexible response' advanced in the writings of General Maxwell Taylor (notably the book he had published in 1959, *The Uncertain Trumpet*) and now espoused by Senator McNamara. This doctrine, in origin a reaction against the theory of 'massive retaliation' preached by Dulles in 1954, demanded the broadest possible span of responses by the United States to any conceivable level of Soviet threat: a small conventional incursion should be answered by slightly superior conventional forces, and a scale of deterrence should proceed by graduated steps up to all-out nuclear retaliation. If this strategy was to be credible it obviously demanded the strengthening of the West's conventional forces—in contrast to the reductions envisaged in the Radford Plan of 1956.[33]

The views contained in Maxwell Taylor's book were taken very seriously in Germany; by the time its German edition appeared in 1962, the author had been Kennedy's military adviser for over a year, and his appointment as Chairman of the Joint Chiefs of Staff was announced in July 1962.[34] The book, and the author's new position, made it appear uncertain that American nuclear weapons would be used except in the event of a nuclear attack on the United States, and thus—as de Gaulle and his strategic advisers were already arguing, not to mention the less publicized arguments for the British independent deterrent—the European members of NATO could no longer count on the automatic protection of the American nuclear umbrella which Dulles had offered them, at least verbally, in the 1950s.

Although American spokesmen, including Secretary McNamara and Assistant Secretary Nitze, tried to reassure Europeans that their security was not in any way diminished, since the Soviet government clearly had no aggressive intention,[35] the German view was not so optimistic, especially after the building of the Berlin Wall. From Bonn it seemed as if Washington and Moscow were moving towards a tacit agreement not to use nuclear weapons against each other, which could only mean—if Soviet intentions continued to be expansionist—that the exposed outposts of the Western alliance, in particular Germany, were in greater danger of a Soviet attack.

As de Gaulle was not slow to remind the Germans, the new American strategic doctrine potentially created a serious distinction between the security of the United States herself and that of her European allies. When de Gaulle attempted to correct this possible imbalance by creating a French nuclear force, he did so against strong American disapproval: it even appeared to some European critics of Kennedy that he wished to establish a division of labour within the alliance, whereby America would produce the nuclear forces and Europe the conventional ones. When Kennedy met Adenauer in April 1961 and assured him that he intended to strengthen America's commitment to NATO, he left no doubt that her European partners were in return expected to bring their own conventional forces up to the levels desired by Washington.[36]

The Norstad/Herter proposals were not discussed in Kennedy's talk with Adenauer,[37] and in the following month, when Kennedy delivered a speech in Ottawa, he made it clear that the five submarines to be allocated to the NATO theatre of operations would be kept under close American command, and that the development of a NATO nuclear force 'multilateral in the true sense' could be considered only if NATO as a whole brought up its conventional strength to the agreed goals.[38]

In November 1961 Kennedy took an initiative which the Germans regarded as tactless, if not insulting: true to his policy of seeking a dialogue with the Soviet Union on world security, he gave an interview to Khrushchev's son-in-law Alexey Adzhubey, Editor of *Izvestiya* in which he went out of his way to say that West Germany 'for the moment' represented no threat to the Soviet Union, since she had no nuclear weapons and her conventional forces were firmly integrated within NATO. He went on to tell his interlocutor, however, that 'if this situation changed, if Germany developed an atomic capacity of its own, if it developed many missiles or a strong national army that threatened war, then I would understand your concern and I would share it.' Kennedy went on to speak of possible common American and Soviet interests in such a situation.[39]

From the American point of view it was therefore not surprising that emphasis was laid on Germany's increasing her conventional forces,[40] and that the Norstad/Herter plan should have been finally buried at the NATO ministerial meeting in Athens in May 1962. Until then Strauss and Norstad had hoped to carry out at least three objectives: that the *Bundeswehr* should be fully equipped with the small-scale nuclear weapon 'Davy Crockett'; that the European members of NATO should receive medium-range ballistic missiles (as envisaged by Herter at the end of 1960) to counter-balance the Soviet rockets targeted on Western Europe; and that the McNamara-Maxwell Taylor concept of 'flexible response' should not be adopted as NATO's official strategic doctrine. There was a fourth point on which Strauss sought American assurances: that the European NATO governments should be given more information about the atomic weapons based on their soil, and an assurance that they would be neither fired nor withdrawn without full consultation.[41] The Athens meeting and the ensuing discussions failed to give Germany satisfaction on any of these points—except for a slight improvement in the degree of consultation [42]—and the lesson was underlined by Secretary McNamara's speech at Ann Arbor on 16 June. This speech, stressing Washington's determination to achieve centralized (i.e. American) control of all the nuclear forces of the alliance, denounced other independent nuclear forces as costly and provocative, and invited its European members to concentrate on contributing conventional forces. Great alarm was caused in Germany.[43] It should be said that Germans were not used to the style of government practised by Kennedy and his leading officials, which included trying out explosive new ideas in public and awaiting reactions. Also neither the government in Bonn nor the German embassy in Washington at that time possessed the knowledge of strategic theory necessary to follow the sophisticated logic of the McNamara Doctrine in all its detail,[44] so its impact was more alarming to Germans than it might otherwise have been.

In any case, Adenauer had for some years been perturbed about America's declining concern with Western Europe—in a talk with de Gaulle in Baden-Baden in February he had unburdened himself of a long discourse on the subject [45]—and for him the McNamara speech did no more than complement the painful impressions created by American behaviour on many other issues. As for Strauss, who was in America immediately before the Ann Arbor speech but was given no warning of it,[46] McNamara's action marked a clear failure for his policy of associating Germany with some form of nuclear 'hardware' through a NATO force. It was to make Strauss deeply sceptical of the MLF version of this idea as it developed during 1963 (by which time, however, the *Spiegel* affair of November 1962 had forced him to resign as Defence Minister).

The first eighteen months of the Kennedy administration were thus a period when several factors within the Atlantic Alliance—of which disagreements about nuclear strategy and the rise of de Gaulle were the most obvious—imparted a new degree of tension into the German-American relationship.

Relations with the Adversary: Washington's Worst Berlin Crisis

Even before the Wall divided the two parts of Berlin in August 1961 the Western allies faced a most serious situation there. Khrushchev's threat to sign a separate peace treaty with the German Democratic Republic, handing over Soviet authority in Berlin, had still not been withdrawn, and the Kennedy administration made it clear from the start that the negotiations broken off by the fiasco of the 1960 summit conference would one day have to be resumed. In March 1961, while the administration was working out its position on Berlin (in particular, attempting to assess how the problem fitted into the broader perspectives of an improved East-West relationship dear to the President and his advisers) Averell Harriman, Kennedy's Ambassador-at-large, announced that the negotiating positions adopted in 1959 and 1960 were withdrawn, and that 'all discussions on Berlin must begin from the start.' [47]

When Khrushchev and Kennedy met in Vienna at the beginning of June, Khrushchev produced a forcible reminder that the 'abnormal' situation of West Berlin needed to be regularized, and pressed on Kennedy an *aide-mémoire* reiterating the Soviet views of 1958 onwards.[48]

Kennedy, basing his reply on a paper worked out by Dean Acheson in April, replied that in the American view the essential elements of a settlement were: freedom for the West Berliners to choose their own political system; the presence of Western troops in West Berlin as long as the Berliners wanted them, and unimpeded travel between the West and West Berlin by means of the *Autobahn*, railway, canal, and air lanes. Kennedy reminded Khrushchev that the United States presence in West Berlin had existed for fifteen years. 'He had not,' he said firmly, 'assumed the office of the presidency to accept arrangements totally inimical to American interests.'[49]

In response to Khruschchev's demands officials in Washington prepared a reply which was discussed in July and early August. The State Department's working paper of 18 July is said to have been a dull reiteration of the standard Western view that any weakening on Berlin would demoralize West Germany and encourage the Soviet Union to make further demands,[50] whereas some of the President's less conventional advisers urged the need to explore ways of preventing the situation from escalating into acute conflict. Senators, Fulbright, Humphrey, and Mansfield were pressing for accommodation with the Russians—the last-named suggested placing the whole of Berlin under United Nations control as a 'free city', while the White House advisers Carl Kaysen, Arthur Schlesinger, and Henry Kissinger also favoured 'a more aggressive canvas of diplomatic possibilities.'[51]

In considering Washington's approach to the Berlin problem it is important to note that the central issue, as indicated by Kennedy's statement to Khrushchev, was the status of *West* Berlin. American attention was concentrated on preserving the position of the *Western* part of the city, whereas Bonn, quite naturally, wanted to keep the way open for German reunification—which meant that the legal unity of *the whole* of Berlin should be stressed as strongly as possible. Bonn also believed that the ultimate disappearance of the GDR would be facilitated by a firm refusal to have any official dealings with it, and thought that negotiations would strengthen its position by implying diplomatic recognition.

These differences between Washington and Bonn were to come sharply to the surface after the Soviet and East German governments made their next move, the building of the Berlin Wall on 13 August; the Americans—and still more the British, though their position was less important—took the view that negotiation with the East (including at some stage the GDR) was a logical and necessary way to 'de-fuse' the situation, whereas for Bonn, any negotiation with or concerning the GDR as a government could only have the consequence of hardening the division of Germany.

The Bonn government was thus profoundly perturbed at the correspondence that Kennedy began with Khrushchev in September 1961: its existence was known in Bonn, though not its contents, and it lent credence to the belief that Washington had prior knowledge of the East German intention to build the Wall, and had tacitly encouraged it.[52]

In his letters to Khrushchev, Kennedy appears to have tried to dissuade the latter from signing a peace treaty with East Germany—which, he said, would only provoke violent resentment in Bonn—but he and his officials made numerous suggestions for changing the situation so as to reduce the tension. These suggestions provided for the establishment of East-West technical commissions on access and contacts (a revival of the 1959 'Western Peace Plan'); adjudication of the Berlin issue by the World Court; agreement to make all Berlin a 'free city'; agreement to preserve the status quo for a fixed term, five or ten years; the transfer of the United Nations headquarters to Berlin; a security plan for all of Central Europe; and the setting-up of an International Access Authority controlling the routes between West Berlin and the West.[53]

It was this last-mentioned proposal that particularly antagonized the Bonn government, since every variant of the scheme included East Berlin and/or the GDR as partners in the proposed international authority, and such upgrading appeared likely to foreclose the changes of reunification. Kennedy is said to have realized, in retrospect, that he was making a serious mistake in committing 'the folly of pressing upon the Germans and other allies solutions which were not really negotiable [to the Russians] anyway,' but his approach was that by trying out a variety of ideas an acceptable compromise for the problem of Berlin could be found, as it had been for that of Austria in 1955.[54] In Bonn such an approach aroused horror, which became more acute as detailed negotiations between Washington and Moscow began at the end of 1961.[55]

Kennedy had discussed the internationalization of the access routes to and from West Berlin with Gromyko in September and Adzhubey in November, and he and Rusk apparently accepted the view expressed by the new German Foreign Minister Gerhard Schröder that the forthcoming talks should be limited to Berlin alone, without bringing in the broader question of European security which would inevitably have raised that of the status of East Germany.[56]

Early in 1962 the talks on Berlin were being pursued in Moscow by Gromyko and the American Ambassador Llewellyn Thompson, and it was arranged that they should be continued by Rusk and Dobrynin (the new Soviet Ambassador to Washington) in mid-April. The American government worked out two position papers, which were presented to Bonn via Ambassador Grewe on 10 April, with a request for any German comments to be made within twenty-four hours.[57] Adenauer insisted on more time, called a meeting of CDU leaders, and then, on 12 April, declared his agreement in principle with the American suggestions (on the assumption that the Soviet government would turn them down).[58]

The Chairman of the CDU/CSU parliamentary group, von Brentano, then transmitted the essence of the American paper to a group of Bonn journalists, and it was published the next day.[59] This action unleashed the worst storm in German-American relations since the war. The Department of State complained of a 'flagrant breach of diplomatic usage' which had caused 'incurable harm' to relations between the two countries, the more so as this was not the first German indiscretion of the kind.[60] Adenauer is said to have wished to return Rusk's telegram of protest because of its violent tone,[61] and the content of Adenauer's counter-protest is said to have been diluted by the Embassy in Washington before transmission to the State Department.[62]

The document which had caused this unprecedented rift between Washington and Bonn contained three main proposals: that the United States and the Soviet Union should undertake not to hand over nuclear weapons to third parties; that NATO and the Warsaw Pact should exchange declarations of non-aggression; and that a number of all-German committees should be established to deal with technical contacts and agreements between the two parts of Germany.[63] These points, together with the particularly delicate suggestion of an international control authority for Berlin (including neutral states and also East Germany), were the substance of the German 'leak' to the press in mid-April.[64]

Despite Bonn's indiscretion, Rusk's talks with Dobrynin began on 16 April and this exchange of views was still in progress when Rusk met Schröder at the NATO ministerial meeting in Athens at the beginning of May. Schröder apparently expressed no objection to the continuation of the Rusk-Dobrynin talks (it is said that not even Couve de Murville took exception to them)[65] and American diplomats were still congratulating themselves on the 'reasonableness' of Adenauer's new Foreign Minister when the old Chancellor made a series of public statements in Berlin which were unprecedentedly critical of American policy. He had apparently brooded for three weeks in his Italian retreat at Cadennabia, then flew to Berlin, and, in the words of one commentator, 'smashed as much alliance-policy porcelain as he possibly could.'[66] Adenauer's Berlin statements dismissed Kennedy's idea of a Berlin access authority as unworkable; poured open sarcasm on Rusk's attempts to negotiate an agreement with the Soviet Union; urged the United States to break off the talks before any more harm was done; and finally dropped a hint that British membership of the EEC—on which Kennedy set great store—was not necessarily desirable.[67]

Adenauer told the American journalist James Reston that the text of Rusk's complaint to Schröder was more 'wounding' than anything he had experienced as Chancellor, and the American government also took the matter very seriously: on 8 May, the day after Adenauer's outburst in Berlin, it was announced that Ambassador Grewe—with whom the American administration had refused to communicate since the indiscretions of April—was being recalled to Bonn at Washington's request.

The exchange of views between Washington and Moscow continued, though with no immediate result. The Cuban crisis of October was to reduce Soviet pressure on Berlin, with the result that none of the suggestions for Berlin access-arrangements were to be discussed in any detail; and the notion of non-aggression agreements between NATO and the Warsaw Pact was only to be revived—and even then not implemented—in connection with the Test Ban Treaty a year later.

By the summer of 1962 German-American relations had reached their worst condition since the war: at every level—incompatibility between the two regimes, disagreement about their mutual obligations, deadlock about arrangements in the alliance, and discord about dealings with the adversary—it was time for a new start.

NOTES

1 Theodore C. Sorensen, *Kennedy* (1965), p. 584; Arthur Schlesinger, Jr, *A Thousand Days* (1965), pp. 380–4.

2 USA, President, *Public Papers of the Presidents of the United States: John F. Kennedy . . . January 20 to December 31, 1961* (1962), p. 1.

3 Schlesinger, pp. 299 ff.

4 Richard E. Neustadt, *Presidential Power: the Politics of Leadership* (1968 edn.), p. 198.

5 Joseph Alsop, *Washington Post*, 23 May 1962, quoted by Marshall, p. 84. The way in which Kennedy in 1961 ' tossed into the ashcan most of the national security machinery created by his predecessors ' is described in a most informative article by a participant, John C. Ausland, ' Crisis Management: Berlin, Cyprus, Laos ', *For. Aff.*, Jan. 1966, pp. 290–303.

6 D. C. Watt, *Survey of International Affairs 1961* (1965), p. 67.

7 Adenauer, *1959–1963*, pp. 91, 101. Adenauer was wrong in thinking that any of these three men would have any substantial influence on the new President's policy.

8 Private information, Washington. This group's view on the need for consultation with Bonn was expressed by Acheson in an article in the *New York Times*, 15 Dec. 1963: ' unexpected or unexplained action nearly always causes consternation in Germany.' There was to be plenty of such action during the Kennedy presidency.

9 This slogan is the title of a perceptive Adelphi Paper by Curt Gasteyger (1966), *The American Dilemma: Bipolarity or Alliance Cohesion?*

10 See above, pp. 79–81.

11 Grosser, *Germany in Our Time*, p. 129; Sorensen, p. 591, says the German government was visibly unable to take decisions during the summer of 1961, as the election approached.

12 H. von Borch, ' Kennedy und Deutschland ', *Die Welt*, 19 Nov. 1960; Bandulet, pp. 148–52.

13 Sorensen, p. 597, reports that this expression was used even by one of the Bonn government's ' admirers ' in Washington.

14 Ibid. p. 559.

15 Ibid. p. 597, and private information, Washington. An instance of a German ' leak ' in 1959 is recorded in Bandulet, p. 155, following F. von Eckhardt's ' confession '.

16 *New York Herald Tribune*, 16 Mar. 1961, cited by Watt, *Survey of International Affairs 1961*, p. 49.

17 Private information, Bonn.

18 Television appearance, 22 Sept. 1961: for German text, see Bandulet, p. 169.

19 Private information, Washington.

20 See below, p. 114.

21 Sorensen, p. 559. An instance of Adenauer's ' astonishing influence ' over Eisenhower is cited by Bandulet, p. 257.

22 This claim was made by Heinrich Krone, the Minister in question: see Bandulet, p. 278.

23 See above, p. 83.

24 The above account is based on Mendershausen, pp. 73–6.

25 Robert E. Osgood, *NATO, the Entangling Alliance* (1962), p. 356.

26 Bandulet, p. 157, and sources there given.

27 See above, pp. 61, 66.

28 Bandulet, p. 157.

29 Watt, *Survey of International Affairs 1961*, p. 47.

30 See e.g. his article in *Aussenpolitik*, Feb. 1961, cited in Watt, *Survey of International Affairs 1961*, p. 47.

31 Bandulet, p. 147.

32 On 20 Dec. 1961, quoted ibid. p. 152.

33 See above, pp. 63–5.

34 Bandulet, p. 137.

35 J. L. Richardson, pp. 73–83; Bandulet, pp. 137–8 and 277.

36 Adenauer, *1959–1963*, pp. 92–3; Watt, *Survey of International Affairs 1961*, p. 49.

37 Adenauer, *1959–1963*, pp. 91–9; for the communiqué, see D. C. Watt, ed., *Documents on International Affairs 1961* (1965), pp. 151–2.

38 Bandulet, p. 158, and sources there given.

39 *Public Papers of the Presidents of the United States: John F. Kennedy . . . January 20 to December 31, 1961*, p. 751.

40 Bandulet, p. 158, reports Strauss's reactions to this pressure.

41 Ibid. pp. 151 and 159.

42 Ibid. pp. 159–60.

43 Ibid. pp. 139–40; text of speech in *Survival*, 4/5 (1962), pp. 194–6.

44 Private information, Washington.

45 Adenauer, *1959–1963*, pp. 136–50.

46 Bandulet, ch. e.

47 Schlesinger, p. 341.

48 See above, p. 98 and sources there given.

49 Sorensen, pp. 583–5.

50 Ibid. pp. 587 and 596; Schlesinger, pp. 383–4.

51 Schlesinger, p. 384: even Acheson is said not to have excluded the idea of negotiation with the Russians.

52 Bandulet, p. 161, quotes Senator Fulbright's (legally incorrect) statement of 2 Aug. 1961 that the East Germans would have a right ' to close their frontier ', and underlines Kennedy's failure on 10 Aug. to disavow this statement. On Kennedy's correspondence with Khrushchev, and Bonn's knowledge of this, see Bandulet, p. 282.

53 Sorensen, p. 599.

54 Ibid. pp. 598 and 600.

55 The differences in perspective between Bonn and Washington are analysed in a perceptive article by William Griffith, ' Die Bundesrepublik in Amerikanischer Sicht ', *Aussenpolitik*, 13/3 (1962), pp. 157–64.

56 H. von Borch, ' Anatomie einer Entzweiung ', *Aussenpolitik*, 13/6 (1962) pp. 357–60.

57 This chronology, given by von Borch, ibid., varies slightly from that given by Bandulet, p. 166.

58 Bandulet, p. 166.

59 Ibid. p. 282, supplemented by private information, Bonn.

60 Bandulet, p. 166, and sources there cited.

61 Smith, p. 335.

62 von Borch, *Aussenpolitik*, 13/6 (1962), p. 359.

63 Bandulet, p. 167.

64 Ibid. p. 283.

65 von Borch, *Aussenpolitik*, 13/6 (1962), p. 360.

66 Ibid.

67 Ibid.; Bandulet, p. 168. The last point shows clear traces of the influence of de Gaulle, but Adenauer's (unfinished) memoirs for this period make no direct reference to this matter.

CHAPTER SEVEN

The Thousand Days: Phase II 1962–1963

Background: from Cuba to the Test Ban Treaty

THE period from mid-1962 to the death of President Kennedy in November 1963 witnessed the gravest episode of the Cold War, the Cuban missile crisis of autumn 1962: yet before it ended, the super-powers had formalized their intention of stabilizing their relationship and starting to settle their differences by signing the Partial Test Ban Treaty of August 1963. The Cuban crisis, in fact, precipitated the search for a modus vivendi: in the frequently quoted words of Dean Rusk, when the two super-powers had confronted one another 'eyeball to eyeball' over Cuba they recoiled together from the brink of the abyss; the dialogue which led to the Test Ban Treaty (and to the 'hot line' linking Washington and Moscow) was an attempt to prevent such crises from occurring again.

The Cuban missile crisis began with the American discovery in August 1962 that substantial numbers of Soviet missiles, capable of reaching targets in the United States, were being installed in Cuba. This act was of course perfectly legitimate in international law, but in substance it was a provocative challenge to the balance of power in the American hemisphere, which the Kennedy administration decided was intolerable. The 'Thirteen Days' in October during which the United States forbade the Soviet Union to send more missiles to Cuba, imposed a naval blockade to prevent this, and ran a considered risk of nuclear war, have been fully described and documented:[1]

the outcome of the crisis was a clear moral victory for Kennedy, in that Khrushchev agreed to remove the Soviet missiles already in Cuba, and not to instal any more. One effect of this duel, on the Soviet Union's international posture as a whole, was a relaxation of pressure on West Berlin: by the end of the year, no more was heard of the demands of 1958–62 that the West must accept East German control of access to the city, and Khrushchev made this brutally clear to the East Germans themselves in January 1963.

Another important element in the international system by now was China. The rising tension between Peking and Moscow, expressed in ideological tirades but at the same time a clear case of power-rivalry, was perhaps one reason for Khrushchev's original adventurousness over Cuba and for his subsequent retreat: in the first phase he was determined to keep ahead of the Chinese in the world Communist movement by actively supporting Cuba, and in the second he may have withdrawn all the more hastily for fear of being in difficulties on both flanks simultaneously. The Chinese were themselves involved in military action shortly after the Cuban crisis: in the autumn of 1962 their forces crossed the border of India—at least the border claimed by the Indian government—in an attempt to establish control over a disputed piece of territory. The fighting was bitter but short-lived: the Chinese withdrew after inflicting a telling defeat on the Indian army and causing the great powers to fear an escalation that might endanger the peace globally as well as regionally.

In the meantime, dramatic events were under way in the Atlantic alliance. President Kennedy's speech of 4 July 1962 at Philadelphia, delivered on the anniversary and the site of the Declaration of Independence, sketched out a 'Grand Design' for a programme of interdependence between the United States and a united Western Europe. This design—known alternatively as the 'two pillars' or 'dumb-bell' concept—envisaged a successful outcome of Britain's attempt to enter the European Community, and the development of the latter into a political unit capable of speaking with one voice and of sharing the burdens of world leadership with the United States.

In matters of strategy, it was assumed that the European component of the 'Atlantic Community' would remain closely linked with the United States through NATO, but this view was strongly opposed by another Grand Design, that of President de Gaulle. The latter, by now relieved of the burden of Algeria and closely supported by his neighbour Adenauer, had abandoned the notions he had advanced in 1958 of an Anglo-Franco-American directorate of the Western alliance and was insistent that Europe ' from the Atlantic to the Urals ' should make herself independent of the United States. Thus, when Macmillan and Kennedy signed the Nassau Agreement of December 1962—providing for Britain's acquisition of Polaris missiles—de Gaulle used the occasion to denounce America's attempt to perpetuate her ' hegemony ' over NATO, and vetoed Britain's entry to the EEC on the grounds that she had confirmed that she was not truly ' European '. Out of the ruins of Kennedy's ' Grand Design ', shattered in January 1963 by de Gaulle's action, was to grow [2] a new American attempt to keep the loyalty of West Germany by offering her access to NATO nuclear weapons in a new form—the Multilateral Force, or MLF.

Another constant preoccupation of Western governments during this time, particularly of Washington, was the problem of economic development. Kennedy and his advisers were determined to alleviate the poverty of the Third World; they not only provided substantial American aid for programmes like the Latin American ' Alliance for Progress ' (though here the aim of social change was somewhat stultified by local conservatism and American business influences) but also pressed their European allies repeatedly to make a bigger contribution to the ' have-nots '. The situations in Cuba, the Congo, and Vietnam (where fighting between North and South was beginning to arouse American concern by the end of 1963) gave Washington policy-makers the picture of a world in which the West must make greater efforts to compete with Communist influence throughout the Third World.

The attenuation of the Cold War by direct dealings with the Soviet Union, however, remained a principal concern of the American administration in the months after Cuba. By August 1963 the two super-powers, together with Britain, had worked out and signed the Partial Test Ban Treaty renouncing nuclear testing above ground and under water. This was accompanied by the installation of a telephonic 'hot line' linking Washington and Moscow, and was followed in October by a UN resolution, jointly sponsored by the two super-powers, against the sending of nuclear warheads into space.

Even though President Kennedy undertook a successful trip through Western Europe in June 1963 to reassure his allies about Washington's intentions, there was no doubt that a serious dialogue between the two super-powers was changing the shape of world politics by the time Adenauer retired in October and Kennedy was assassinated in November.

Internal Politics: Relative Compatibility

In 1962–3 the political machines in both Washington and Bonn became more capable of operating smoothly, and co-operated with each other better, than in the previous eighteen months. Although both the Kennedy and Adenauer administrations had many and pressing domestic problems, none of them imparted particular tension into German-American relations.

In Washington, for a start, governmental routines were working more smoothly than in the somewhat anarchic days of the 'New Frontier' of 1961. In the view of several senior officials who had seen administrations come and go, the young President and his advisers, having shown in their first year or so of office, that they were capable of making mistakes, were now showing their capacity to learn from them.

Some of these advisers themselves were to admit that they had acted hastily, and according to one of them, Kennedy himself regretted trying to force the Germans to accept suggestions on Berlin and other matters that were unacceptable to the Russians anyway.[3] Another of Kennedy's advisers, looking back a few years later, admitted that he had been wrong in 1961–2 in expecting the problems of Berlin, Germany, and Central Europe to be resolved by bursts of diplomatic activity: he now realized that the status quo then in force was the best state of affairs that could be obtained for some time.[4]

The men in the White House with Kennedy had by now overcome their irritation with the officials in the State Department when the latter produced standard arguments against excessive attempts to pursue détente with the Soviet Union at the expense of relations with allies, notably Germany. In 1961 the argument that high priority must be given to conciliating Germany—or at least not upsetting her—had been treated with some scorn in the White House. By late 1962, once the Berlin storm of the spring had blown over,[5] the President's advisers treated such arguments with a good deal more respect. For one thing, the Soviet Union was proving more intractable than the White House staff had imagined—and it was to prove more so by the time of the Cuban crisis; and for another, the alliance was beginning to be seriously shaken by de Gaulle. These considerations, combined with Germany's growing power, brought out the desirability of encouraging friendly relations with the government in Bonn: as we shall see, that government did in fact seem much easier to cultivate in Adenauer's last year than during the period just past.

A striking development within the Washington machine during 1962—reflecting the new international constellation and particularly the realization that Western Europe (particularly Germany) needed to be cultivated—was the growing power of a group of ' Europeans ' located in strategic positions in the State Department. Theirs was not to be the only voice in the making of Kennedy's European policy in 1962–3, but by the time of his replacement by Johnson it was distinctly the ascendant one. This group included Gerard Smith, Director of the Policy Planning Staff until 1961, then an adviser; Henry Owen (a member of the Policy Planning Staff); Robert Bowie (former Assistant Secretary for Policy Planning and special adviser from 1960); Robert Schaetzel (Deputy Assistant Secretary of State for Atlantic Political Affairs from late 1962); Thomas Finletter (Permanent Representative to NATO from 1961 to mid-1965); and Livingston Merchant (former Under Secretary of State under Eisenhower and an adviser under Kennedy). This group was associated with the project for a NATO multilateral force, which took up some of the ideas evolved by Norstad and Herter in 1960.[6] As we shall see, the position of influence held by this group in Washington brought the MLF to the forefront of debate between allied capitals in 1963 and 1964.[7]

In Bonn, also, the distribution of political power was one which favoured better German-American relations than in the immediately preceding period. Here, where the institutional hierarchy was more formal than in Washington, and the opportunity for a group of officials to take and hold influence less, changes in the composition of the cabinet itself were of more importance. Adenauer was still Chancellor, but the crisis of 1959 had seriously weakened his position,[8] and the FDP's price for joining his cabinet in 1961 had been to insist that he promise to retire in 1963. This was a price which many of his CDU colleagues were glad he had to pay: they included Ludwig Erhard, who had been deprived of the succession in 1959 but was certain to get it now. This represented a further weakening of Adenauer's position, but it strengthened his government's ties with Washington, since Erhard was well liked there, and regarded as an easier man to deal with than Adenauer. The Foreign Minister Gerhard Schröder, again, was regarded more highly in Washington than his predecessor von Brentano: no blame for the German-American upheavals of April-May 1962 was ascribed to him, and he was usually very welcome to participate in official discussions in Washington.[9] A press report from Washington in October 1962 which said that 'the impression is held here that Schröder knows, more closely than many holders of power in Europe, how highly to value the degree of commitment undertaken by the USA in the East-West confrontation'[10] was typical of much comment in the American capital.

An unexpected event in Bonn also led to the departure from office in December 1962 of one of Adenauer's ministers who had got on least successfully with the Kennedy administration. Franz Josef Strauss, the Minister of Defence, was strongly criticized in parliament for his part in the arrest of members of the staff of *Der Spiegel* in October 1962, and was forced to resign.[11]

His successor, Kai-Uwe von Hassel, was a man with whom the Pentagon, State Department, and White House found relations much easier, as was shown by the close understanding on MLF and other matters reached during his three-day visit to Washington in February 1963.[12]

A Washington in which the White House was readier to listen to a powerful group of State Department 'Europeanists', and a Bonn in which Adenauer, von Brentano, and Strauss were being replaced by Erhard, Schröder, and von Hassel, appeared capable of conducting a more harmonious relationship than that of 1961 and early 1962.

Bilateral Relations: Harmony Maintained

Transactions concerned with bilateral German-American affairs during this period were marked by a substantial measure of agreement, in contrast to the transactions involving alliance matters or relations with the East. The smooth running of this part of the relationship was due in part to the changes in political personnel just noted, but much more to the fact that no particularly divisive issues arose between the two governments.

The agreement of November 1961 on German purchases of American military equipment [13] provided, for the time being, a solution to the problem of troop stationing costs which for different reasons fully satisfied both parties. It should be added that the continuing deficit in the overall American balance of payments was considerably alleviated in 1962 by the 6 per cent revaluation of the Deutschmark at the end of the previous year. The combination of the arms-purchase agreement and the revaluation made it possible for the administration to respond to the Berlin crisis by sending 50,000 additional American troops to Europe, without any Congressional disapproval.[14] The 1961 agreement was renewed in 1963; the moment when such an arrangement could no longer suit the two parties, and offset costs would acutely divide them, was still in the future.[15]

The direct balance of trade between the United States and the Federal Republic also remained stable and generally satisfactory in 1962 and 1963: in the former year, American exports to Germany amounted to $1,061m., and imports from Germany to $961m.; in 1963, the figures were $1,103m. and $1,003m. respectively.[16] This, however, was relatively small compensation for America's overall deficit, and certain problems were in fact created by the German application of increased tariffs, in accordance with the EEC's policy, to individual American food products. The most politically conspicuous of these proved to be chickens, whose American producers claimed that the increased tariff had damaged their exports to Germany to the extent of $46m. The American government accepted this figure, and raised the issue with the authorities of the EEC, who estimated the loss at the much more modest figure of $19m. After much argument both parties agreed to seek the opinion of the consultative committee of the GATT, which was given on 21 November 1963. The GATT estimate of

$26m. was nearer to the EEC estimate than to the American one, and the American side only accepted it with a reservation to the effect that American import duties on European goods would be raised by an equivalent amount, unless the EEC gave compensation elsewhere.[17]

The impact of this kind of commercial issue on the political relationship between Washington and Bonn was to become more acute as the American balance of payments worsened during the later 1960s. In the meantime the possible ramifications of such issues, in stimulating American irritation with Europe, were indicated by remarks made to the West German minister Heinrich Krone on his visit to Washington in the early summer of 1963: as Adenauer told de Gaulle shortly afterwards, Krone was warned by three prominent Senators that if Germany cut her imports of American chickens, she might have to do without American soldiers too.[18]

The generally trouble-free nature of the bilateral dimension of German-American relations during this period, except for specific problems of which the 'chicken war' was the worst, was not enough to ensure that the relationship as a whole would be harmonious. Alliance problems and relations with states outside the alliance subjected the partnership to considerable tension, and these dimensions—particularly the latter—were clearly more influential determinants of the relationship than its strictly bilateral component.

Alliance Politics: from the Ann Arbor Speech to MLF

One branch of Washington policy-making in which the changes of 1962 were not welcome either in Bonn or in some other European capitals was defence policy. As we have seen, General Maxwell Taylor, who appointment as Chairman of the Joint Chiefs of Staff was announced in July 1962, was a strong believer in the doctrines of unified control and flexible response which were enunciated, after Taylor had written about them, in McNamara's speech at Ann Arbor.[19] General Lemnitzer, again, who replaced Norstad as NATO's Supreme Commander in Europe at the same time, was no believer in the kind of NATO nuclear force Norstad had supported.[20] German disappointment at this setback was ill-concealed by Strauss, but not felt so keenly by his successor von Hassel.

In the meantime, President de Gaulle was busily impressing on the German government his view of the unreliability of the United States and the suitability of France as an alternative partner. Although he appears to have made no suggestion that Germany should be associated with the French nuclear force or with research to develop it (the Fourth Republic's hints of 1957–8 thus remaining without an echo under the Fifth),[21] he lost no opportunity of putting forward the idea of close political consultation among the six members of the European Community (Franco-German co-operation forming the kernel) which was currently being discussed by the so-called Fouchet Committee.[22] These matters were discussed during Adenauer's state visit to France in July 1962 and during de Gaulle's visit to Germany, which was a triumphant success, two months later.[23]

By the autumn of 1962 it had become clear that there were two quite divergent views about the future of the Atlantic alliance. On the one hand, the 'Grand Design' adumbrated in Kennedy's Philadelphia speech of 4 July 1962 foresaw an 'Atlantic Community' comprising an American and a European pillar—the latter strengthened economically and politically by British entry into EEC, but preferably not provided with any nuclear weapons independent from those of the United States.[24]

The rival conception to this Anglo-American vision was that of President de Gaulle: for him, British entry into EEC was becoming ever more suspect as an American device for preserving the 'hegemony' of the United States over Europe, and the future West European structure had to be firmly based on co-operation between the six states of the existing Economic Community, particularly France and Germany. A series of events in December 1962 was to bring the conflict between these two opposed concepts of the Western alliance to a head and was to have profound repercussions on the future of German-American relations.

In mid-December Macmillan met de Gaulle at Rambouillet, and it appears to have been made fairly clear to him that Britain's attempt to enter the European Community was doomed to failure.[25] In any event, Macmillan then flew to Nassau in the Bahamas, to engage in critical talks with Kennedy on the future of the British independent deterrent: as the

American administration had decided not to proceed with the Skybolt missile, on which the British government and the RAF depended for the future of Britain's deterrent, Macmillan tried, successfully, to get Washington to return to an earlier commitment to make available a substitute in the form of Polaris missiles for British submarines. The Nassau Agreement provided for Britain to be supplied with these missiles, which were to be placed under NATO command but subject to independent control by the British government in a situation of 'grave national emergency'.

This Anglo-American agreement, prolonging both the British deterrent and the apparent 'special relationship' between Washington and London, was used by de Gaulle as part of the grounds for his statement in a press conference on 14 January 1963, that negotiations for British entry to EEC could not continue. In the same press conference he denounced Kennedy's notion of an Atlantic Community as an ideological mask for American domination of Europe, and insisted again that Europe must be free and independent.[26]

By January 1963 the main elements of Kennedy's 'Grand Design' were thus in ruins: British membership of EEC had been rejected, and France insisted with redoubled force on going her own way in the alliance, including developing her own nuclear force independent of American control. The impact on Washington's thinking about the alliance was considerable, and the impact on thinking about Germany quite dramatic. What if Adenauer followed the example of his friend de Gaulle in demanding a nationally controlled nuclear deterrent for Germany? What if, at the very least, German feelings of unfair treatment—in that Germany was contributing at least as much to the alliance as France or Britain, and unlike them was forbidden to produce nuclear weapons—should surge to the top in German politics, perhaps bringing Strauss or some even more nationalistic figure to the chancellorship? Such fears of what came to be called 'German Gaullism' were rife in Washington, and they led to what one critic called an 'ardent wooing' of Bonn in an attempt to prevent her following the pernicious example of Paris.[27] The courtship had begun during 1962, when the 'Europeanists' of the State Department had been able to make progress with their idea of a multilateral nuclear force (built, as we have seen, on the ideas of 1959–60) which they saw as a tranquillizer for Germany and a cement for the alliance. The plan had appealed to the German government for the same reasons as had the Norstad scheme of 1960—a way of access to NATO's nuclear decision-making through part-ownership and shared control of some of the alliance's 'hardware'. The Germans were therefore glad to hear from McGeorge Bundy (speaking at Copenhagen in September 1962) that the American administration might ultimately, if the multilateral force developed as planned, remove the American veto on its use, thus effectively 'Europeanizing' it.[28] By this time the proposal put forward was for a fleet of surface ships equipped with Polaris missiles, the US Navy having vetoed the original idea of a submarine force; this weakened the interest of London and other European capitals (France had rejected the whole scheme from the beginning), with the result that Germany emerged as one of the strongest European partners of the United States in the MLF discussions.

Kennedy's agreement in December 1962, to let the British have Polaris, indirectly strengthened the hand of the State Department's 'Europeanists', who were alarmed at what Germany might do if she felt discriminated against. Their alarm was increased by the Franco-German treaty signed on 22 January 1963 in which Adenauer and de Gaulle (the latter having by now crushed the idea of British entry to the EEC, and in turn been rebuffed on his project for political consultation by all his European partners except Germany) committed their countries to close collaboration and consultation in all matters of foreign policy.[29]

This presumed evidence of 'German Gaullism' led to counter-measures in Washington. First, the administration encouraged those politicians in Bonn (including Erhard) who wished to add a preface to the recent Franco-German treaty specifying that it would not affect Germany's existing Atlantic commitments, and the point was forcibly put to Adenauer's representative Karl Carstens when he visited Washington from 5 to 7 February.[30] Secondly, the events of January, as we have noted, gave a fresh impetus to the efforts of the 'MLF lobby' in the State Department, and assured them of a favourable hearing in the White House. As early as 14 January, the day of de Gaulle's fateful press conference, Under-Secretary of State George Ball had been sent to Bonn to win German approval for the MLF,[31] and shortly afterwards Livingston Merchant was given a special appointment to work with Ambassador Finletter in developing the plan's details.[32]

An exploratory mission by Merchant and his staff, who toured the allied capitals of Europe in March and April, turned into what has been described as a vast 'sales mission'[33] of thirty-two men, and their selling of MLF was nowhere easier than in Bonn. The German government was interested in the MLF as a way of gaining status in the alliance, and the American government was interested in it (though Kennedy privately doubted if the scheme would ever be put into practice and is reported to have been amazed to hear that Adenauer really liked it)[34] as a way of holding the alliance together against the threat represented by de Gaulle. A close harmony of interests appeared to exist between Washington and Bonn; the cloud on the horizon was whether enough other members of NATO could be persuaded to take an interest so that the MLF did not appear to be a purely German-American undertaking. By October 1963 this aim seemed to have been achieved, when a study-group representing several Allied governments was set up to give more detailed analysis to the MLF proposal.[35]

In the meantime Kennedy had undertaken another important step, his visit to Western Europe in June 1963. Impelled in part, like MLF, by de Gaulle's actions of January,[36] this visit was designed to reassure the European members of the alliance that America's commitment to them was serious, despite all the problems presented both by de Gaulle and by America's own impending talks on a test ban agreement with the Soviet Union.

The time he spent in Germany in June 1963 is chiefly remembered for his dramatic phrase '*Ich bin ein Berliner*',[37] and there is no doubt that he was given a hero's welcome by the German crowds: he remarked to one of his assistants that any future American president feeling discouraged need only be told 'Go to Germany'.[38] A more significant aspect of his speeches, however—particularly that in the *Paulskirche* in Frankfurt—is that he gave the Germans a clear warning not to count on American support for German reunification along the lines conceived in the past by Adenauer and Dulles.[39] This warning was quite clearly in line with the policy pursued by Kennedy since the building of the Berlin Wall two years earlier, and embodied in the abortive negotiating position of spring 1962: that the United States would certainly maintain her own rights in West Berlin, and hence the city's political and other links with West Germany, but that an extension of West German influence to *East* Berlin, and a fortiori to East Germany would *not* be backed by the United States. This American warning to Germany to adjust her expectations to the realities was all the more relevant as Kennedy was now continuing a process—begun in 1962 after the Cuban crisis and explained in his speech at American University, Washington on 10 June 1963—of seeking détente by direct agreement with the Soviet Union.[40]

Relations with the Adversary: Test Ban Treaty, but no Non-aggression Pact

Although the Kennedy administration, as we have noted, was more stable in its functioning in 1962–3 than in 1961–2, a certain tendency to pursue incompatible policies simultaneously still persisted. The American system of government may not differ intrinsically from others in this respect; but the degree of publicity attending governmental deliberations—stimulated by deliberate leaks to the press by one or another faction within the machine—makes the simultaneous pursuit of only partially compatible objectives more obvious than in other systems. As Dean Acheson is reported to have expressed it, the Washington governmental machine resembled a dinosaur, and the answer you got about what American policy was depended which bit of the dinosaur you tapped.

By 1963 at least three American policies on strategic and security affairs were being pursued simultaneously. First, the policy of encouraging at least one ally to maintain a quasi-independent deterrent had been confirmed by the Nassau Agreement of December 1962. Second, the prospect of an inter-allied MLF with a clear American veto had been given ' a modest re-floating ' by the President in January 1963, as an antidote to ' Adenauer's growing fascination with de Gaulle.' [41] And thirdly, the ' eyeball-to-eyeball ' confrontation over Cuba had stimulated the desire to seek a dialogue with the Soviet Union, one aim of such a dialogue being to make the world afer by limiting the spread of nuclear weapons.

Up to a certain point, it could be argued that there was nothing incompatible about these three policies: the Nassau Agreement and existing Anglo-American arrangements left it doubtful whether the British deterrent was in fact 'independent';[42] the MLF would clearly long remain subject to an American veto, even though McGeorge Bundy's Copenhagen speech had envisaged the lifting of this in the very long run; and in the American-Soviet discussions of non-proliferation, as these developed from 1963 onwards, it was made clear that the eventual transfer of the British and French nuclear forces to a West European political union (whether or not in the form of the MLF, and whether or not Germany had a partial say in nuclear policy) would not in American eyes constitute 'proliferation'.[43]

The three lines of policy pursued in 1963 could thus in a sense be reconciled: however, the impression prevailed at the time that rival groups of Kennedy's advisers and officials were pursuing policies of their own without much regard for each other. As a critic with an inside view of the proceedings put it, 'Kennedy used to run government like a seminar: collecting bright ideas from all sides, and carrying pragmatism to the point where his long-range objectives were quite unclear.'[44]

If the MLF activities of 1963 were the work of a 'cabal' of 'Europeanists' inside the State Department,[45] the pursuit of détente with the Soviet Union reflected the views of a different group of advisers: Dr Jerome Wiesner, the President's Scientific Advisor (for some time, as we have noted, an active promoter of the 'Pugwash' conferences with the Russians) and Averell Harriman, the President's Ambassador-at-large, were the most prominent members of this group, but the post-Cuban concern to open a dialogue on world security with Moscow was widely shared thoughout the State Department, White House, and Pentagon.

Early in June 1963 Kennedy's speech at American University indicated the general lines on which détente would be sought by Washington,[46] and later that month, while Kennedy was reassuring the European allies, Harriman went to Moscow to negotiate the details of an agreement banning nuclear testing, accompanied by Carl Kaysen, McGeorge Bundy's deputy.[47] The details of the agreement were worked out in time for its signature on 5 August, but not before fairly serious differences of opinion had developed between Washington and Bonn. These disagreements, although in no way as acute as the explosions of April-May 1962,[48] indicated three fundamental divergences between American and German views about negotiations with the Soviet Union. First, the German government was concerned that the link between arms negotiations and German reunification, established in the 1950s, was now being clearly broken: an agreement on nuclear testing without a corresponding one to change Germany's political status quo could only consolidate the latter.[49] Secondly, the negotiations were being conducted by the two super-powers (and to some extent by Britain) without any effective consultation with Bonn: this meant, for instance, that it was relatively easy for the Soviet Union to bring in the demand that the GDR be introduced as a signatory of the treaty—a demand not too troubling for the United States, but in 1963 profoundly unwelcome to West Germany, since it contributed to consolidating Germany's division. Thirdly, there was some inclination among Americans to accept the Soviet demand that the proposed test-ban treaty should be followed by a general non-aggression treaty, or series of treaties, signed between the members of NATO and the Warsaw Pact: this again would have upgraded the status of the GDR as a signatory to agreements recognized as valid by the Western powers, and would once again have contributed to hardening the division of Germany.

In June 1963, when Harriman and Kaysen saw Kennedy before setting off for Moscow, the President instructed them to explore with Khrushchev the prospects of a general understanding with the Soviet Union—which would of necessity include at least some discussion of the Soviet wish for a non-aggression pact. When Harriman remarked that any American reticence on this point, i.e. concentration on the test-ban treaty alone, would require 'something to sweeten the package', Kennedy's reply was 'I have some cash in the bank in West Germany and am prepared to draw on that if you think I should'.[50]

In the end, the Test Ban Treaty was signed on 5 August without the Soviet demand for a non-aggression pact being met first, but this demand persisted in the aftermath of the treaty. One of the American diplomats concerned in the negotiations described the mood of some of his superiors as one of 'millennial optimism',[51] and it was clear in Washington that one of the purposes of Schröder's visit there in mid-September was 'to block the search for a non-aggression arrangement between NATO and the Warsaw Pact'.[52]

Walt Rostow, in 1963 Chairman of the State Department's Policy Planning Council, later confirmed that West German resistance had been responsible for the fact that 'we resisted in Moscow all pressures to link the nuclear test ban to a non-aggression pact between NATO and the Warsaw powers.'[53] The pressures, however, had been strong, and the temptation to give way to them had been and remained strong too.

In the end the West German government signed the Test Ban Treaty, but its signature was delayed for a few days while Bonn made it absolutely clear that West Germany would not sign the same copy of the agreement as East Germany. The West German signature was deposited in Washington, and the East German in Moscow: Dean Rusk even agreed, on 12 August, after a long and difficult discussion in Bonn, that the United States would officially take no notice of the East German signature, thus denying East Berlin anything that could be construed as recognition.[54]

It should not be thought that the United States had a monopoly, during the summer months of 1963, of envisaging transactions with the Soviet Union which were of a nature to alarm her alliance partners. Adenauer, in his last few months in office, revived a project he had submitted to the Soviet Union in June 1962, for a ten-year 'truce' on the subject of German reunification, by which the status of the two German states would be tacitly recognized even by Bonn, in exchange for some improvements in the situation of the East German population.[55] The Soviet response in 1962 had been very negative (the plan was seen as a trick to bring about reunification and Adenauer had indeed proposed free elections for all Germany at the end of the ten-year period) but in the summer of 1963 Adenauer appears to have mentioned both to Kennedy and to de Gaulle the possibility of reviving it.[56]

It appears that when Adenauer had informed Kennedy of the idea in June 1963—as he tells us, 'not in so much detail' as he gave de Gaulle—the President had at first 'not seemed keen' on the proposal, though he later encouraged Adenauer to try it out.[57]

Adenauer decided against a further démarche towards Moscow on the question. His main aim in East-West relations was to reaffirm the standard West German position on re-unification, and these relations during the period 1962–3 were thus characterized essentially by *American* dealings with the Soviet Union, which aroused more or less sharp feelings of alarm in West Germany. It was a period in which Washington had tried, though not always very attentively, to live up to the precepts laid down by Dean Acheson as the period came to an end:

. . . my thesis is that in making political and military judgments affecting Europe a major—often *the* major—consideration should be their effect on the German people and the German government. It follows from this that the closest liaison and consultation with the German government is an absolute necessity. . . . Unexpected or unexplained action nearly always causes consternation in Bonn. Sensible action after careful consultation, even when there has been some difference of view, rarely does.[58]

NOTES

1 D. C. Watt, *Survey of International Affairs 1962* (1970), pp. 44–70.
2 See below, pp. 128–30.
3 Sorensen, pp. 598 and 600.
4 Schlesinger, p. 384.
5 See above, pp. 110–15.
6 See above, pp. 106–7.
7 See below, pp. 128–30, 148–51.
8 See above, p. 81.
9 Private information, Washington.
10 H. von Borch, *Die Welt*, 23 Oct. 1962.
11 See Ronald F. Bunn, *German Politics and the Spiegel Affair: A Case Study of the Bonn System* (Baton Rouge, Louisiana State UP, 1968).
12 H. von Borch, *Die Welt*, 29 Feb. 1963: the report mentions that Germany's membership of the NATO Standing Group had already been under discussion—a foreshadowing of the idea of the Nuclear Planning Group that evolved in 1965.
13 See above, p. 83.
14 Richard M. Stebbins, *The United States in World Affairs 1962* (1963), p. 131. See also Hanrieder, pp. 170–1.
15 Mendershausen, p. 75. A supplementary German-American agreement, for joint production of a new tank, was reached when McNamara visited Bonn in Aug. 1963: see *l'Année Politique 1963* (Paris, 1964), p. 284.

16 United Nations, *Yearbook of International Trade Statistics* (New York, annually).

17 *L'Année Politique 1963*, p. 311. For a fuller analysis of the 'chicken war' of 1962–3, see George M. Tabor, *John F. Kennedy and a Uniting Europe: the Politics of Partnership* (1969), pp. 141–5.

18 Adenauer, *1959–1963*, p. 226. A similar remark made by Senator Fulbright in Bonn in August is reported in *l'Année Politique 1963*, pp. 285–6.

19 See above, p. 109.

20 See above, p. 109. Because of the Cuban crisis, Lemnitzer and Taylor did not take up their new posts for some months.

21 See above, p. 67.

22 Silj, esp. pp. 13–39.

23 Adenauer, *1959–1963*, 158–84.

24 The British deterrent, whose targeting was planned jointly with the US Strategic Air Command, was not regarded as running counter to the McNamara Doctrine, but the French *force de frappe* was. Kennedy's 'Grand Design' is described in some detail by Sorensen, ch. 20. Other members of Kennedy's staff have suggested that he saw the future of the alliance in very pragmatic terms, and that the concept of 'grand design' meant less to him than it did to Sorensen, who wrote the speech Kennedy delivered in Philadelphia (private information, Washington).

25 Neustadt, *Alliance Politics*, p. 52. This work provides the best account available of the Skybolt crisis, and has been drawn on in what follows.

26 Charles de Gaulle, *Major Addresses, Statements and Press Conferences, May 19, 1958–January 31, 1964* (1964), pp. 208–22.

27 Kissinger, *The Troubled Partnership*, p. 235; see also ibid. p. 74.

28 Schlesinger, pp. 851 ff., Mahncke, *Nukleare Mitwirkung*, p. 133, and A. Buchan, *The Multilateral Force: an Historical Perspective* (1964).

29 For the text of the treaty, see *l'Année Politique 1963*, pp. 404–6.

30 Adenauer, *1959–1963*, pp. 214–15. For the text of the Bundestag's preamble (16 May 1963) to the treaty, see *l'Année Politique 1963*, pp. 406–7.

31 *NZZ*, 11 Mar. 1963, quoted by Bandulet, p. 218.

32 Schlesinger, p. 872.

33 Ibid. p. 873.

34 Private information, Washington.

35 Buchan, *The Multilateral Force*, p. 10.

36 Schlesinger, p. 872.

37 *Public Papers of the Presidents of the United States: John F. Kennedy . . . 1963* (1964), p. 525.

38 Sorensen, p. 601. See also *Public Papers . . . Kennedy . . . 1963*, p. 522.

39 *Public Papers . . . Kennedy . . . 1963*, pp. 520–1. The background of Kennedy's thinking is assessed by Charles R. Planck, *The Changing Status of German Reunification in Western Diplomacy 1955–1966* (1967), esp. pp. 33–48.

40 See below, pp. 132–4.

41 Schlesinger, p. 866.

42 See above, p. 128.

[43] See above, p. 129.

[44] Private information, Washington.

[45] See above, p. 123.

[46] For text, see *Public Papers . . . Kennedy . . . 1963*, pp. 459–64.

[47] Schlesinger, pp. 903 ff.

[48] See above, pp. 110–15.

[49] Bandulet, p. 242.

[50] Schlesinger, p. 904. Private information confirms that Kennedy had in mind giving way to the Soviet demand for a non-aggression pact if necessary: such action would of course provoke protests by Germany, but the President felt his standing there was good enough for this to be unimportant.

[51] Private information.

[52] H. von Borch, 'USA setzen Hoffnung auf Schröder', *Die Welt*, 2 Sept. 1963. According to this exceptionally well-informed observer, American officials were disappointed that Bonn's negative views about a non-aggression pact (Bonn was still insisting on the Western 'reunification' proposals of 1959) blocked the way to a possible understanding that Soviet pressure on West Berlin would be forbidden by the proposed pact. See Planck, pp. 44–8.

[53] W. W. Rostow, *View from the Seventh Floor* (1964), p. 75.

[54] H. Bechtoldt, 'Deutschland und das Moskauer Abkommen', *Aussenpolitik*, 14/19 (1963), pp. 579–82.

[55] Bandulet, pp. 232–4, and sources there quoted.

[56] Adenauer, *1959–1963*, p. 226: record of conversation with de Gaulle, 4 July 1963.

[57] Ibid. This volume is remarkable for the detailed attention Adenauer gives to his dealings with de Gaulle, in contrast to his neglect of those with Kennedy.

[58] *New York Times Magazine*, 15 Dec. 1963. For a detailed analysis of events in the Kennedy-Adenauer period, see Walter Stützle, *Kennedy und Adenauer in der Berlin-Krise 1961–1962* (1973).

CHAPTER EIGHT

President Johnson and Chancellor Erhard 1963–1966

Background: the Period of Détente

LYNDON Johnson and Ludwig Erhard both assumed office late in 1963, and they came to understand each other tolerably well by the time Erhard was forced to resign—ironically, given his background, over issues of economic policy—at the end of 1966. During these three years the development of international relations was characterized by a striking paradox. On the one hand, America was engaged in an increasingly bloody war against the Communist forces in Vietnam; yet on the other, the post-Cuban détente was continued and developed, and was symbolized by extensive East-West negotiations and a number of important agreements.[1]

The war in Vietnam was largely fought by American forces after the episode in the Gulf of Tonking in August 1964, when American warships were fired on by the North Vietnamese. The number of American troops in Vietnam rose from 14,000 in 1963 to 267,000 at the end of 1966; American military and economic resources available for deployment elsewhere, and the attention given to non-Asian problems inevitably began to be somewhat reduced in consequence.

The economic factor—America contined to experience growing balance of payments deficits—was one reason why Washington continued to pursue its dialogue with Moscow on arms control, hoping ultimately to reach an agreement which would allow a levelling-off of the US arms budget. A first step towards such an agreement was seen as being to halt the spread of nuclear weapons to further non-atomic powers (also seen, of course, as a contribution to security in its own right): this was the aim of the non-proliferation treaty on which active bilateral negotiations began with Gromyko's visit to Washington in October 1966, after preliminary debate in Washington about the wisdom of seeking an agreement with the Soviet Union which some at least of America's allies would view with apprehension. The pursuit of a non-proliferation treaty certainly marked a complete break with the principle accepted by Washington in the 1950s, partly at Bonn's insistence, that no agreements concerning arms control or disarmament should be sought without simultaneous agreement on political issues such as the reunification of Germany.

There was, however, a general sense—which by 1966 had developed quite strongly—that the tension between the two Cold War blocs was diminishing (in spite of Vietnam), and that the degree of internal cohesion both blocs had shown in the 1950s was no longer necessary or even desirable. The word 'polycentrism', coined by the Italian Communist leader Palmiro Togliatti, appeared to have some applicability to both alliances. In the Warsaw Pact, Rumania was beginning by 1966 to show marked signs of independence, which were to become more pronounced later. Within the Western alliance, France under de Gaulle carried her independent position of the early 1960s a good deal further; in 1965–6 the functioning of the European Economic Community was seriously disrupted by the refusal of the French government to transfer more power to the Commission in Brussels, and in March 1966 de Gaulle announced that France was leaving the integrated command structures of NATO, whose European headquarters had to be removed from France and transferred to Belgium. This move occurred after various attempts had been made by the United States government to strengthen the cohesion of the alliance: during 1964 President Johnson allowed negotiations on the MLF to continue, before deciding at the end of the year that the project was not supported strongly enough either in the Senate or among the European allies, whereupon he quietly shelved it, and the MLF project was succeeded by a less ambitious means of giving the European allies a larger share in planning the use of NATO's nuclear weapons, NATO's so-called ' McNamara Committee ', later officially entitled the Nuclear Planning Group. (This body, established in 1965, appeared to satisfy Germany's wish for a greater say in NATO's nuclear planning, without the expense and embarrassment entailed in providing NATO with extra ' hardware ' in the form of the MLF.)

A further development in West European affairs was that the Labour government of Harold Wilson, re-elected to office in April 1966 with a comfortable majority, reversed its previous refusal to contemplate membership of the European Community, and let it be understood later in the year—after the Community's internal crisis of 1965–6 had abated—that it wished to reopen the entry negotiations broken off by de Gaulle in January 1963.

The prospect of the two armed blocs in Europe being replaced by a new pan-European security system still seemed remote in 1966, but a proposal for such a system (or at least for a conference on how to achieve it) was put forward by the Soviet Union and its allies at the Warsaw Pact's Bucharest conference early in July.

Meanwhile in Asia a serious conflict between India and Pakistan, over Kashmir, developed early in 1965 and led to a short but sharp war between the two countries that summer. The interest of the Soviet Union in promoting stability in the Indian subcontinent—if only because conflict there might strengthen the position of China at Russia's expense—was shown by the fact that it was the Soviet Union which mediated between the two warring states and brought the conflict to an end. This not only indicated the influence of the Soviet Union as a super-power in Asia, but also confirmed the inability of Britain to maintain the cohesion of the Commonwealth or to sustain an effective military role East of Suez, and thereby accelerated the Labour government's decision to turn towards Europe.

A crisis in Africa also contributed to this decision: when the white regime in Rhodesia issued its unilateral declaration of independence in November 1965 the British government decided not to use military force, but instead (through the United Nations) imposed economic sanctions which totally failed to change the policy of the Rhodesian regime, and confirmed the United Kingdom's declining inability to influence events outside Europe.

In Latin America, in contrast, the United States was able to impose its will by force in the political crisis of 1965 in the Dominican Republic, and the influence of Castro's Cuban regime showed little sign of increasing.

Despite these crises in different parts of the world, and despite even Vietnam, the period 1963–6 remained one of growing détente between the two super-powers: this was its most important characteristic, as far as Europe was concerned.

Internal Politics: Outward Stability but Growing Strains

Vice President Lyndon B. Johnson, when he unexpectedly became President in November 1963, wished to use his new power to carry out a considerable programme of reform in many fields of American policy: education, urban renewal, social services, and civil rights were only a few of the areas where there were strong pressures for change—with which he was personally in sympathy. His whole background as a Democratic Congressman and Senator since the 1930s made the continuation of Roosevelt's reforming legislation his primary concern; and of course, he had been associated with the continuation of some of these policies in the office of Vice President. He had dealt very little with foreign affairs, except when Kennedy sent him on special missions, for instance to Asia early in 1961 and to Berlin after the building of the Wall, and had not wished for closer involvement with them.

The paradox—and the tragedy—of Johnson's presidency was that circumstances forced him to expend enormous resources on the war in Vietnam: resources not only of men and money, but also of his attention and his personal skill and experience in getting his way with Congress. Despite the Vietnam war, the President was determined to enact as much domestic legislation as possible, and this reduced his ability and inclination to seek Congressional approval or even indulgence for some matters concerning America's European allies: for instance, Johnson's realization that the Senate would resist the MLF was one reason for his abandonment of the idea at the end of 1964, and the Senate's disapproval of West German commercial transactions with China strengthened the administration's own condemnation of them.[2]

The preoccupation of the White House with domestic policy and with Vietnam meant that the attention given to Europe was intermittent, and tended to be provoked only by problems of a fairly spectacular kind: for instance, France's withdrawal from NATO in the spring of 1966 or Germany's unhappiness about the scale of offset payments later the same year. It was characteristic that a visit to Washington in May 1964 by the German Opposition leader Willy Brandt occasioned almost the first discussion of German affairs in the American press since Erhard's talks with Johnson in Texas the previous December;[3] thereafter, although Erhard came to Washington much more frequently than Adenauer before him, many of these visits were occasions only for brief and unproductive exchanges of view, in part because of Johnson's other preoccupations.[4]

Other changes in Washington contributed to a diminution of the attention given to America's allies in Western Europe. Early in 1966 McGeorge Bundy was replaced as the President's Special Assistant for International Security Affairs by Walt Rostow, previously Chairman of the State Department's Policy Planning Council. By all accounts, Rostow was less active in pressing advice on the President, and shared his inclination to deal with foreign policy issues one at a time, instead of trying to keep several in play simultaneously, as Bundy had tended to do.[5]

By the end of 1966 Rostow, despite his concern for keeping Germany firmly aligned with the United States,[6] had decided that negotiations with the Soviet Union should have priority, and was accordingly giving more attention to the non-proliferation talks than to NATO affairs.

The same was inevitably true of another increasingly powerful official in the Washington machinery, the Director of the Arms Control and Disarmament Agency, William C. Foster. Although Foster, a former Deputy Secretary of Defense, had occupied this post since 1961 (when he had narrowly failed to become Under-Secretary of State), his influence was held in check until the MLF was shelved at the end of 1964; he began to exercise a really strong influence as non-proliferation became a dominant objective of the administration in 1965–6. An article by Foster in the July 1965 issue of *Foreign Affairs* categorically stated that, in the case of a conflict of objectives, détente with the Soviet Union should have priority over solidarity with America's allies; this provoked understandable concern in Bonn, but it was an indication of the shift in the balance of Washington's thinking.[7]

Attention should be given to a further important element in the American political scene, the mood of Congress. As the burden of the Vietnam War mounted, as the balance of payments deficit grew (from $1.3 (US) billion in 1965 to $2.3 billion in 1966), and as some European allies became difficult—particularly de Gaulle—the reluctance of Congress to maintain large American forces in Germany increased, and this reluctance was a factor which had to be kept seriously in mind by the Johnson administration.[8]

If there were thus many developments in Washington which presented or portended problems for Bonn, the state of things on the Rhine was also uncertain, and somewhat disturbing, as seen from the Potomac. With Adenauer, American policy-makers had had their problems, but had at least known where they stood; with Erhard, life was less predictable and hence less comfortable. Particularly by 1966, as Erhard's authority visibly weakened, as the Neo-Nazi Party (NPD) began to grow in strength, and as eminent Germans increasingly spoke of the need for a CDU/SPD 'Grand Coalition',[9] the future evolution of German politics became a matter of concern in Washington. Officials dealing with West European affairs there, whether in the State Department or the White House, became increasingly likely to take the view that American policy must concentrate on maintaining the conditions for domestic stability in Germany, rather than on her international status or relations with the East: this policy was of course likely to be threatened, to some extent, by Washington's simultaneous pursuit of détente with the Soviet Union.

This view of Germany's importance—which had, of course, been a basic determinant of American policy ever since 1945, but now became strikingly prominent—was articulated in a book by Walt Rostow published in 1964:

> Germany is located astride the balance of power in Europe. It represents a critically important area, population and concentration

of resources between the East and the West. In the past, some Germans have been able to dream of using that position to dominate Europe. From the Communist point of view, in the pursuit of world power Germany remains the greatest possible prize.[10]

The central uncertainty in Germany's political system was the position of Ludwig Erhard. Adenauer, having predicted that Erhard would be an unsatisfactory successor and having tried in vain to prevent him from becoming Chancellor,[11] was now doing his best to ensure that the prophecy was fulfilled and that Erhard was removed from office. Although Adenauer had combined the posts of Chancellor and CDU Party chairman, he now argued that it was unsuitable for one man to hold the two posts: still trying to keep the chairmanship out of Erhard's hands he retained it until March 1966, well over two years after he had ceased to be Chancellor.[12] From this position of influence, and with his authority enhanced by his position as the Federal Republic's only ex-Chancellor, Adenauer kept up a barrage of criticism of Erhard's policies. In this he was seconded by another powerful ex-Minister, Franz Josef Strauss, and by other articulate lieutenants including Baron von und zu Guttenberg.[13] This group of 'German Gaullists' attacked the policies pursued by Erhard, Schröder, and von Hassel—particularly those towards the United States—and they began by denouncing the MLF as a device that would give Germany only the appearance, not the reality, of a say in NATO's nuclear policy. When the MLF was abandoned at the end of 1964 the 'German Gaullists' redoubled their pressure for Bonn to turn towards Paris and away from Washington—ironically, de Gaulle himself was by this stage turning away from Bonn towards the East—and the 'Atlanticists', Erhard and his colleagues, were forced on to the defensive.

Erhard's position was further weakened by disputes with his coalition partners, the Free Democratic Party. Although the CDU emerged from the election of September 1965 the largest party, as usual,[14] Erhard still depended on an alliance with the FDP, and its demands proved increasingly onerous. At the end of October 1966, when an economic crisis of alarming proportions threatened West Germany, the four Free Democratic Ministers in Erhard's cabinet resigned in protest against proposed tax increases. This episode, which led directly to

Erhard's fall, was in reality only the culmination of a long-drawn-out crisis, in which his freedom of action in foreign policy had been seriously hampered by the weakness of his political base in Germany.[15]

Bilateral Relations: from Concord to Disaster

Chancellor Erhard was justly proud of his good personal relations with President Johnson, who said of the Chancellor to a reporter from *Der Spiegel* 'I simply like everything about him.'[16] Erhard went even further, confiding to one of the journalists who accompanied him to America in 1963, 'I love President Johnson, and he loves me.'[17]

Unfortunately for Erhard, he steered the course of German policy—following the line taken by his Foreign Minister Schröder from early 1963 onwards, in reaction against Adenauer's treaty with de Gaulle—into a relationship of open dependence on Washington, which ultimately contributed to his downfall.[18] In the words of one commentator:

> Bonn was unable to stabilize its gains with the United States. The Federal Government's assiduous cultivation of Washington in the aftermath of the Franco-German treaty had not produced the hoped for special relationship. Despite the Government's perpetual pledges of Atlantic solidarity, despite its support of American policy in China, Vietnam, and Santo Domingo, and despite its extensive arms purchase commitment, these *Vorleistungen* [advance payments] had failed to pay off. The MLF, held out as a concrete promise in 1963, did not materialize. Bonn's reunification initiative of December 1964 had foundered against the wall of American preconditions. And the troop issue, latent throughout the Sixties, loomed more dangerously than ever before . . . 15,000 American troops were withdrawn in April 1966.[19]

Even this degree of neglect of Bonn's general interests by Washington might not have been too damaging to the German government as Erhard made it plain that he had no intention of following de Gaulle's kind of 'deviation' and as Johnson's European policy came to focus on East-West détente.

The issue which was in fact to do irreparable harm to Erhard's political standing was that of the financial burden of American troop-stationing, which reached crisis-point in the summer of 1966. As we have seen,[20] the German-American agreement signed in 1961, providing for extensive German purchases of American military equipment to offset the balance of payments costs of troop-stationing, appeared to correspond to the interests of both parties: there were several reasons, including the economies of increased production-runs, why the United States welcomed this market for weapons and equipment, which in turn were actively desired by the German armed forces. The agreement was renewed in November 1964, when Germany undertook to purchase approximately 1.35 (US) billion dollars' worth of military goods in the United States during the two-year period ending on 30 June 1967.[21]

By the spring of 1966, however, German orders had in fact met only a modest proportion of the agreed total, and Bonn was put under very strong American pressure to fulfil the agreement. The Secretary of Defense Robert McNamara, who personally led the effort to develop American arms exports (a few years earlier such matters had been left to the Assistant Secretary, William Bundy, who had thus earned the nickname 'Basil Zaharoff Bundy'),[22] did so with particular zeal at a time when America's balance of payments deficit was in process of growing from $1.3 billion (1965) to $2.3 billion (1966) and the Vietnam War was becoming steadily more onerous. When McNamara confronted his German opposite number, however—at a meeting in the Pentagon on 13 May 1966—he faced the representative of a government which had economic and other problems of its own: for the first time for several years, Germany's national output in 1966 was failing to rise, and a further complication was that the German armed forces were now reasonably well equipped with the standard weapons America had provided, and were less than enthusiastic to purchase the long-distance troop transport aircraft and the new helicopters which McNamara and his advisers now pressed on them. (There had also been fifty-six crashes of the *Luftwaffe*'s Starfighter jets since January 1965.) Several weeks of hot argument ensued, during which the German government attempted to divert part of the promised orders from military equipment to space research requirements or equipment for its aid programme for developing countries, but by mid-June Bonn had agreed to purchase the original quota of armaments in full.[23]

There was no doubt that a determining reason for Bonn's compliance was the unprecedented warning given by McNamara to von Hassel on 13 May: Washington would henceforth reserve the right to reduce its forces in Germany 'proportionally' should Bonn's lagging purchases of American arms fail to offset US troop costs.[24]

When Erhard visited Johnson late in September his aims included the preliminary negotiation of a new type of offset agreement to replace arms purchases in 1967. Moreover he quite unrealistically hoped, in view of the critical situation of his government's finances, to obtain some alleviation of the burden Germany had assumed under the 1964 agreement and confirmed in June. President Johnson showed no pity to his visitor, whose political standing in Germany had slipped catastrophically since his election victory a year earlier and who had disastrously neglected to prepare the ground before going to Washington: Johnson is said to have treated Erhard with a certain degree of consideration until the existing offset agreement was confirmed, and then to have callously dismissed him.[25] When Erhard returned to Bonn he was forced to ask his cabinet to accept an increase of $1.05 (US) billion in the 1967 budget, designed in large part to enable the government to carry out its bargain with Washington. The revolt of Erhard's Free Democratic coalition partners against this measure at the end of October brought about his downfall and his replacement by the Grand Coalition under Kurt-Georg Kiesinger at the beginning of December.[26]

Erhard might well have undergone a premature fall in any case—he had powerful enemies in Adenauer and Strauss, and showed himself an irresolute and ineffective head of government—but his end was certainly precipitated by his ill-judged dependence on Washington in the financial as well as the political aspects of the bilateral relationship. His successors in the post of Chancellor were to take care not to make the same mistake.

Alliance Politics: from the Sinking of MLF to the Nuclear Planning Group

With Chancellor Erhard, as we have seen, Washington appeared to have a German head of government who would give a clear priority to relations with Washington and would not be tempted into the Gaullist deviationism characteristic of Adenauer's last years—even though ' Der Alte ', Strauss, and others were urging Bonn to remain faithful to the pro-French alignment symbolized in the treaty of January 1963.[27] At the end of 1963 Johnson and Erhard met on two occasions: first at President Kennedy's funeral at the end of November and then when Erhard visited the Johnson ranch in Texas in mid-December. As far as developments within the alliance were concerned—as distinct from the essentially bilateral question of offset costs—the main topic for discussion was Germany's role in NATO's nuclear affairs, and particularly in the MLF.

As we have seen, Kennedy had given the State Department's MLF lobby a ' hunting license ' to pursue the project early in 1963, and an inter-Allied study-group had begun to examine it by the time Johnson took over.[28] President Johnson is said to have given little thought to the proposal for the whole of his first year of office—he was of course hard-pressed with other matters—and there were plenty of authoritative voices to confirm that the project at least deserved further study. Dean Acheson, for instance, went on public record at the end of 1963 to urge close collaboration with Germany in ' the nuclear arm ', saying:

> the most helpful road to this end, both militarily and politically, is the multilateral force, where all willing to come in are to man the ships and join in the planning and command. The German Government is eager to get on with the job, willing to pay its share of the cost and to provide its share of the crews. . . . The greatest incitement to interest is to get the project under way, if only on a trial basis. To do this, we would be wise to work closest with the most enthusiastic, those most eager to have the plan succeed.[29]

In view of the lack of interest of America's other main allies, the discussions on the MLF became largely an American-German matter: France refused to participate, and the British government was seriously divided on the issue.[30] The American-German consultations which developed on strategic affairs during 1964—McNamara and von Hassel building up a very close working relationship—covered not only the MLF but also such matters as the possibility of limited nuclear war in NATO's forward areas (in Germany), the limitation of damage in Germany in the event of such a war, and means of enhancing the credibility of the Western deterrent in general.[31] This dialogue, whereby German officials came to share American thinking on the strategic issues of the alliance, was ultimately to prove of more significance and lasting value than the discussion of a ' hardware solution ' to Germany's demands embodied in the MLF.

By October 1964, by the time the new Labour government in Britain took office, likely to be more hostile to the MLF than its Conservative predecessor (of the departments, the Foreign Office had been sympathetic to the idea for diplomatic reasons, while the Ministry of Defence opposed it for strategic and economic ones), the German government was ready to state that if no other allies were interested, they would proceed with the project on a purely German-American basis.[32] Matters remained thus until late in November, when Johnson, now triumphantly re-elected to the presidency, faced the imminent visit of Harold Wilson and the demand for an American reaction to the new British proposal for an Atlantic Nuclear Force, widely seen as an attempt to sabotage the MLF.[33]

The situation which Johnson found, when he at last gave his mind to the problem, was that Washington and Bonn had each proceeded with the MLF plan on the assumption that the other was strongly attached to it, whereas in reality neither of them was. In November, after Wilson's election and while the new British policy was being decided, emissaries of Johnson had returned to Washington with the news that the CDU in Bonn was seriously divided on the MLF: the pro-MLF faction—Erhard, Schröder and von Hassel—were strongly opposed by Adenauer, Strauss, Jäger, and others. This German hesitancy, which the State Department had apparently not hitherto fully reported to the White House,[34] was confirmed by a meeting of the CDU parliamentary group on 11 November, which decided in effect to take no action until a clearer demand for the MLF was made by Washington.[35] The report of this decision was considered by Johnson and McGeorge Bundy on Sunday 6 December, the day before Wilson's arrival; on this same Sunday the President made some telephone calls to establish whether the MLF was popular in the Senate. The response he got from Capitol Hill was distinctly negative—liberal Senators opposed the sharing of nuclear secrets with Germany, and conservatives opposed sharing them with anyone—and this was enough to settle the matter. The establishment of the MLF would entail the signature of a treaty requiring a two-thirds majority in the Senate, and as the President was going to need senatorial approval for a great range of domestic reform legislation in 1965, there was no question of his wasting his standing there in aid of a project which not even Bonn now appeared to want. The British delegation was therefore told on 7–8 December that the ANF proposal would be considered (though not, it is said, before Johnson had forced Wilson to agree at least in principle to the MLF); [36] and the President then sent a National Security Council memorandum to all agencies of his government insisting that pressure for the MLF was no longer the policy of the administration. In order to make quite sure that this injunction was obeyed even by the 'MLF lobby' in the State Department, the President ensured that a copy was transmitted to James Reston of the *New York Times*, whose resulting article made the administration's shelving of the MLF clear and unmistakable.[37]

For several months the MLF was still spoken of as a possible solution to NATO's nuclear problems, and there was even talk of an alliance force under German-American co-ownership; [38] however, the 'denouement' of November-December 1964—the almost simultaneous realization in both Bonn and Washington that the other was not seriously interested—in fact brought an end to the MLF with only a moderate degree of strain in relations between the two capitals.

At this point the Pentagon took an active hand in the game: the MLF had of course stood in some conflict with the principle of unified command which formed a central part of the McNamara Doctrine, and McNamara was now determined that no new scheme for the decentralization of 'hardware' should be developed which might jeopardize both unified control in the alliance and the non-proliferation negotiations with the Soviet Union. The solution thus evolved by the Pentagon was the consultative one—based on the inter-allied exchanges of view on strategic doctrine already under way—which provided for the establishment of a new forum for discussion in the alliance. This so-called 'McNamara Committee', later officially entitled the Nuclear Planning Group, included Germany as one of its permanent members, thus reviving in a new form the earlier suggestion that Germany should become a member of the alliance's Standing Group in Washington.[39] The Committee was formally proposed in May 1965 and held its first session in November: thereafter, the Nuclear Planning Group (NPG), meeting every six months at Defence Minister level, provided a useful device for associating Germany with the nuclear policy of the alliance, and overcoming the feeling that as a non-nuclear power she was the victim of 'discrimination'. The 'hardware' solution to Germany's wish for equality of status was not formally abandoned at this stage: it was constantly discussed in the press, and also during Erhard's visit to Johnson in December 1965 (when Erhard raised it, despite American advice that the President would not be receptive), but it was effectively dead after the end of 1964.

A cement for German-American relations in NATO was all the more necessary at this point, since the alliance was seriously shaken in 1965–6 by the policies pursued by France. President de Gaulle's Government regarded the NPG, like the MLF, as a sign of American hegemony, and refused to have anything to do with it. Moreover, after disrupting the workings of the European Economic Community by his boycott in 1965–6, he struck a serious blow against NATO by announcing in March 1966 that France was withdrawing from the integrated command structure of the alliance, and insisting that the European headquarters of NATO must be removed from French territory. (It went to Brussels.) The fairly close harmony of view between Bonn and Washington in their respective responses to Paris in part reflected the fact that there was a certain symmetry in de Gaulle's dealings with them: Bonn was damaged by his treatment of the European Economic Community, and Washington by his treatment of NATO. Both were also somewhat perturbed by his overtures to the Soviet Union in 1964–6; there was in any case, of course, a deep underlying identity of American and German interests with respect to NATO.

The EEC recovered from the crisis of 1965–6 well enough to function almost as before, though the impetus towards integration was broken in the process. At the end of 1966, as noted above,[40] there was a revival of British interest in membership, an issue on which Washington and Bonn again found they had common interests: Erhard in particular welcomed the prospect of an enlarged European Community, orientated towards freer transatlantic trade by British membership, as an alternative to the narrower grouping of the Six under French leadership.

One reason why Bonn and Washington continued to see fairly closely eye-to-eye during the strategic debates of 1965–6 was because both capitals, not just Washington as hitherto, were now turning with increased interest to the prospects of détente with the East.

Relations with the Adversary: Détente with Russia, but not with China

For Washington, the search for a dialogue on international security with the Soviet Union showed the continuation by Johnson of one of Kennedy's central concerns in the post-Cuban phase of international relations. As far as Europe's future went, the American belief that acceptance of the territorial status quo was essential in the short run, as a way of changing it in the longer run, peacefully and with general consent, remained as firm under Johnson as under Kennedy. This meant that America increasingly accepted the existence of the German Democratic Republic as a state, and at times pressed Bonn to do so too, in the confident hope that this process would bring about 'change through contact' (i.e. internal liberalization through external recognition) and ultimately allow reunification by consent. This view was to some extent shared by Willy Brandt—the Mayor of West Berlin until the end of 1966, when he was to become Foreign Minister in Kiesinger's 'Grand Coalition'—since the SPD in Berlin on the whole held a more flexible view on East-West contacts than the Party in Bonn.[41] This meant that there occasionally appeared to be a tacit coalition between Washington and West Berlin, against the rather harder line still taken in Bonn, even though Brandt was careful to deny when he visited Washington that he had any intention of trying to use Johnson against Erhard.[42] In a world where all states seemed to be in process of abandoning some at least of the rigidities of the Cold War, American policy under Johnson appeared to espouse the cause of détente through negotiations, flexibility, and multiple East-West contacts with particular interest.[43]

Johnson summarized his view of Germany's role in East-West relations in an interview with the Munich weekly *Quick* in April 1964. He repeated what he had told Erhard in Texas the previous December: ' Put yourself in the place of the Russians. Try to understand their feelings. They are worried about the Germans and that is understandable.' [44] Such words, accompanied by Washington's marked reluctance in 1964–5 to put pressure on the Soviet Union to discuss German reunification in the old sense, created some disappointment in Bonn.[45] This disappointment was very slight, however, in comparison with the sense of outrage and betrayal which Bonn had felt during Kennedy's dealings with the Russians in 1961–2. Bonn itself, as will be seen, was going through a process of modifying its views on détente, and took a much more confident view of Washington's intentions. Even an American statement like William C. Foster's article of July 1965 on disarmament, which explicitly gave détente with the Soviet Union priority over relations with allies,[46] failed to arouse the degree of alarm in Bonn which similar statements a few years earlier would have provoked.

In 1965–6 the crisis caused in NATO by de Gaulle's policies gave rise to a considerable debate in America about the function of the alliance. Several witnesses testified before various Senatorial bodies (notably Senator Jackson's Subcommittee of the Committee on Government Operations and Senator Fulbright's Committee on Foreign Relations) to the effect that the alliance should concentrate on becoming a force for stability in Europe. This stability, it was argued, should be based on a rough equality of military force between the two sides, and an acceptance of the political and territorial status quo, at least for the immediate future.[47]

One particularly important witness, whose testimony before the Senate Foreign Relations Committee in June 1966 was taken very seriously in Bonn, was McGeorge Bundy. Bundy, who had just been appointed President of the Ford Foundation, had spent five years as Special Assistant for National Security Affairs to Presidents Kennedy and Johnson. When he firmly called on West Germany to contribute to détente by a categorical renunciation of all claims to territory beyond the Oder-Neisse Line—' a clear statement on the record of what we all know off the record '—German opinion naturally realized that this reflected the views of the White House. When Bundy went on to declare that the ultimate purpose of Western policy in Europe was ' not strength, but settlement ', and that West

Germany and the United States carried a ' special responsibility ' in this task (Bonn's responsibility including the permanent renunciation of nuclear weapons), German leaders again knew that this analysis could not be ignored.[48]

Washington's thinking on the future of East-West relations in Europe was summarized in an important speech delivered by President Johnson in New York on 7 October 1966. The President argued the need for ' peaceful engagement ' between the two halves of Europe, rather than the more passive concept of ' peaceful coexistence ', and placed German reunification (as Kennedy had done) clearly at the end of a process of détente, not as its precondition or first step: ' We must improve the East-West environment in order to achieve the unification of Germany in the context of a larger, peaceful and prosperous Europe.' [49] Such warnings that America saw the road to German unification as leading through all-European ' re-association ' neither fell on deaf ears nor provoked cries of rage in Germany. As we have noted, the SPD under Willy Brandt was moving firmly towards a more flexible position on East-West relations.

One reason why this evolution led to harmony rather than discord with Washington was precisely because it constituted a deliberate effort to adapt German policy to lines of thought which had been current in Washington since Kennedy's arrival in power. Egon Bahr, one of Brandt's closest associates, has confirmed that the proposal for a new relationship with the GDR which he put forward as early as July 1963, the programme of ' change through contact ', or *Wandel durch Annäherung*, was based on a point-by-point examination of the Kennedy administration's ideas on East-West relations.[50]

It was not only the SPD Opposition that adjusted its views on the possibility of improved relations with the East. Gerhard Schröder, who had been Foreign Minister since 1961, found more scope for flexibility under Erhard's chancellorship than he had in the last two years of Adenauer's. In the spring of 1964 he expressed his belief that ' in some East European countries there is a growing understanding for the German problem . . . It appears to me that our desire for true relaxation of tensions is meeting with more understanding in those countries than with the Soviet government for the time being.' [51]

Schröder acted on this analysis by setting up trade missions in Poland, Hungary, Bulgaria, and Rumania, and was even prepared to abandon the Hallstein Doctrine by establishing diplomatic relations with the last-mentioned of these states, despite Bucharest's relations with the GDR. This proposal, however, went too far for some of the more conservative members of Erhard's cabinet, and diplomatic relations with Bucharest were established only in 1967, after his replacement by the Grand Coalition.[52]

In January 1965 the Opposition spokesman Fritz Erler, Vice-Chairman of the SPD, argued that the time had come for West Germany to discuss with Poland the recognition of their mutual frontier; and two months later Erich Mende, the leader of the FDP, who was Erhard's Vice-Chancellor and Minister for All-German Affairs, asserted that there was a danger of the two German states' growing ever further apart, and recommended the establishment of joint commissions representing the two Germanies (nominally acting as agents for the Allies) to overcome this tendency.[53]

Fritz Erler's support for the suggestion that the Oder-Neisse Line should be recognized (an idea already advanced by many eminent Germans, including the philosopher Karl Jaspers and the historian Golo Mann) reached a new level of popularity when it was incorporated in a memorandum issued by the Evangelical Church in October 1965. The memorandum attacked one of the basic tenets of Bonn's existing Eastern policy—the ' right to the homeland ' as a basis for German claims in the East—by pointing out that, in the areas taken over by Poland, this right must clearly extend to the rights of the Poles born there in the intervening twenty years.[54]

The growing readiness in Germany for a more conciliatory attitude towards the East was momentarily stilled during the election campaign of late 1965, but by the beginning of the following year another of Erhard's ministers was deviating from the accepted policies. In January 1966 Johann-Baptist Gradl, the CDU Minister for Refugee Affairs, stated that East Germany would have to make ' sacrifices ' over the Oder-Neisse Line as the price of reunification, ' since no-one could expect it to take place within the 1937 boundaries.'[55]

In March 1966 the government as a whole took the further step of addressing a ' Peace Note ' to the East European states, offering to sign mutual agreements renouncing the use of force.

This step was welcomed in Washington, but its effect was blunted by some unconciliatory wording and by references to the German frontiers of 1937—these were the work of diehards in the Cabinet [56]—and two months later the Bonn government issued a comprehensive White Book reasserting the traditional claim to reunification. It is noteworthy that, among the officials responsible for compiling this document, there was a feeling that it represented a point of view which Bonn was in fact already being forced to recognize as untenable.[57]

As the *Landtag* election in North Rhine-Westphalia approached (this vote, in July 1966, was to be the first large-scale test of German opinion since the general election of September 1965), it was clear that public feelings about Germany's Eastern relations had become distinctly more flexible since the previous autumn. Instead of taking an ultra-cautious line about relations with the GDR, the SPD began to apply Egon Bahr's doctrine of 'change through contact' by trying to negotiate with the East German Socialist Unity Party an exchange of speakers that would allow Ulbricht and other East German leaders to address public meetings in West Germany, in exchange for invitations to Brandt, Erler, and Wehner to speak to audiences in the GDR. The project was eventually called off by the East German authorities, who had taken fright, but the SPD won a striking degree of popularity for the idea, as the North Rhine-Westphalia voting results showed.[58]

Determined not to leave a monopoly of flexibility to the other parties, an active spokesman of the CDU—Rainer Barzel, a potential rival to Erhard—made a controversial speech during a visit to the United States, in which he argued that Soviet troops should be allowed to remain in a reunified Germany to represent legitimate Soviet interests. This notion, and Barzel's endorsement of Mende's earlier proposal for East-West commissions representing the two German governments, went too far for the majority of the CDU leadership at this stage, and he was forced to explain that it was only a 'personal contribution' to the discussion.[59]

It was probably no coincidence that the scene of Barzel's détente-orientated speech was Washington, where many an ambitious European politician aspired to build up his domestic prestige by making remarks calculated to please his hosts. German and American leaders increasingly agreed in their search for accommodation with the Communist world: the one significant East-West issue on which American actions still upset German sensibilities was the non-proliferation of nuclear weapons. Informal consultations between the American and Soviet governments for a pact limiting the spread of nuclear weapons had begun at the time of the Test Ban Treaty in 1963, and had become fairly active by 1965.[60] The consultations took place in the context of the Eighteen-Nation Disarmament Conference in Geneva, where West Germany had only observer status, and German concern about the issue was quite slow to develop. The American Permanent Representative to the NATO Council at the time has testified that ' alliance interest ' in the projected Non-Proliferation Treaty was only ' desultory ' until the US-Soviet talks became concrete in the winter of 1966–7, and a draft treaty committing signatories not to make, receive, or transfer nuclear weapons was worked out.[61]

As West Germany had no intention of abrogating her undertaking not to acquire a nuclear force (dating back to 1954), it was at first sight surprising, and to some observers worrying, that the Erhard government reacted with increasing alarm as Washington's attention, in 1965–6, switched from the MLF to the proposed NPT. A perceptive analysis of Bonn's concern, written in the spring of 1966, suggested that it had four grounds.

To begin with, the German government was still not satisfied with its role in NATO's planning of nuclear strategy and peacetime decision-making (still being worked out in the ' McNamara Committee '), and was alarmed at the Soviet view that such consultations should be included in the nuclear ' dissemination ' which the proposed treaty was to ban. Secondly, the idea of a NATO nuclear force along the lines of the MLF, with an American veto, had still not been finally abandoned, and the German view was that this matter, like NATO's arrangements for consultation, should be settled between the Allies rather than in treaty negotiations with the Russians. Thirdly, some Germans, particularly Strauss and his Bavarian colleagues, had still not given up the idea of a European nuclear force. They—and also the ' Atlanticists ' who still hoped to see a European nuclear force developing through the MLF's ' European clause '—wished to ensure that ' proliferation ' was not defined in such a way as to foreclose this option. Finally, many Germans saw a German renunciation of nuclear weapons as a bargaining counter which should be used only in exchange for Soviet concessions on the question of reunification, not as an unreciprocated gift.[62]

As we shall see, the main focus of German objections to the NPT was to shift from these somewhat unrealistic strategic and political calculations to more concrete issues concerning the industrial uses of atomic energy and the role of Euratom,[63] but it was already clear by the end of the Erhard administration that the approaches of Washington and Bonn to the problem diverged substantially.

As a final factor in the role of extra-alliance relations in this period, it should be noted that the Erhard government itself embarked on certain ventures of collaboration with the alliance's adversaries, only to abandon them under American pressure. In January 1964 an agreement for a large sale of steel pipes by West Germany to the Soviet Union was cancelled in response to American protests about the export of strategic materials, and later the same year a drafted German-Chinese trade agreement was called off; [64] early in 1966 an even more controversial project, the building by West Germany of a $150 million steel plant in China, was also cancelled after strong protests in the Senate.[65]

Washington's wish to see Bonn committed to 'peaceful engagement' in Eastern Europe clearly did not extend to acts likely to strengthen America's main adversaries—particularly in view of the Vietnam War—and the Erhard government, unlike its successors, was unwilling to persist in forms of Ostpolitik which incurred American displeasure.

NOTES

1 President Johnson proudly observes in his memoirs *The Vantage Point* (1971), p. 476, that during his presidency more 'significant agreements' were signed between the American and Soviet governments than during the whole of the thirty years since the establishment of diplomatic relations by Franklin Roosevelt in 1933.

2 See below, p. 159.

3 *NYT*, 19 May 1964.

4 Adenauer had visited the United States ten times between 1953 and 1963, an average of once annually. Erhard was there in Nov. and in Dec. 1963, June 1964, June and Dec. 1965, and Sept. 1966.

5 Private information, Washington.

6 See below, pp. 144–5.

7 'New Directions in Arms Control and Disarmament', *For. Aff.*, 43/4, pp. 587–601. Private information in Washington indicates that the article seriously irritated the Secretary of State—who, through an oversight, had not cleared it for publication—but it reflected White House thinking.

8 Johnson's interview with the Munich weekly *Quick*, reported in the *NYT*, 8 May 1964, gives a good reflection of this mood.

9 This idea was publicly supported in 1965–6 by President Lübke and ex-Chancellor Adenauer: *NYT*, 28 Dec. 1965; *Die Welt*, 3 Jan. 1966.

10 Rostow, pp. 70–1. Similar views were frequently expressed in private conversations in Washington in 1965 and 1966.

11 See above, p. 80.

12 See Morgan, 'The Federal Republic of Germany', in S. Henig and J. Pinder, eds, *European Political Parties* (1969), pp. 49–50.

13 See Strauss's article 'An Alliance of Continents', *Int. Aff.*, Apr. 1965. For Guttenberg's views, see his book *Wenn der Westen Will: Plädoyer für eine mutige Politik*, 2nd edn (1965).

14 Grosser, *Germany in Our Time*, p. 129.

15 See Morgan, 'The Scope of German Foreign Policy', in *Yearbook of World Affairs 1966*, pp. 78–105.

16 See *Der Spiegel*, 1 May 1967.

17 Count Finck von Finckenstein, quoted in Prittie, p. 307.

18 On the course of German policy faced with divergence between Washington and Paris, see J. Joffe, 'Germany and the Atlantic Alliance', in W. C. Cromwell, ed., *Political Problems of Alliance Partnership* (1969), pp. 365–80.

19 Ibid. p. 380.

20 See above, p. 105.

21 *NYT*, 15 Nov. 1964, quoted in Cromwell, p. 112.

22 *NYT*, 6 June 1966.

23 *Die Zeit*, 24 May 1966; *NYT*, 6, 10, 11, 12 and 15 June 1966. On the economic and political background, see Mendershausen, pp. 94–8.

24 Robert Kleiman, *NYT*, 6 June 1966. As noted above, 15,000 of America's 225,000 ground combat troops in Germany had recently been removed, for transfer to Vietnam.

25 Private information, Washington and Bonn. See *Der Spiegel*, 1 May 1967. As *l'Année Politique 1966* observes (p. 281), Johnson's suggestion that a telephonic hot line be installed between Washington and Bonn was 'une faible compensation'.

26 Cromwell, in idem, ed., p. 113. See also Morgan 'The Federal Republic of Germany', in Henig and Pinder, eds, pp. 52–3, and Johnson's account of the episode (pp. 307–8).

27 See above, p. 129.

28 See above, pp. 128–30. The expression 'hunting license' was used by a critic of the plan in Washington.

29 *New York Times Magazine*, 15 Dec. 1963.

30 A perceptive analysis of British opinion in the summer of 1964—not intended for publication—is Richard E. Neustadt's 'Memorandum on the British Labour Party and the MLF', printed in *New Left Review*, Sept.-Oct. 1968, pp. 11–21.

31 See U. Nerlich, 'Die nuklearen Dilemmas der Bundesrepublik', *Europa-Archiv*, vol. 17 (1965), pp. 637–52, and John Newhouse, *De Gaulle and the Anglo-Saxons* (1970), pp. 269–70.

32 *NYT*, 9 Oct. 1964.

33 A. Buchan, *The Multilateral Force*, pp. 10–11. H. Wilson, *The Labour Government 1964–1970* (1971), pp. 39–50.

34 Private information, Washington.

35 Mahncke, *Nukleare Mitwirkung*, p. 194.

36 Private information, Washington.

37 J. Reston, 'President urges full U.S. effort to reunify NATO', *NYT*, 21 Dec. 1964, supplemented by private information, Washington. For further details, see Joffe, in Cromwell, ed., p. 417, footnote; and Mahncke, *Nukleare Mitwirkung*, pp. 200–1.

38 See Hanrieder, *The Stable Crisis*, pp. 23–9, and sources there given.

39 See above, p. 141.

40 See above, p. 141.

41 See A. Ashkenazi, *Reformpartei und Aussenpolitik* (1968). The American version of the policy of changing the status quo through accepting it is exceptionally clearly stated in one of J. Kenneth Galbraith's letters to President Kennedy: *Ambassador's Journal* (1969), p. 211.

42 Reports appeared in *Die Welt*, and other German newspapers throughout May 1964.

43 A penetrating assessment by H. von Borch, 'Amerika und der europaische Status Quo', *Aussenpolitik* 15/2 (1964), pp. 81–91, characterizes this Kennedy-Johnson approach as 'sociology transposed into diplomacy'. For a more detailed account, see the same author's *Friede trotz Krieg: Spannungsfelder der Weltpolitik seit 1950* (1966).

44 *NYT*, 29 Apr. 1964.

45 *Le Monde*, 5 Jan. 1965, reporting remarks by Dean Rusk. See Karl Kaiser, *German Foreign Policy in Transition* (1968), p. 37.

46 See above, pp. 43–4.

47 See, e.g., Henry M. Jackson, ed., *The Atlantic Alliance: Jackson Subcommittee Headings and Findings* (1967).

48 *NYT*, 21 June 1966; private information on reactions in Bonn.

49 Quoted in Johnson, pp. 474–5; for the complete text, see *DOSB*, 24 Oct. 1966, pp. 622–5. The speech was largely inspired by Prof. Zbigniew Brzezinski, who was then serving as a member of the State Department's Policy Planning Council. For two contemporary assessments of Germany's role in détente, see Pierre Hassner, 'German and European Reunification', and W. E. Griffith, 'The German Problem and American Policy', *Survey*, no. 61, Oct. 1966.

50 See Kaiser, *German Foreign Policy in Transition*, p. 90. Bahr, who in 1963 was press secretary and an adviser to Mayor Brandt in Berlin, was to implement his programme for Ostpolitik as Head of the Planning Staff

in the Foreign Ministry from 1967 and as State Secretary in the Chancellor's office from 1969. For a controversial presentation of his views, see Walter F. Hahn, 'West Germany's Ostpolitik: the Grand Design of Egon Bahr', *Orbis*, 16/4 (1973), pp. 859–80.

51 Quoted by Hanrieder, *The Stable Crisis*, p. 104.

52 See Kaiser, *German Foreign Policy in Transition*, pp. 86–90; and, for a more detailed account of this phase of Bonn's diplomacy, Morgan, 'The Scope of German Foreign Policy', *Yearbook of World Affairs 1966.*

53 Kaiser, as preceding note, pp. 36, 95.

54 Ibid. p. 38.

55 Gradl interview in *Der Spiegel*, 17 Jan. 1966, cited by Kaiser, p. 40. Cf. *NYT*, 18 Jan. 1966, for an American reaction.

56 Kaiser, *German Foreign Policy in Transition*, pp. 39, 88.

57 German Federal Republic, Auswärtiges Amt, *Die Bemuhüngen der deutschen Regierung und ihrer Verbündeten um die Einheit Deutschlands 1955–1966* (1966); private information, Bonn.

58 Kaiser, *German Foreign Policy in Transition*, pp. 26, 102–4.

59 Ibid. p. 91, n. 99 and p. 95, n. 105; and *New York Times*, 16 and 17 June 1966.

60 See the discussion of Foster's article of July 1965, above, p. 144.

61 Harlan Cleveland, *NATO: The Transatlantic Bargain* (1970), p. 68.

62 Theo Sommer, 'The Objectives of Germany', in Alastair Buchan, ed., *A World of Nuclear Powers?* (1966), esp. pp. 48–9, presents these arguments in greater detail. See also Joffe, in Cromwell, ed., pp. 418–21.

63 See below, pp. 181–4.

64 Joffe, in Cromwell, ed., pp. 370–1; *Der Spiegel*, 1 May 1967; private information, Washington.

65 *NYT*, 18, 22 and 25 Mar. 1966.

CHAPTER NINE

The Period of the Grand Coalition 1966–1969

Background: the late Sixties

THE Grand Coalition under Kurt Georg Kiesinger and Willy Brandt held office for almost three years, from the downfall of Erhard at the end of 1966 to the general election which took Brandt from the vice-chancellorship to the chancellorship in October 1969. Most of this period coincided with the closing phase of the Johnson presidency; the Nixon administration which took office in January 1969 spent most of its first year in a reassessment of the main aspects of American policy, in which the new President was aided, as far as external affairs were concerned, by his Special Assistant Henry Kissinger.

In the world of the late 1960s both the opposing power-blocs of the Cold War continued to show an increasing decentralization of some forms of power, and détente between them was still expected and practised, despite the persistence of some serious armed conflicts.

The gravest of these was in Vietnam, where a vast increase in America's ground forces (she had over half a million troops there by mid-1968) failed to halt the spread of Communist control in the South, and the United States had recourse to increasingly massive aerial bombardments of the North. By 1968 it was widely felt in the United States (and certainly by America's European allies, whose attitudes varied between open disapproval in France and reluctant support in Britain and Germany) that an attempt should be made to end this appallingly costly war by negotiation. At the end of March President Johnson announced his readiness to embark on peace talks with the North Vietnamese government and at the same time published his decision not to accept re-nomination for a further term as President, in order to give the peace talks a better chance of success.

The overriding importance of the Vietnam War in American politics—indicated by this gesture—was confirmed by the prominence of the issue in the ensuing election campaign, when both the Democratic candidate, Vice President Humphrey, and his Republican opponent, the former Vice President Richard Nixon, emphasized their intention of bringing the war to an end. At the peace talks which began in Paris in May 1968, however, no reconciliation between the American and North Vietnamese positions had occurred by the end of 1969.

One of the striking features of the Vietnam War was that despite its military escalation and the accompanying public attacks on American 'imperialism' by the Soviet Union (and China), it did not appear in practice to have any detrimental effect on the process of détente between the two super-powers, which continued to gather momentum. Their common interest in preventing conflicts in any part of the world from spreading so as to involve themselves, and in developing a basis of mutual understanding and co-operation, was shown in the aftermath of the Six-Day War in the Middle East in June 1967.

This clash, the worst crisis in the Middle East since the Suez affair of 1956, began with a pre-emptive attack by Israel's air force against her Arab neighbours, and ended with Israel in possession of large tracts of territory beyond her previous frontiers, comprising the Sinai Peninsula and Gaza Strip (from Egypt), the strategically crucial Golon Heights (from Syria), and the west bank of the River Jordan (from Jordan). Considerable diplomatic effort in and around the United Nations, including the untiring mediatory attempts of the Organization's Special Representative Gunnar Jarring from 1968 onwards, failed to resolve the conflict, but one of its immediate and most evident consequences was to bring together President Johnson and the Soviet leader Leonid Brezhnev. They met at Glassboro, New Jersey, on 23 June 1967 and made clear their common intention to refrain from exploiting the crisis to each other's disadvantage. They also discussed other international issues of mutual concern which had been explored when Gromyko visited Washington the previous October; for instance, the Soviet-American conversations about a bilateral arms control agreement, which President Johnson had suggested in January and which were by now under way.

A similar prudence on the part of the super-powers was evident in the case of a conflict in another part of the Third World: the civil war in Nigeria, which resulted after much bloodshed in the failure of secessionist Biafra to establish its independence. In marked contrast to their behaviour during the Congo crisis at the beginning of the decade, Washington and Moscow carefully refrained from any involvement in this dispute.

It was perhaps more surprising that even a conflict entailing military force in the heart of Central Europe—the area of direct confrontation between NATO and the Warsaw Pact—failed to occasion any interruption of the progress the two super-powers were making towards measures of détente, marked by the treaty on non-proliferation of nuclear weapons which they signed early in 1968. This crisis came in August 1968 with the invasion of Czechoslovakia by the Soviet Union and her Warsaw Pact allies, after a tense period of several months in which it had seemed possible that the Russians would, despite everything, tolerate Czechoslovakia's experiments in liberalization under Alexander Dubcek. In the event, the Soviet invasion led only to a passing moment of apprehension in Western Europe—which was, not surprisingly, most marked in the Federal Republic; and although it considerably retarded progress towards more independence for members of the Soviet bloc, except for the somewhat remote and persistently idiosyncratic Rumania, it did much less to disrupt progress towards détente at the super-power level. The American-Soviet bilateral talks on arms control, for instance, were briefly interrupted after the invasion, but resumed in earnest by 1969.

Within Western Europe the period from 1966 to 1969 was marked by the further development of the European Community—notably the completion of the customs union and the merging of the three Executives into the united Commission in whose presidency Jean Rey succeeded Walter Hallstein—

and also by a further French veto, at the end of 1967, on Britain's second attempt to join. This veto was in fact almost the last of President de Gaulle's acts of individualism in European and Atlantic affairs (it came after his controversial support of the Arab states in the June War and his dramatic pronouncements on world affairs in Moscow, Warsaw, and Quebec): his government, weakened by an electoral setback in March 1967, was severely shaken by the turbulent events in France in May 1968, and he left office in April 1969.

The economic and monetary problems of the Western world were in these years matters of more pressing concern than in the earlier years of the decade. The most significant aspect of these problems, in terms of the relations between states in the area, was the consistent strength of the West German economy and currency as the coalition government overcame the recession that had defeated Chancellor Erhard. Throughout the British balance of payments difficulties which led to the devaluation of sterling in November 1967, the problems of the dollar and other currencies leading to the IMF's establishment of Special Drawing Rights in June 1968, and the French monetary crises of 1968–9 the Deutschmark remained the most solid currency of the Western economic system. The German government was repeatedly urged to revalue its currency (as it had done in 1961), but Kiesinger refused to help other countries solve their balance of payments problems in this way. It was only during the election campaign of September 1969 that the Mark was 'floated' to counteract speculation, and only in October that the new government under Brandt and Scheel agreed to a revaluation—as we shall see, in circumstances which suggested that the 'economic giant' was no longer a 'political dwarf'.

Internal Politics: Uncertainty in Washington, Confidence in Bonn

We have already remarked that Lyndon Johnson, when he was precipitated into the presidency by Kennedy's assassination, was mainly interested in using the office to promote a programme of domestic reforms. Even after his electoral victory against Goldwater a year later, when America's commitment to the Vietnam War was beginning to escalate, Johnson still hoped to devote his time and the country's resources to the problems of civil rights, educational opportunities, and urban renewal. As the intensity of the war continued to mount, however, and the number of American troops in Vietnam rose from 385,000 in January 1967 to 540,000 in June 1969,[1] the attention of official Washington was inevitably drawn towards Asian problems and away from others. As well as the military prosecution of the war, considerable importance was attached to the peace talks with the North Vietnamese government, held in Paris from May 1968 onwards, the American delegation being led first by Averell Harriman, then, after the change of administration, by Henry Cabot Lodge. President Nixon, who came into office in January 1969 committed to finding an honourable end to the conflict, shortly afterwards announced at his first news conference: 'We have a new sense of urgency with regard to these negotiations. There will be new tactics. We believe that those tactics may be more successful than the tactics of the past.'[2] By the end of his first term of office nearly four years later, these hopes had not been fulfilled.

By the latter part of the 1960s the cost of the war was making a marked impact on the United States' balance of payments. Although the private sector of the balance remained constantly in credit (at least until 1969, when it showed a deficit for the first time), the military and other expenditure of the United States government abroad led to a large and increasing deficit in the public sector: the overall deficit thus went from \$2.9 billion (US) in 1964 and \$1.6 billion in 1966 to \$4.2 billion in 1967, \$1.7 billion in 1968, and \$6.9 billion in 1969.[3]

With the balance of payments in this condition, and with the burden of spending on the fairly impressive programme of domestic reforms which the Johnson administration was none the less able to accomplish, it was not surprising that powerful voices on the American political scene increasingly called for a curtailment of America's costly military support for Europe. Although both the Johnson and Nixon administrations repeatedly reaffirmed the strength of the American commitment, anxious West Europeans—particularly Germans—could not ignore the mounting pressures on Capitol Hill. Senator Stuart Symington, for instance, an influential Democrat who had served under Truman as Secretary of the Air Force, complained in 1966 that the European members of NATO had consistently failed to fulfil their military obligations throughout the seventeen-year history of the alliance, and that the United States had been forced to make good the deficiency of several tens of thousands of troops.[4] Symington argued that since the United States was bearing an unfair economic burden, and since even the large numbers of conventional forces she maintained in Europe could not deter any Soviet attack without nuclear escalation, their number should be reduced to 50,000.[5]

An even more persistent critic of the scale of America's military presence in Europe was Senator Mike Mansfield of Montana. He repeatedly introduced resolutions into the Senate, from 1966 onwards, calling for 'substantial reductions' in American forces in Europe. The number of Senators supporting these resolutions fluctuated—Mansfield scored 44 in the vote of August 1966, and was estimated to have 42 supporters in January 1967, 49 in July, and 'more than a third of the Senate' a year or two later.[6]

German political leaders concerned at the spectacle of such views gaining ground in Congress could feel safe as long as the possible outcome of the Mansfield Resolution remained uncertain—even if successful, its effect would have been recommendatory, not mandatory—and the administration was not forced to give it too much weight in formulating policy towards Europe. There was much more cause for alarm when the administration itself recruited men with views unwelcome in Bonn. Even Henry Kissinger, well known for his sympathy with Germany's views,[7] occasioned a moment of concern in Bonn when it became known, shortly after he took office as President Nixon's Special Assistant for National Security Affairs, that he had been a member of a study group on European security organized by the United Nations Association of the United States, whose recommendations included a Standing European Security Commission with both German states as full members.[8]

In general, however, Germany's political leaders in 1966–9 had no reason to fear that American administrations, either Democratic or Republican, would take any steps—as, for instance, such a 'premature' diplomatic recognition of the GDR—which would be positively opposed to Bonn's views of the German national interest. The most serious sources of conflict, within the American political system, appeared to be

Washington's continuing preoccupation with Asian and domestic affairs, and the mounting Congressional pressures represented, among others, by Senators Mansfield and Symington.

In Bonn, similarly, there was a clear tendency after the economic and political crisis of 1966 for the new government to give most of its attention to Germany's own problems, and relatively little to the concerns of its major ally: in this it contrasted markedly with the Erhard government. The very composition of Kiesinger's cabinet, reflecting an elaborate series of compromises made for reasons of party political, regional, and religious representation, made it plain that Washington would no longer be dealing with quite such a docile partner as before. The government's leading figures included—as well as the Chancellor himself, who was known to favour an active rapprochement with Gaullist France—the Vice-Chancellor and Foreign Minister, Willy Brandt, who had helped the SPD to overcome its neutralist attitude in foreign affairs, but who currently shared Kiesinger's inclination to turn first to Paris rather than to Washington; Franz Josef Strauss, whose support for Kiesinger in the CDU's internal disputes gave the latter the chancellorship, but only at the price of bringing back into the cabinet a man whose distrust of American policy was quite explicit; and Herbert Wehner, the SPD's tactician, whose policy as Minister for All-German Affairs might well be influenced, as Washington observers saw it, by his Communist past. Several proven friends of the American connection remained in the cabinet, though in some cases their influence was reduced: the 'Atlanticist' Foreign Minister Gerhard Schröder, for instance, had to move to the Defence Ministry in order to make room for Willy Brandt.[9] Two of the most powerful figures under the new dispensation in Bonn were Rainer Barzel and Helmut Schmidt, chairmen respectively of the CDU and the SPD parliamentary groups: they were both committed to the American alliance, but also showed a strong and pragmatic feeling for Germany's national interests.

The Grand Coalition, based on an impregnable parliamentary majority of 447 seats out of 496, confronted Washington with a new self-confidence which demanded a change in the nature of the relationship. A well-informed observer, after noting that 'while the principle of alliance remains undisputed its modalities are certain to come under close and critical scrutiny', summarized the *Zeitgeist* in a passage which deserves quotation at some length:

It would be dishonest, in this context, to deny that a heretofore unknown resentment has built up with regard to the Johnson Administration and its handling of both bilateral relations and alliance affairs. It is generally accepted by now that Dr. Erhard's fate was sealed after he returned empty-handed from his last visit with President Johnson, having failed to move the Americans from their currency offset demands. Even those who were content to see Erhard go regretted that, in the last analysis, it was American insensitivity which brought him down. Prominent 'Atlanticists' gave vent to their irritation, and inevitably it was Secretary McNamara who came in for most of the criticism. The Secretary of Defense has long been rubbing even staunch friends of the United States the wrong way. He has frequently ruffled German feelings by not only being right but being rudely so; he appears to many as a tireless arms merchant with shockingly high-pressure sales techniques, and there are leading figures in both coalition parties who blame the present disarray of NATO as much on him as on General de Gaulle. To all this must be added the agitation over recent Soviet-American negotiations for a non-proliferation treaty. American handling of this issue created the impression in Bonn that Germany was to be stampeded into signing a document about whose previous history it had been informed only spottily and belatedly and the implications of which remain unclear. Suspicions were aroused that the Johnson Administration was putting its common interests with the Soviet Union above the common interests of the Western Alliance.

Germany is not about to take up a Gaullist attitude toward the United States. Opinion polls bear out the belief that America is still regarded as an indispensable and reliable partner. But the government of the Grand Coalition will no doubt take a more independent stance in defining Germany's national interest. The Federal Republic no longer feels like a ward of Washington. It will not hesitate to disagree with, and if necessary to deviate from, American-sponsored policies.[10]

In the words of a political scientist who served as a foreign policy adviser to Chancellor Kiesinger during this phase, what Germany needed was to correct the self-denying policy of the Adenauer era by 'a conscious *Wille zur Selbstständigkeit* (will for autonomy)'.[11]

One reason why the Federal government adopted this more independent stance towards its allies was that the increasing ' will for autonomy ' among sections of German public opinion was bringing unprecedented support to an extreme right-wing party, the National Democratic Party of Germany, or NPD. The NPD's success in more than one *Landtag* election during the economic doldrums of 1966 had been one of the reasons for the coming-together of the two main democratic parties to form the Grand Coalition, but this cure for the disease was slow to take effect: in the short run, the very fact that the CDU and SPD could be presented as ' ganging-up ' together to stifle all opposition had the effect of bringing even more support to the NPD, which achieved scores of up to 10 per cent of the votes in a further series of *Landtag* elections in 1967 and the spring of 1968.[12]

Even with the German electorate in this mood, American policy-makers had of course no serious reason to fear a militantly nationalistic attitude on the part of the new administration in Bonn. There was, however, no doubt that the combination of American over-commitment elsewhere, and Germany's new-found sense of political maturity demanded a clear change in the nature of their relationship. The West German decision in December 1968 to hold the presidential election of March 1969 in West Berlin, despite Allied requests not to provoke the Russians by doing so, was only one indication of the new situation.[13]

Bilateral Relations: New Terms for Offset Bargaining

During the animated negotiations on offset costs which preceded the fall of Chancellor Erhard in 1966 his government had made it clear to the United States that agreements on the pattern of those reached since 1961—providing for extensive German purchases of American military equipment—would not be acceptable in the future.[14] The situation early in 1967 when the Kiesinger government began to bargain for something better (the current agreement was due to expire in June) was rendered precarious by the serious financial problems of both governments. It was worsened by the considerable tension arising from Bonn's concern at the progress of Washington's discussions on the prevention of nuclear proliferation with the

USSR, conducted, so Kiesinger complained, without consultation with the allies directly affected by the projected treaty banning the acquisition of weapons by non-nuclear states.

As Kiesinger put it, criticizing American behaviour in a talk with reporters at the end of February 1967, on the eve of new offset negotiations: ' It can't go on like this. We talk nowadays only about matters in dispute, not about our common problems.' [15] The well-informed Washington correspondent of *The Times* was, in the event, exaggerating when he commented that there was an American-German crisis ' the like of which has not been seen since Dr Grewe, who was West German Ambassador to Washington, left here under a cloud ', and that ' there certainly seems little use in discussing force levels and nuclear strategy, and certainly not support costs, while Dr Kiesinger, the Chancellor, is in his present mood.' [16] However, the offset talks which began in London on 3 March 1967 threatened to be hard-fought and protracted. It was partly for this reason that Washington and Bonn had agreed to tripartite talks including Britain, the third NATO power involved in the question—though its Anglo-German dimension was somewhat different in kind from the German-American—and that President Johnson had appointed as the chief American negotiator the former High Commissioner John J. McCloy, whose reputation as a staunch friend of Germany was calculated to make German acceptance of a hard bargain easier.[17]

The background to the talks included the determination of the West German armed forces to curtail their purchases of American equipment (in which they were backed by German manufacturers), and an apparently equal determination of the Pentagon (though not the State Department) that these should be continued. It was in fact clear that some at least of the American balance of payments costs would be met by German investment in United States government securities, and also that Germany would probably have to accept a limited redeployment of American service units from Germany to the United States.[18] The negotiations were preceded by well-publicized salvoes from the respective parties, designed to improve their bargaining positions. In mid-February the German Finance Minister Franz Josef Strauss announced that Germany's budgetary problems would not permit her to make any further offset payments to the United States until ' the end of 1968 at the earliest',[19] and a few days later it was reported in Washington that, in view of Bonn's inability to continue offset payments, the withdrawal of a whole American division by mid-1968 was being considered.[20]

Despite these threatening words, the London talks proceeded quite amicably, thanks in part to the early American abandonment of the demand that stationing costs should be met by arms purchases. With this concession (representing a victory for McCloy and the State Department over the Pentagon view), and with a well-publicized visit by McCloy for talks with Kiesinger both in Bonn and in his home state of Baden-Württemberg, the way was open for discussion on the details of a new solution to the problem.[21] The most important feature of this new agreement—which in fact consisted of a complex triangle of agreements, committing the United States, the United Kingdom, and Germany to a number of military, commercial, and financial transactions over a twelve-month period from July 1967—was that Germany's main obligation to the United States was henceforth monetary, not commercial: only a small part of America's estimated D-Mark outlay of $800 million would be covered by arms purchases, and the bulk of Germany's contribution would be through a new device, the purchase of $500 million-worth of special medium-term US government securities. The German Federal Bank, in the so-called 'Blessing Letter', also confirmed its intention not to convert its dollar holdings into gold, thus literally adopting a 'dollar standard' and greatly helping Washington.[22]

A potentially very disruptive source of trouble between Washington and Bonn has thus been contained—significantly, mainly through concessions made by the former. At the same time the broader issue of faulty consultation between the two governments, which had provoked the new Chancellor's ire in February, also became less serious as the German coalition settled down in office. Kiesinger is reported to have complained to Johnson about lack of consultation at the end of April 1967, when the President came to Bonn for Adenauer's funeral, and by the time the Chancellor paid his first official visit to Washington in August, accompanied by his Foreign Minister Brandt, he had reason to declare himself 'very satisfied' with the state of the German-American relationship.[23]

During the remaining part of Johnson's presidency, and the

first year of Nixon's, the financial agreements reached in spring 1967 were shaken by major upheavals in the international monetary system. In particular, the crisis brought on by the weakness of the pound, and only partly allayed by its devaluation in November 1967, aggravated the American balance of payments problem and led President Johnson to call in January 1968 for ' prompt negotiations with our NATO allies to minimize the foreign exchange costs of keeping our troops in Europe '.[24] The negotiations for a renewal of the 1967 agreement, when they began in March 1968, took place against the background of strict American controls on the export of capital to Europe, and of the hectic international negotiations leading to the establishment of a double price for gold.[25] The new US-German agreement, concluded on 10 June 1968, reflected Germany's financial strength, that is, her capacity to lend money to meet the costs incurred by her allies. This time the agreement—to cover the year 1968–9—provided not only for a further purchase of $500 million-worth of medium-term US Treasury Bonds by the *Bundesbank*, but also for a purchase of $125 million-worth by a German banking consortium. In combination with German orders for military goods and services worth $100 million, and the renunciation of an earlier American Export-Import Bank credit worth $60 million, these payments were enough to ' neutralize ' the American balance of payments costs of $800 million.[26]

The renewal of this agreement for the period after mid-1969 was to prove more difficult. The overall American balance of payments deficit had been somewhat less acute in 1968 than in 1967, but the United States trade balance with Germany had taken a dramatic turn for the worse. Although the exports and imports of the two countries from and to each other had been roughly in balance since the beginning of the 1960s (in 1967, for instance, the United States imported $1,955 million worth of goods from Germany, and exported $1,706 million worth to her), American imports from Germany in 1968 rose to the new record level of $2,721 million, while exports to Germany dropped slightly to $1,702 million.[27]

This trade imbalance of $1,000 million, combined with a deficit on capital account, appears to have been one of the reasons why the United States spokesmen, in the renewal negotiations of early 1969, took the line that Germany must meet the whole of America's balance of payments costs in Germany, which they now estimated at $900 million per annum.[28] They requested a renewal of arms purchases, whereas the Germans preferred to continue investing in United States government securities, and they disputed the German estimate of the American balance of payments costs. At the beginning of the year the German estimate was stated as $625 million, and in the first round of talks, held early in May in Washington, the German offer of payment was still only $700 million.[29]

Two further sets of talks, in June and July, were needed before an agreement was concluded in Washington on 9 July. This time it was to run for two years. Its most notable feature was that, instead of any further purchase of securities, the German government made a ten-year loan of $250 million to the United States. The part played by military procurement in the agreement was also much larger than in previous years: $800 million. Non-military purchases were to amount to $150 million (an effort being made to ensure that these were additional purchases, not ones which would have been made anyway), and various smaller commitments were added to make a total payment of $1,250 million for the two-year period.[30]

The most prominent and deep-seated problem in Bonn's bilateral relations with Washington was thus again resolved in a manner satisfactory to both governments, and the acrimony which had attended it a few years earlier was not allowed to recur.

Alliance Politics: Monetary Conflicts and Strategic Détente

In the perennial bargaining between Washington and Bonn about offset costs the two partners were thus fairly successful in finding a basis for agreement by the end of the period 1966–9, despite the fact that during these years the international monetary system was in a state of recurrent crisis. The disagreements between Washington, Bonn, London, and Paris about policies to rectify balance of payments deficits and insecure parities came to have something in common with the conflicts between the same allies about strategic guarantees and the control of nuclear weapons earlier in the decade.[31] The alignments among the Western capitals varied according to the economic and financial pressures with which governments were trying to deal; although Bonn and Washington were in agreement on many issues, there was at least one occasion—the crisis of November 1968—when the German Economics Minister Karl Schiller and the American Secretary of the Treasury Henry Fowler firmly adopted diametrically opposing views.

Two of the constant factors underlying the agitation of this period, whether the immediate point at issue was the devaluation of the pound or the non-devaluation of the franc, were the strength of the Deutsche Mark and the weakness of the dollar. It was the combination of these factors which lent a degree of irritation to German-American relations as the multilateral arguments proceeded. As early as 1967, while the West German economy was still recovering from the recession of 1966, a study by the OECD urged Bonn to diminish its impressive balance of payments surplus by relaxing governmental controls over expansion, undertaking other inflationary measures, and even—this the study recommended only implicitly—revaluing the D-Mark upwards, as in 1961.[32] Such a policy would have been warmly welcomed by the United States—the revaluation of 1961 had been undertaken partly in response to American pressure, and a further revaluation now would have benefited American exports to Europe—but the German authorities reacted with their usual hostility to any idea of deliberate inflation (a course which the lessons of the 1920s and 1940s were held to debar), and refused to handicap German exporters by revaluing. At the end of the same year the growing difficulties of the dollar, aggravated by the devaluation of the pound in November, indicated a distinct risk of serious German-American disharmony, though Johnson's emergency measures of January 1968 (including a curtailment of American investment abroad) provoked more criticism in other European countries than in Germany.[33] Again, the next phase of the monetary crisis, the 'gold rush' of March 1968 provoked by speculation that the convertibility of the dollar might be suspended, was not marked by any particularly controversial action concerning Germany, and the 'two-tier' system of gold prices which provided a temporary solution met the wishes of Bonn as well as Washington.[34]

It was during the second major monetary conflict of 1968

(the massive inflow of capital into Germany which reached its peak in November)[35] that a very clear division of views emerged with the West German government confronting simultaneously those of the United States, Britain, and France, all suffering from balance of payments deficits. All three pressed the German government to revalue the Mark, as a means of resolving these difficulties, and the Germans had to undergo long and acrimonious arguments before they prevailed in their refusal to comply. The fact that the critical sessions took place in Bonn (from 22 to 24 November) under Schiller's chairmanship indicated the power of the West German 'economic giant'. Although Bonn's partners were unable to enforce a revaluation of the Mark the West German government agreed to take a series of measures to counteract the international payments imbalances, including fiscal changes to encourage imports and discourage exports, and a substantial loan to France. However, it was clear that considerable friction between Germany and her partners had been provoked by the crisis.[36] A senior Bonn official commented on the talks that the outcome showed that Germany was 'no longer a political dwarf', and it was reported that both Schiller and Strauss had firmly resisted the demands made by Fowler.[37]

There appears to have been a distinct improvement in the atmosphere surrounding German-American monetary relations when the Republican administration took office in the United States—Schiller openly stated in an interview with the London *Times* that he found the new Secretary of the Treasury, David Kennedy, more flexible and easier to deal with than his predecessor[38]—but the underlying difficulties arising from the strength of the Mark and the relative weakness of the dollar persisted. A further vast influx of speculative funds into Germany in May 1969 again both reflected, and increased, the considerable disorder in international monetary affairs, and it was only after several months of confusion (during which, in August, the franc was devalued by de Gaulle's successor Georges Pompidou) that a temporary return to order occurred. This was achieved largely by Germany's action, in response to renewed international pressures, in first allowing the Mark to float (this was the last decision taken by the Grand Coalition, during the election campaign of September 1969), and then re-fixing it at a revalued parity 9 per cent higher than the previous one (almost the first decision of the new Brandt government, taken on 24 October 1969).[39]

This German action put an end, at least for a time, to a source of conflict within the Western alliance which had exercised a quite damaging influence on Bonn's relations with Washington. In the strictly military and security aspects of the relations in the alliance, there were in contrast relatively few sources of discord, a situation very different from that prevailing a few years earlier.

The Multilateral Force which had caused so much controversy in the previous phase of NATO's history was never formally abandoned. The American Permanent Representative to the NATO Council during the late 1960s, Harlan Cleveland, has recorded that 'my first task on arrival in Paris in September 1965 was to help set up a "continuing committee" [on the MLF] designed never to meet again.'[40] However, after President Johnson's decision at the end of 1964 not to press the project, enthusiasm for it even in Germany waned considerably, and by the end of 1966 the wish of Germany and other non-nuclear NATO countries to participate in strategic planning—the problem the MLF had been designed to overcome—was on the way to being solved by the formal establishment of the NATO Nuclear Planning Group. This body, which developed from the so-called McNamara Committee of 1965, was given an official status at the NATO Ministerial meeting in December 1966, by which time the prominent role of Germany in NATO's affairs was evident,[41] and German fears of 'discrimination' by the nuclear powers were progressively allayed by her position as one of the four permanent members in the seven-member Group. During the ensuing years, the German Defence Ministry under Gerhard Schröder played an active part in affairs of the Group, which included among other activities the working-out of guidelines for the use of tactical nuclear weapons, a study conducted in 1967–8 under the joint leadership of Schröder and his British colleague Denis Healey. German participation in such exercises, and the full discussions in the NPG of such issues as the implications of the American project of the same period for the building of an anti-ballistic-missile (ABM) system, laid the foundations for a much more harmonious relationship between Bonn and Washington, in defence matters, than at any previous period of their alliance.[42]

German confidence in the credibility of the American guarantee, despite some reductions of American ground forces in Europe, was reinforced to the point where NATO's Ministerial meeting of May 1967 was able to adopt the 'McNamara Doctrine' of flexible response without any German opposition: a remarkable contrast to the situation of five years earlier, when the idea had aroused deep hostility and distrust in Bonn.[43]

Another issue which had previously been a source of great tension, the precise scale of American ground forces in Europe, could also be approached more calmly in the new framework of systematic consultation in NATO. Between 1966 and 1968 the number of American troops in the European theatre was reduced from 366,000 to just over 300,000, without raising significant German protests: this was made possible by a combination of reduced apprehension of a Soviet attack, enhanced belief in the strength of the American commitment, and the useful doctrine that certain American units 're-deployed' to Kansas and Idaho in 1968 were still 'committed' to the European theatre and could be flown back there in the event of a crisis. The last-mentioned device was due to John J. McCloy, whose employment by President Johnson early in 1967 as a negotiator on offset costs also included the task of making a slight de facto reduction of American ground forces acceptable to the European allies.[44]

A problem of broader dimensions, to which the German and American approaches were in full harmony, was the future role of NATO in a period when East-West détente was increasingly being taken for granted and when France's withdrawal from the Organization in 1966 had been widely seen as the precursor of a general 'unravelling' of the alliance: in 1969, twenty years after the signing of the North Atlantic Treaty, any member-state would be entitled to renounce it after giving one year's notice, and in 1966 it seemed possible that several of them would do so. In order to deal with a number of inter-related problems—this potential 'unravelling' of the alliance, the propaganda effect of the Warsaw Pact's proposal for a European Security Conference made at Bucharest in June 1966, and the generally unco-ordinated responses of NATO countries to such Eastern overtures—the Ministerial meeting of December 1966 decided to commission a Study of the Future Tasks of the Alliance, which was entrusted to a committee under the Belgian Foreign Minister Pierre Harmel. The Harmel Committee and its sub-groups, whose members included the German Klaus Schütz (a close associate of Willy Brandt's who was soon to leave the German Foreign Ministry to become Mayor of West Berlin) and the senior State Department officials Eugene Rostow and Foy Kohler, presented the Ministerial meeting of December 1967 with a comprehensive report. This document emphasized that the dual function of NATO was to preserve the security of its members by maintaining effective deterrent forces and simultaneously to seek for 'progress towards a more stable relationship in which the underlying political issues can be solved'. The report, in asserting that 'military security and a policy of détente are not contradictory but complementary,' reflected both American intentions of pursuing a dialogue on arms control with the Soviet Union, and the attempts of Bonn's Grand Coalition to seek a more relaxed relationship with Germany's Eastern neighbours.[45]

The message of détente contained in the Harmel Report was to be rudely tested by the Soviet invasion of Czechoslovakia eight months later, but the search for East-West understanding was to be renewed by 1969 in the SALT talks and in NATO's soundings on the subject of Mutual and Balanced Force Reductions. The Harmel exercise reflected, as well as doing a good deal to cement, the degree of common purpose between NATO governments in the pursuit of the dual objectives of deterrence and détente, but it could not hide the fact that certain reservations still existed between allies about some of each others' specific intentions and actions, particularly in this field of détente. Most notably, Bonn was perturbed by Washington's pursuit of arms control agreements—above all the NPT—with the Soviet Union.

Relations with the Adversary: the Pursuit of Détente

If the preparation of the Harmel Report showed that détente with the adversary was a goal on which all the members of NATO could in theory agree, it remained uncomfortably true that this area of activity was the one most likely, in practice, to produce discord between them. As our analysis of the history of the Washington-Bonn relationship has shown, the moments of most serious friction were occasioned by hints of German neutralism in the early 1950s; by the apparent 'softness' of Dulles and subsequently of Kennedy on the Berlin problem; and by the latter's pursuit of détente, in the form of the Test Ban Treaty, unaccompanied by what Bonn regarded as due consultation.[46]

The issue of the Non-Proliferation Treaty, the greatest single source of German-American discord in the period from 1966 to 1969, took a form which had become very familiar throughout the history of arms control and détente negotiations since the efforts of Harold Stassen ten years earlier:[47] once again, the United States government attached considerable importance to an agreement on a specific issue of arms control (in this case the non-proliferation of nuclear weapons), whereas the West Germans, as well as protesting that an East-West treaty on this subject would constitute a form of discrimination against them, argued—as so often before—that arms control agreements could bring real détente only if they were accompanied by the removal or mitigation of the underlying political sources of East-West tension, notably the division of Germany.[48] The clash between German and American views was not nearly so sharp in 1966–9 as it had been on similar issues during the Kennedy period, partly because inter-allied consultation was considerably better and partly because the Germans themselves were seriously revising their views about what kind of relationship with the East they could in practice hope to achieve,[49] but something of the old acrimony was distinctly perceptible.

At the turn of the year 1966–7, when Soviet and American negotiators in Geneva agreed on the draft text of a non-proliferation treaty, which was then put to America's allies for comments, the German comments were harshly critical. As we have seen, Chancellor Kiesinger went on record with the words 'it can't go on like this',[50] and he also accused the United States of embarking on 'a form of atomic complicity' with the Soviet Union.[51] Other members of Kiesinger's party were even more outspoken, and invoked dramatic historical parallels: ex-Chancellor Adenauer, in one of his last political comments, compared the NPT to a 'Morgenthau Plan squared', and Franz Josef Strauss, now Finance Minister, called it 'a new Versailles of cosmic dimensions'.[52]

As we have noted,[53] Germany's four main arguments against

the NPT in 1966 were that it might curtail Bonn's still unsatisfactory role in NATO's nuclear planning, that it might finally end the lingering chance of a NATO force along the lines of the MLF, that it might bar the way to any form of European deterrent, and that it would nullify a bargaining counter—the threat of a German national nuclear force—which should be relinquished only in return for Soviet concessions on German reunification. There was thus, except among a small group on the extreme right wing, no serious desire that Germany should actually acquire a national nuclear force, and even the government's wish to participate in owning ' Atlantic ' or European ' hardware ' was markedly diminished now that the CDU was sharing power with the SPD. The four objections noted in 1966 thus dwindled in importance as NATO's Nuclear Planning Group resolved the consultation problem, as the hopes of Atlantic and European hardware either faded or were accepted as being ultimately not incompatible with the treaty, and the threat of a German national force was revealed as devoid of any effective bargaining value. By the spring of 1967 the main emphasis in Bonn's continuing opposition to the NPT was being placed on the dangers entailed in inspection of Western nuclear installations by Soviet and other potentially hostile employees of the International Atomic Energy Authority: not only would the role of Euratom be seriously downgraded by the inspectorial function allocated to IAEA under the Treaty, but there was a serious risk of damage to German interests in the form of industrial espionage in her substantial civilian nuclear-power installations.[54] However, the Soviet Union continued, despite German objections, to insist on full inspection of all non-nuclear signatories by the IAEA, arguing that ' self-inspection ' by Euratom would be inadequate. As this strong Soviet line was accompanied by threats of intervention in German internal affairs, which the Soviet Union argued might be necessary to curb the rising power of the neo-Nazi movement, and which she claimed was legitimate by virtue of the universally forgotten Articles 53 and 107 of the United Nations Charter,[55] Germany felt dangerously exposed, and her objections to American policy on the treaty were redoubled. The Soviet invasion of Czechoslovakia, by slowing the tempo of Soviet-American negotiations, brought something of a respite, and the change of administration in Washington extended it, particularly as President Nixon and his advisers had only a lukewarm interest in the treaty negotiated by their predecessors, who had signed it and invited other powers to sign, on 1 July 1968.

Early in 1969 the Senate Foreign Relations Committee conducted hearings on the treaty—whose ratification the President decided in March to demand—and these brought some concessions, at least in principle, to Bonn's wishes. For instance, the administration confirmed that the ending of the North Atlantic Alliance, then thought to be quite possible at some date after 1969, would count among the 'extraordinary events' releasing signatories from their obligations under the Non-proliferation Treaty.[56] This concession was due partly to the determined lobbying by representatives of the CSU, who went to Washington for the purpose.[57]

The German response to the prospect of American and Soviet ratification of the treaty—which must inevitably increase the pressure on Bonn to sign and ratify in its turn—was to press harder than ever for clarification of the issues important to Germany, notably the dispute between IAEA and Euratom, for inspection rights.

When the Russians let it be understood that their ratification would not be forthcoming until Germany signed—the perpetuation of Germany's non-nuclear status was the main Soviet interest in the treaty—the Nixon administration responded, not by applying the strong pressure on Bonn that Kennedy or Johnson might have exerted but by urging the Soviet Union to ratify the treaty simultaneously with the United States, in order to induce West Germany to sign. This approach proved much more productive than direct pressure on Bonn would have been: such pressure, in an election year when not only the NPD but also Strauss and other members of the cabinet were violently opposed to the treaty, could have had only a negative effect.

In the event, the United States and Soviet Union discreetly announced in November 1969, shortly after the Brandt government had taken office, that their 'ratification procedures' were completed (though actual ratification had still not occurred), and this was enough for the new German government, 'almost conspiratorially',[58] to sign the treaty. The American and Soviet instruments of ratification were deposited on 5 March 1970, when enough ratifications (forty) had been assembled to bring the treaty into effect, but by tacit agreement Germany was allowed to make her own ratification dependent on a satisfactory outcome of the negotiations on inspection rights still proceeding between the IAEA and Euratom. It was accepted by Washington that Bonn's order of priorities in relations with the East would be firstly the negotiation of an agreement on Berlin, secondly the conclusion of treaties with the Soviet Union and Poland, and only thirdly the ratification of the NPT. This formula effectively postponed Germany's ratification for some time (the issue was to become important again only in 1973), and in any case the NPT was before long pushed out of the first place in American arms-control concerns by the SALT negotiations with the Soviet Union.

The story of the NPT as an issue in German-American relations can be seen, in retrospect, as one of those on which the zealous pursuit of a line of policy by the United States began by arousing deep German suspicions, since the crucial dimension of security against the East was involved; but in this case the wise decision of the Nixon administration to bow to German opposition, and not to force the issue, successfully defused it.

The American approach to détente in the period of the Grand Coalition thus provoked a certain tension, at least in its earlier stages. The other aspect of détente policy in this period—the Grand Coalition's own pursuit of better relations with its Eastern neighbours—did very little, by contrast, to arouse discord in the German-American alliance. The policy of the Kiesinger-Brandt government in fact represented an acceleration and development of certain lines of policy already pursued under Erhard, and, as we have noted, the promoters of these policies, including Schröder and Barzel in the CDU and Brandt and Bahr in the SPD, were conscious that their views on détente were close to those prevailing in Washington.[59]

There was of course a sense in which this harmony with American thinking was purchased at a high and even painful price for Germans: on the central issue of whether the two German states could be reunited, it was now clear that American support for reunification along the lines promised by Dulles and enshrined in the agreements of 1954–5 was no longer to be expected. Even if Dulles himself had taken the American commitment to German reunification fully seriously in operational terms—which was itself open to some doubt—the warning issued by Kennedy in 1963 had been solemnly confirmed by Johnson in 1966: the Germans could expect reunification only as the *end result* of a long process of détente between the two parts of Europe, and should no longer expect their allies to insist on reunification as a *first step* to détente, as they had done in the 1950s.[60] The way in which influential American opinion was coming to terms with the idea of recognizing East Germany was confirmed a little later by the recommendation of the US United Nations Association study-group of 1968–9, already mentioned, that both German states should be represented in a European Security Commission.[61]

Senior officials of the American Embassy in Bonn were making it quite clear, during the early months of the Kiesinger-Brandt coalition, that more contact between the two Germanies would be welcomed by the United States. The thought in itself was not new: for several years Washington had been pressing Bonn to promote contacts with East Germany,[62] and even Dulles had tried hard to persuade Adenauer that such contacts could only be to the advantage of the Western side—though his American optimism in the superior attractions and the 'radiation' capacity of democracy failed to convince the sceptical German, who had seen democracy undermined in 1933 and feared that Communist techniques of infiltration and propaganda would be strong enough to contaminate West Germany.[63] What was new in the late 1960s was that as the German political leaders themselves became fully aware that the old doctrine of 'reunification from strength' was dead, and began to explore alternatives, their American allies reminded them more clearly than before that a new attitude to the East German state ought to become a central ingredient of their Ostpolitik. Although Moscow still supported East Berlin in implacable hostility to Bonn, Bonn clearly could no longer count on Washington's support for reunification.

The Grand Coalition thus worked out (of course, only in part in response to American wishes), in the early part of 1967, a line of approach to the East which for the first time included amicable moves towards all three of the relevant 'targets': Moscow, the Warsaw Pact countries generally, and East Germany specifically. Instead of concentrating largely on Moscow (which even Adenauer had regarded as important), or making approaches mainly to the East European states lying between the Soviet Union and Germany (as Erhard and Schröder had done in 1963–6), the Grand Coalition—politically much stronger, of course, than its vacillating predecessor—deliberately combined with these policies a conciliatory posture towards the East German regime. Although it was made clear in Bonn that there could be no question of giving diplomatic recognition to East Germany, there was a distinct change of attitude: abusive propaganda notes from East Berlin were not answered in kind, West German spokesmen gave up Bonn's claim to be the sole legitimate representative of the German people, and in 1967 Chancellor Kiesinger directly acknowledged East Germany's statehood by sending a letter to his East German counterpart Willi Stoph in which he addressed the latter as 'Herr Minister-Präsident'.[64]

This change of approach in Bonn was denounced in East Germany as no more than an ill-disguised form of Bonn's congenital *revanchisme*: the East German regime clearly felt threatened by Bonn's continued advance in improving relations with the other members of the Warsaw Pact, even though Pankow was no longer explicitly excluded from this process of détente as it had been during the Erhard period. In 1967 Bonn opened diplomatic relations with Rumania, and re-established those with Yugoslavia, broken off in 1957 under the Hallstein Doctrine (which was now drastically modified to allow relations with East European states—which had been virtually obliged to recognize the GDR), and shortly afterwards set up a trade delegation in Prague.

West Germany's increasing economic and financial presence in Eastern Europe, and specifically in Czechoslovakia, appears to have played a certain role (together with a number of other and more important factors, including Soviet distrust of liberalization generally) in leading Moscow to use military force against the Dubcek regime in August 1968. The Soviet pretext—that supplies of NATO weapons had been brought into Czechoslovakia by West Germans and others, in preparation for a counter-revolutionary uprising—was clearly false. However, there was a little in the argument that the Soviet Union had been perturbed by the general effects of Bonn's Ostpolitik in unsettling the Warsaw Pact—perhaps, so it was now argued in Bonn, not enough had been done to reassure the

Russians and East Germans that a drastic change in the status quo was *not* part of the West German design—and in any case the prospects for further détente in the aftermath of the Czech invasion looked very poor.

In 1968–9, therefore, the Grand Coalition apparently had to face the total collapse of the more flexible Ostpolitik it had initiated with quite high hopes (though not without a good deal of disagreement between Kiesinger and Brandt about the proper tempo for the operation) during 1967.

The Czech crisis, however, only slightly interrupted the progress of détente at other levels of East-West relations: in Paris, de Gaulle's Foreign Minister Michel Debré dismissed the Czech affair as a mere 'traffic accident' on the route to détente,[65] and, at the super-power level, American interest in both NPT and SALT was only momentarily reduced. American advice to Bonn continued to take the line that détente with the East offered the best hope of solving Germany's problems. By this the Americans meant détente with the USSR and Eastern Europe, but not with China. The perennial hopes of some Germans of using China as an ally to put pressure on Russia, forcing her to disgorge territory in the West, were firmly discouraged by the American Embassy in Bonn, which took the view that any improvement in China's international standing would aggravate America's problems in the Far East, and further that for Germany to encourage China—a Communist power with a crusading ideological grudge against the Soviet Union—would only have the effect of reviving the militancy of the world Communist movement as a whole, to Germany's disadvantage.[66]

Vis-à-vis Eastern Europe, however, Bonn found herself in 1968–9 in a situation of apparent deadlock. The policy of détente, adopted in 1967–8 with Washington's approval, appeared to have led nowhere, and no alternative but the consolidation of the Western alliance was in sight. The right-wing Christian Democrats in the cabinet—notably Franz Josef Strauss—appeared to have been proved right in their sceptical views on the prospects for a more flexible Ostpolitik: it was to require a new German government, without representatives of this school of thought, before Bonn's foreign policy could make a fresh start on Ostpolitik.

NOTES

1 George McTurnan Kahin and John Wilson Lewis, *The United States in Vietnam* (rev. edn, 1969), pp. 343, 402.

2 Ibid. p. 391.

3 US Dept of Commerce, *Survey of Current Business*, June 1969, pp. 26, 34, and Mar. 1971, p. 44, quoted by Timothy Stanley, ' Atlantic Security in the Seventies ', paper presented to 17th Assembly of the Atlantic Treaty Association, London, Sept. 1971.

4 Quoted in John Newhouse and others, *U.S. Troops in Europe* (1971), p. 12.

5 Ibid. p. 10, quoting statements of 1966 and 1969.

6 *Washington Post*, 27 May 1966; 16 Mar. and 12 July 1967; 20 Apr. 1968. *FAZ*, 21 Jan. 1967. See Cromwell, in idem, ed., p. 111 and Cleveland, pp. 113–17, and the useful short history of the Mansfield Resolution from 1966 to 1968 in Thomas W. Wolfe, *Soviet Power and Europe, 1945–1970* (1970), pp. 462–3.

7 See above, pp. 2–3 and Kissinger's essay ' Central Issues of America Foreign Policy ', in Kermit Gordon, ed., *Agenda for the Nation* (1968), pp. 585–614: this essay prefigures what came to be known as the ' Nixon Doctrine '.

8 *Toward the Reconciliation of Europe: New Approaches for the US, the UN, and NATO* (report of a National Policy Panel established by the UN Assn of the USA, released 2 Feb. 1968) cited by Cleveland, pp. 188, 198.

9 Hanrieder, *The Stable Crisis*, pp. 173–82.

10 Theo Sommer, ' Bonn Changes Course ', *For. Aff.*, 43/3 (1967), pp. 483–4.

11 Waldemar Besson, ' The Conflict of Traditions ', in Kaiser and Morgan, eds, *Britain and West Germany*, p. 80.

12 For details, see Morgan, ' The Federal Republic of Germany ', in Henig and Pinder, eds, *European Political Parties*, pp. 56–8.

13 *L'Année Politique 1968*, p. 313: there was to be a further sign that times had changed when, in the presidential election of 5 Mar. 1969, a coalition of SPD and FDP representatives gave the presidency to Gustav Heinemann, who had resigned from Adenauer's cabinet in 1950 in protest against German rearmament.

14 See above, p. 148.

15 *The Guardian*, 28 Feb. 1967.

16 *The Times*, 28 Feb. 1967; on the circumstances of Grewe's recall, see p. 114 above.

17 *Washington Post*, 2 Mar. 1967; *The Times*, 3 and 14 Mar. 1967.

18 Mendershausen, p. 100.

19 *Financial Times*, 16 Feb. 1967.

20 *NYT*, 24 Feb. 1967.

21 *The Times*, 4 Mar; *The Guardian*, 6 Mar.; *FAZ*, 7 Mar. 1967.

22 Mendershausen, pp. 101–5.

23 *NYT*, 27 Apr., 16 and 17 Aug.; *Der Spiegel*, 1 May; *NZZ*, 19 Aug. 1967.

24 *NYT*, 2 Jan. 1968.

25 On this background—merely sketched here—see Mendershausen, pp. 111–15, and Hanrieder, *The Stable Crisis*, pp. 78–85.

26 Mendershausen, pp. 116–17.
27 *United Nations Yearbook of International Trade Statistics*, 1969.
28 *Daily Telegraph*, 8 Nov. 1968; *NYT* and *Daily Telegraph*, 20 Feb. 1969.
29 *NYT* and *Daily Telegraph*, 20 Feb.; *International Herald Tribune*, 3 and 4 May 1969.
30 *Financial Times*, 10 July 1969 and *DOSB*, 4 Aug. 1969, cited by David Calleo, *The Atlantic Fantasy: the US, NATO and Europe* (1970), pp. 161–2; see also Thiel, ' Truppenstationierung und Devisenausgleich ', *Europa-Archiv*, 24/7 (1969), pp. 221–8.
31 See Edward Morse, ' Crisis Diplomacy, Interdependence, and the Politics of International Economic Relations ', in R. Tanter and R. Ullman, eds, *Theory and Policy in International Relations* (1972), esp. pp. 131–2.
32 *OECD Economic Surveys: Germany 1967*, pp. 24–31, cited by Hanrieder, *The Stable Crisis*, p. 82.
33 See above, p. 167, and *l'Année Politique 1968*, pp. 208–9.
34 See *l'Année Politique 1968*, pp. 226–30.
35 Ibid. p. 303, where a figure of $250 million for the week ending 9 Nov. is given.
36 Ibid. pp. 303–4; Hanrieder, *The Stable Crisis*, pp. 77–80.
37 *NYT*, 22 and 23 Nov. 1968.
38 *The Times*, 4 June 1969.
39 Hanrieder, *The Stable Crisis*, pp. 83–6. See also Lawrence Krause, ' Private International Finance ', in R. O. Keohane and J. S. Nye, Jr, eds, *Transnational Relations and World Politics* (1972), pp. 173–90.
40 *NATO: the Transatlantic Bargain*, pp. 52–3.
41 *NYT* report, cited by Edward Heath, *Old World, New Horizons* (1970), p. 71.
42 Details of the NPG's work are given by Cleveland, pp. 53–65, and Mahncke, *Nukleare Mitwirkung*, pp. 219–52.
43 *NYT*, 10 May 1967, cited by Cromwell, p. 114. On German reactions in 1962, see above, p. 109.
44 See above, p. 172; Cromwell, pp. 114–18; Cleveland, pp. 110–17.
45 The Harmel Report and its background are usefully summarized by Cleveland, pp. 138–47.
46 See above, pp. 38, 88–91, 110–15, 133–5.
47 See above, pp. 56–7.
48 On the American approach to the issue, see William B. Bader, *The United States and the Spread of Nuclear Weapons* (1968), esp. pp. 48–9 and 60–1.
49 See below, pp. 185–6.
50 See above, p. 172.
51 *The Times*, 1 Mar. 1967.
52 *Der Spiegel*, 27 Feb. 1967, cited by Joffe, in Cromwell, ed., p. 423.
53 See above, pp. 158–9.
54 See Theo Sommer, ' Germany's Reservations ', *Survival*, May 1967, pp. 144–5; Carl von Weizsacker, ' Nuclear Inspections ', ibid. pp. 146–8; Arnold Kramish, *The Watched and the Unwatched* (1967) and *Die*

Zukunft der Nichtatomaren (1970); Beate Kohler, *Der Vertrag über die Nichtverbreitung von Kernwaffen und das Problem der Sicherheitsgarantien* (1972), esp. pp. 109–44.

55 *NYT*, 20 Sept. 1968, cited by George Quester, *The Politics of Nuclear Proliferation* (1973), ch. 3. The following summary of German attitudes to the NPT draws heavily on this work. See also G. Quester, 'The Nonproliferation Treaty and the International Atomic Energy Agency', *Int. Org.*, 24/2 (1970), pp. 163–82.

56 US Senate, Foreign Relations Committee, Hearings, cited by Quester, *The Politics of Nuclear Proliferation*, ch. 10.

57 Hanrieder, *The Stable Crisis*, p. 33.

58 Quester, as n. 56, above, ch. 10.

59 See above, pp. 157–8. Statements by Under Secretary of State Eugene Rostow in 1967 and 1968, expressing strong support and admiration for the Ostpolitik of Kiesinger and Brandt, are quoted by Calleo, p. 162.

60 On Kennedy's and Johnson's statements, see above, pp. 130 and 155.

61 See above, p. 168.

62 See above, p. 92.

63 Private information, Bonn.

64 Among the best discussions of this phase of Ostpolitik are Sommer, 'Bonn's New Ostpolitik', *Journal of International Affairs*, 22/1 (1968), pp. 59–78; Kaiser, *German Foreign Policy in Transition*, esp. ch. 7; and Hanrieder, *The Stable Crisis*, esp. pp. 110–27.

65 *L'Année Politique 1968*, p. 272.

66 Private information, Bonn.

CHAPTER TEN

Into the 1970s: SALT and Ostpolitik 1969–1972

Background: the Era of Negotiation

WILLY Brandt's accession to the chancellorship of West Germany in October 1969 marked a significant turning-point in German history. Not only was the head of government a Social Democrat for the first time since 1930, but the formation of the ruling coalition between Brandt's SPD and the FDP, led by Walter Scheel, banished the CDU to the Opposition benches for the first time in the twenty-year history of the Federal Republic. It was clear that the new German government, although faced with a heavy agenda of domestic reforms, would also try to move faster than its predecessor in the improvement of Germany's relations with the East. The change was thus one of great international as well as internal significance, more particularly since the Brandt government took office in a period which President Nixon shortly afterwards described, in the first of the annual foreign policy reports soon baptized ' state of the world messages ', as ' the era of negotiation '.[1]

By the time the third of these annual reports was issued two years later an unprecedented group of highly significant East-West agreements was about to be concluded: the first strategic arms limitation agreement between the United States and the

Soviet Union, the treaties of friendship between West Germany on the one hand and Poland and the Soviet Union on the other, and an agreement between the Soviet Union and the three Western powers on the question of Berlin.

When Willy Brandt spoke at Harvard University on 5 June 1972 as guest of honour at the commemoration of the twenty-fifth anniversary of the Marshall Plan—an occasion which was in a sense his moment of greatest triumph, but ironically also one of grave political weakness—all these agreements had been concluded. President Nixon's visit to Moscow in May 1972 saw the signing of a group of detailed Soviet-American undertakings on strategic weapons, including defensive (ABM) and offensive systems, and also a comprehensive Soviet-American declaration agreeing on the general principles of détente and coexistence. The German-Soviet and German-Polish treaties, signed respectively in August and December 1970 and ratified amid unprecedented parliamentary conflicts in Bonn shortly before the American President's visit to Moscow, enshrined West Germany's acceptance that the German frontier with Poland (the Oder-Neisse Line) would in effect be recognized as permanent, as well as the division of Germany into two states. And the third agreement negotiated in 1970–1 and confirmed in June 1972, the four-power agreement on Berlin, included several important concessions made by the Soviet Union at the expense of East Germany, confirming West Berlin's right, under allied responsibility, to enjoy easier access and links of all kinds (except constitutional ones) with the Federal Republic. This treaty was followed by an intensification of negotiations between the two German states on matters of transport, trade, and closer relations generally, preparing the way for the Basic Treaty which they were to sign in December 1972.

The conclusion of this group of agreements—SALT, Germany's Eastern treaties, and the Berlin settlement—in May-June 1972 was generally regarded as only one landmark, though an important one, on the way to a more comprehensive détente in Europe. As the NATO powers had made the Berlin agreement a condition for their participation in a Conference on Security and Co-operation in Europe, proposed for several years by the Soviet Union, it seemed likely that the conclusion of the agreement would allow the conference to go ahead. From May 1971 onwards there had also been indications of Soviet willingness to accept the West's proposal for a discussion of mutual and balanced force reductions, presumably in the context of the proposed conference.

Europe was not the only scene of activity in the 'Era of Negotiation'. Another of its significant manifestations was in the relations between the United States and the People's Republic of China. It was announced in July 1971, after a preliminary visit to Peking by President Nixon's Special Assistant Dr Kissinger, that the President himself would go there early in 1972, and the United States shortly afterwards dropped her objections to the admission of Communist China to the United Nations, where she duly took her place at the 1971 General Assembly. President Nixon's visit to Peking in February 1972 symbolized a new start in Sino-American relations, and prepared the way for a closer relationship with Peking on the part of several of America's Asian allies, notably Japan.

A further indication that a fair degree of stability and calm prevailed in international relations was that even the Middle East, the scene of repeated conflicts ever since 1945, was by now relatively peaceful. The efforts of the UN mission under Gunnar Jarring produced a one-year cease-fire in August 1970, and this was not violated when its term expired. The United States government had to continue to give careful attention to the Middle East, as also to the growing naval presence of the Soviet Union in the Mediterranean; and the countries of Western Europe did so too, particularly Britain and France who were participants in the Four-Power discussions concerning the area. The Middle East was also one of the regions towards which the foreign ministries of the six member-states of the European Community attempted to co-ordinate their policies in the framework of the so-called 'Davignon Committee' established in 1970.

Western Europe itself was another area where in these years discord appeared to be giving way to agreement. The summit conference of the Six held at The Hague in December 1969 agreed on the further development of the European Community, including the renewal of entry negotiations with Britain and the other applicants. The British negotiations were begun by Harold Wilson's Labour government in the spring of 1970, and continued by Edward Heath's administration after the Conservative Party's election victory in June of that year.

By June 1971 the terms of British entry had been agreed; they were confirmed by the House of Commons late in October, and by mid-1972 Britain's final accession to the European Community could be assumed to be virtually certain.

There were two significant exceptions to the picture of harmony and agreement epitomized as the Era of Negotiation: the Vietnam War dragged bloodily and expensively on, and these years also saw alarmingly sharp conflicts on economic and monetary issues among the advanced nations of the capitalist world.

In Vietnam, despite President Nixon's electoral promise in 1968 to end the fighting, the Republican administration remained committed to the regime of President Thieu in Saigon, with which the North Vietnamese resolutely refused to compromise. The peace negotiations in Paris thus continued to be the scene mainly of public accusations of hostility and bad faith between the two sides, and even the repeated visits of President Nixon's emissary Dr Kissinger failed to find any way of overcoming the deadlock. President Nixon carried out his undertaking of 1968 to reduce America's fighting forces in the ground-war in Vietnam (all but about 50,000 of them were removed by the early summer of 1972) but American aerial bombardment of Vietnam continued with a greater intensity than ever. One of the striking features of the war was that, although it was locally very violent, its diplomatic repercussions were less damaging than might have been feared. The persistence of the conflict was clearly one reason why America's rapprochement with China was so long delayed, and was very circumscribed even when it eventually came in 1971–2, but the growing understanding between the United States and Russia, on a number of matters from SALT to Berlin, hardly appears to have been inhibited at all by the fighting in Vietnam.

The other type of international conflict in 1969–72—renewed and accentuated monetary and economic crises—although it was without military violence was perhaps an equally disconcerting feature of the world system. Although the floating and subsequent revaluation of the Deutsche Mark in 1969 did a good deal to stabilize the system of international payments, renewed trouble built up during 1970, partly but not entirely associated with the balance of payments deficit of the United States. This deficit, which reached alarming proportions in the spring of 1971, accentuated the weakness of the dollar and precipitated a torrential speculative movement into the Deutsche Mark in early May. The renewed floating of the Mark acted only as a palliative, and on 15 August 1971 President Nixon announced a programme of emergency measures whose main features, internationally, were a 10 per cent surcharge on imports and a freeing of the dollar from the gold standard. This abrupt ending of the Bretton Woods monetary system, which had worked with increasing difficulty but without total collapse for twenty-five years, led to dramatic confrontations between the United States and her trading and financial partners in Western Europe and Japan. A conference of the Group of Ten, held at the Smithsonian Institute in Washington in December 1971, agreed on a temporary solution to the international payments crisis, including a devaluation of the dollar by 8.57 per cent and corresponding revaluations of other currencies, but the first half of 1972 continued to be marked by financial strains which showed that a really stable solution had yet to be found.

It was widely argued, as the period 1969–72 came to an end, that the world had now finally left the bipolar system of the Cold War years and was well on the way to a more complicated five-power or ' pentapolar ' one. President Nixon even went so far as to assert that the world would be safer and better ' if we have a strong, healthy United States, Europe, Soviet Union, China, Japan, each balancing the other, not playing one against the other, an even balance.' [2]

It was easy to dispute the accuracy of the view that the world system was in any strict sense composed of five poles: the United States and the Soviet Union, for instance, were clearly very far ahead of the other three ' poles ' in strategic capacity; Western Europe and Japan might be economic giants, but were clearly political and military dwarfs; and China, though militarily powerful within its immediate regional surroundings, was clearly very far from being a world power like the United States or the Soviet Union.[3] Even though the notion of pentapolarity was far-fetched, however, the governments of the United States and West Germany clearly had to conduct their external relations, in these years, in the framework of an increasingly complex and mobile international system.

Internal Politics: Pragmatism brings Harmony

It might have been expected that a right-wing Republican administration in Washington and a left-wing Socialist-led government in Bonn would have many points of difference, and that their approaches to a number of policy issues would be so divergent as to bring them into serious conflict. In fact, however, by the end of the 1960s both the Republican Party and the Social-Democratic Party had evolved very markedly from the ideological positions they had respectively held, even ten years earlier, so that their approaches to economic and foreign policy alike were not difficult to reconcile.

One possible source of conflict arose from the fact that both the Nixon and the Brandt administrations were confronted with serious and intractable domestic problems—inflation, stagnation, and, in the case of the United States, rising unemployment, deteriorating race relations, and an increasingly alarming balance of payments deficit. Faced with this situation, both governments attempted to alleviate some of the most pressing social and economic problems by devoting more resources to domestic spending and relatively less to defence: in the United States the amount spent on defence was even reduced in absolute terms, the defence budget for 1971 being 7 per cent less than its predecessor, and 1971 being the first year since 1950 when the United States had spent more on social and domestic programmes than on defence. The American public concensus which had sustained a vast commitment in Vietnam was beginning to crumble, in a way which portended trouble for the commitment to Europe too: and the pressure for the administration to concentrate on domestic policies was rising.

There was also a pressing temptation for both governments to take dramatic and well-publicized initiatives for international détente, in part because these offered the prospect of some palpable success to offset their unsatisfactory performances in the realm of economic issues.(It should be added that the Bonn government believed in any case in keeping up a considerable momentum in negotiation with the East: Brandt's experience of East-West dealings ever since his days in Berlin had convinced him that this was the best way to win concessions from the Russians.)

Such a situation, with two allied governments both anxious

to appear to take dramatic initiatives for peace, might have led to grave misunderstandings and tensions between them, and there were moments, as will be seen, when this was the case. However, one of the striking features of the performances of both the Washington and Bonn governments, during this intensive 'Era of Negotiation', was the degree to which effective inter-allied consultation and co-ordination was maintained.

This was in part due to the fact that the relevant posts in each of the two governments were occupied by men who knew the other country well, and had a deep appreciation of its problems. In Washington, for instance, President Nixon's most influential adviser on foreign policy, Henry Kissinger, was of German origin, had a good knowledge of the political situation in Bonn, and had been notably perturbed by what he regarded as the insensitive handling of Germany by the Kennedy administration.[4]

In the State Department, the important post of Assistant Secretary for European Affairs was now occupied by Martin Hillenbrand, who had acquired an extremely close understanding of Germany in the course of many years' work on German matters both in Washington and as Counsellor of the American Embassy in Bonn. It should be added that the Nixon administration's Ambassador to Bonn, Kenneth Rush, although new to diplomacy (he was a former professor of law, a president of the Union Carbide Company and a friend of Attorney-General John Mitchell), proved to be an extremely able promoter of German-American co-operation, particularly during the difficult Berlin negotiations of 1971: his close relations with President Nixon were of great importance at this stage.[5]

There were of course some powerful figures in the American political system whose attitudes and policies were not so conducive to amity with Germany. The most important of these was perhaps Senator Mansfield, who persistently raised in the Senate his resolution calling for a reduction of American troop levels in Europe: in May 1971, senatorial support for this view was in fact only strong enough for the Mansfield resolution to obtain 26 votes against 63, but this result was largely due to very strong opposition to the resolution by the administration, and to its success in getting Soviet agreement to negotiate on Mutual and Balanced Force Reductions (MBFR).[6]

Although the Mansfield resolution was thus defeated on this occasion, it was clear that pressure to reduce American troops in Europe would be a factor of growing importance for both the American and the German administrations.

Another influential group whose attitudes portended difficulties for Germany was made up of some of the men responsible for economic policy in the Nixon administration. Although, as we have seen, the German Minister of Economics had publicly praised Nixon's original Secretary of the Treasury, David Kennedy, for his sympathetic view of European problems,[7] Kennedy was replaced during 1970 by John Connally, the former Governor of Texas, whose approach to economic policy placed a much more uncompromising emphasis on America's national interests. In the great international monetary crisis of 1971, although there were moments when Connally showed a disposition to treat Germany favourably,[8] the administration's general posture was one of impatience with the problems created for others by America's drastic solutions for her own problems. This attitude was reinforced by the fact that one of the more influential advisers in favour of the provocative measures of 15 August 1971, Peter Peterson, had been president of Ball and Howell, a mid-Western photographic manufacturing company severely hit, like many other American firms, by Japanese competition. (In 1972 he left the post of Executive Director of the President's Council on International Economic Policy to become Secretary of Commerce.) At a time when the economic and monetary issues between the group of states in the European-Atlantic area were coming to play the central role occupied by strategic questions ten years earlier[9] it was a matter of concern to Germany that some of the American officials in charge of economic affairs took such an emphatic view of American interests. However, the American political system as a whole contained relatively few powerful elements of a nature to cause misgivings in Bonn.

The same, broadly speaking, was also true in reverse. The predominantly Social-Democratic administration led by Willy Brandt might have been expected to pursue economic or foreign policies unwelcome to the Republicans in Washington, but in fact the SPD had entirely dropped its collectivist economic policies of the early post-war years: Karl Schiller, an academic economist of neo-liberal convictions, represented something very different from Kurt Schumacher, and Willy Brandt himself was, of course, very well known and trusted in Washington, as were the Defence Minister Helmut Schmidt and other leading members of the Cabinet. Some doubts persisted about Egon Bahr, the Chancellor's personal adviser in charge of policy towards the East, who was thought in Washington to attach too little importance to West European integration and the Atlantic alliance: as a Berliner, he seemed to be too exclusively concerned with Germany's Eastern relationships for a man occupying his very influential position. In the event, however, he developed very close working relationships with his American colleagues during the long negotiations with the Soviet Union in 1970–2.[10] The German Ambassador in Washington at this time, Rolf Pauls, was also a particularly effective exponent of his government's policies and an able interpreter to Bonn of the American political scene.

More generally, there was serious concern in Washington than Chancellor Brandt's government might be too insecurely based to carry through the ambitious programmes of domestic and external changes which in 1969 it had promised to undertake, and even that it might fail to survive at all: the Coalition had a parliamentary majority of only 12 when its life began, and defections reduced this to vanishing-point by the beginning of 1972.[11] The very fragility of the parliamentary majority, coupled with disagreements between the SPD and its Free Democratic allies about the programme of domestic reforms, gave the Brandt government a further inducement to try to achieve quick successes in foreign affairs, particularly in relations with the East. The unexpected readiness of the Soviet Union and its allies to negotiate with Bonn also helped to make it possible for Brandt, within a year of taking office, to have signed a treaty with Moscow, to have held two meetings with his East German opposite number, and to be on the point of concluding a further treaty with Poland.

The Ostpolitik in itself—the facing by the Germans of facts long faced by Americans—was distinctly welcome to Washington, but there was considerable concern less Brandt's occasionally precipitate search for agreement, and his apparent concessions to the Russians, might provoke domestic dissent in Germany to the point where the stability of the Federal Republic itself would be endangered, and with it the whole of

Western Europe. These fears mounted as the Christian Democratic Opposition led by ex-Chancellor Kiesinger, and after October 1971 by his successor Rainer Barzel, mounted a violent campaign of opposition to the Ostpolitik, and the parliamentary crisis of spring 1972 appeared to suggest that there was at least some substance to these fears. It was ironical that after seeing the Federal Republic preserved from extremists of the Right and the Left (the NPD, the most serious neo-Nazi force, had been decimated at the Bundestag election of 1969), Americans now had cause to fear lest the regime fail to survive a constitutional crisis provoked by a moderate Chancellor's pursuit of a policy of which the United States on the whole approved.

Bilateral Relations: American Problems, German Concessions

After Chancellor Brandt's two-day meeting with President Nixon at Key Biscayne, Florida, on 28 and 29 December 1971, the Chancellor, replying to public comments to the effect that the meeting appeared to have covered American-European, rather than American-German relations, confirmed:

> The talks at Key Biscayne did indeed center on the American-European partnership rather than on German-American relations. This will not surprise anyone who knows to what extent bilateral relations between West European countries and the United States are overlaid by a network of multilateral relations which is steadily getting more dense. In the Federal Republic of Germany there is not a single question of any importance that could be treated outside the context of American-European relations. This applies to international currency and trade affairs as well as to security policy and above all to efforts to decrease tensions between East and West.[12]

Despite the general truth of this disclaimer of any German-American 'special relationship' in economic or strategic affairs, there remained one or two issues in which the German and American governments were more directly concerned than their other NATO allies or EEC partners. The most notable example of such an issue remained, as for the whole of the preceding decade, the question of American troop levels in Germany and the German contribution to offsetting their cost.

It is true that there was also a similar and related Anglo-German problem, as we have noted,[13] and by 1970–1 serious efforts were being made to spread the costs of American troop stationing among the allies (Chancellor Brandt's disclaimer of a bilateral relationship was no doubt in part intended to contribute to this aim); however, the hard core of the problem remained West Germany's wish to retain the American divisions stationed on her territory, and the American wish that Germany should offset a larger proportion of their cost to the US balance of payments.

The motives for these wishes were also familiar, particularly on the American side. Whereas the West German position was undergoing a perceptible change, in that simple fears of Soviet invasion were giving way to the serious wish to negotiate a new relationship with the East from a position of reasonable strength, the American viewpoint was powerfully influenced by the familiar but increasing concern with the balance of payments: whereas Eisenhower had been unconcerned by the incipient deficit, and Kennedy rather more concerned, Nixon was very aggressively concerned indeed.

The overall payments deficit reached $6.9 (US) billion in 1969 and $5.5 billion in 1970;[14] in the first quarter of 1971, when negotiations began for the renewal of the offset agreement due to expire on 30 June, the deficit was the worst America had ever experienced.[15]

Senator Mansfield and other critics of American force levels in Europe did not fail to point out the contribution of defence costs to the deficit. As Mansfield put it in April 1970:

> In 1969, our direct outlays in Europe reached a new high of over $1.6 billion and, in Germany alone, a new high of almost $950 million. . . . These expenditures . . . represent a drain on the dollar and act to weaken its international position. Salaries and other indirect costs eat heavily into U.S. tax resources, leaving less for essential purposes at home and adding severe inflationary pressures to the economy.[16]

A year later, when the offset negotiations were in progress, Mansfield's colleague Symington argued during the debate on the Mansfield Resolution that military spending in Western Europe accounted for 46.1 per cent of the overall US payments deficit. He added: ' If military sales to Western Europe, which

I am informed totaled $599 million in 1970, are deducted from the $1.77 billion of military expenditures in Western Europe, net military expenditures still constitute 30.5 percent of the total balance-of-payments deficit in 1970.' [17]

Against this background of congressional pressure for troop withdrawals as a means of curing the payments deficit—which was also the aim of the Mills Bill promoted by Representative Mills and others to curtail foreign imports into America [18]—the administration inevitably adopted a fairly tough posture in the negotiations with Germany. Under Secretary of State Elliott Richardson, in a speech in Chicago early in 1970 stated that American troops would not stay in Europe 'at present strengths for ever and ever', despite the unchanging nature of the guarantee itself, and suggested clearly that their future levels might have a relationship with European purchases of American exports.[19]

On the eve of Brandt's first visit to the United States as Chancellor, in April 1970, his Defence Minister Helmut Schmidt created a stir by a statement, widely reported in the American press, which served notice that renewed German purchases of American military equipment, at least, were unlikely: 'We have reached the end of the build-up phase in our armed forces . . . there are no longer any large arms orders that we might place in the United States, so further offset agreements are going to be difficult. Budgetary contributions . . . would have to come out of the German defence budget. We would mend one hole by opening up another.' [20]

During his visit—whose importance to the Nixon administration may have been symbolized by the unusual handing-over of Camp David as a base where Brandt and his colleagues could spend three days before reaching Washington—the Chancellor reiterated Germany's concern that American troop levels should not be reduced, but indicated that she would not be in a position to continue payments on the current scale under the new agreement. American spokesmen confirmed that the present level of 310,000 men would be maintained until June 1971, but suggested clearly that reductions might then be necessary.[21]

The situation was summarized by a *New York Times* editorial on the results of Brandt's visit. This suggested that one contribution the Bonn government could make towards solving the American balance of payments problem would be to restrain the European Community's policy of high farm prices and surpluses which competed with American output, although such a policy would be politically difficult because of the farm lobby in Bonn. The article also underlined the connection between two of the main subjects discussed by Nixon and Brandt—American troop levels and Bonn's Ostpolitik—by arguing that Brandt needed strong American military backing for his Eastern negotiations and hinting that Germany might find it worth paying a higher price for this backing.[22] In the agreement that was finally to be reached late in 1971 Germany would indeed act on this calculation. In the meantime, the need for America also to make concessions, and to preserve her current troop levels to provide the backing for Germany's Ostpolitik, was strongly argued by critics of Senator Mansfield. For instance, Leslie H. Gelb and Morton H. Halperin, who had both served in the Pentagon during the 1960s, argued in an important article at the end of 1970 that Germany's adjustment to the realities of East-West relations was unquestionably in the interests of the United States, and that it should be encouraged by the maintenance of American forces: any significant reductions, they said, would suggest that a complete withdrawal was imminent and might prevent German ratification of the non-proliferation treaty, stop German support for the SALT negotiations, worsen the forthcoming trade war between America and Europe, and generally de-stabilize the European balance in conventional forces.[23]

The American position when formal negotiations began in March 1971 was somewhat influenced by such arguments that continued troop stationing was in America's interests as well as in Germany's, but the financial and congressional pressures resulted in a strong demand by Nathaniel Samuels, the Under Secretary of State, that Germany increase her contributions, including covering part of the local costs incurred by the American forces in Germany.[24]

The negotiations were complicated by the floating of the Mark in May 1971, which added 3 or 4 per cent to American costs,[25] and by the renewed financial crisis of August. It was only in December that Washington and Bonn concluded a new agreement, which, despite all Germany's protestations the previous year that no increase in payments could be afforded, was considerably more favourable to the United States than the previous arrangement. It was agreed that German payments for the two-year period from July 1971 to June 1973 would total $2,034 (US) billion—an increase of $400 million on the previous figure. They would consist of $1,200 million in purchases of military equipment (notably Phantom fighters), which the German forces fortunately needed; $600 million in purchases of US Treasury Bonds, to be repaid, it was hoped, when the American balance of payments improved; and, for the first time, a contribution of $184 million towards the modernization of barracks and other American facilities in Germany.[26] This last provision indicated a new German willingness to participate in 'burden-sharing' in a literal sense, and the German concessions in the whole agreement suggested that the Bonn government, despite some internal disagreements, was willing to pay a substantial price for American support at a time when Germany's Ostpolitik was arousing a certain degree of tension and controversy.

Alliance Politics: the End of Bretton Woods

By the end of the 1960s there was abundant evidence that economic issues would be the main sources of conflict in the relations between the world's advanced capitalist nations, playing a similar role to that of military problems in the early years of the decade.[27]

The main issues of an economic nature which affected the Atlantic area at the turn of the decade were two: the structural question of the enlargement of the European Community and the substantive problem of international payments and monetary arrangements. Both these very large topics can be considered here only in so far as they presented problems for the relations between Washington and Bonn:[28] in this aspect of each of them, the striking feature was the way in which the German government took considerable pains (and withstood a good deal of domestic and European pressure) to minimize conflict with the United States. The result of these efforts was that a range of international activities and policies which might have injected very severe strains into the Washington-Bonn relationship did so only within limits: at a time when the United States felt marked irritation at the actions and policies of several other European states, and also at the posture of the EEC in the European-American trade negotiations in 1971–2, it was often clear that the Bonn government was still regarded with favour as distinctly well-disposed towards American interests. This was on the whole an accurate perception: the Federal Republic, by now second only to the United States in the volume of its external trade, had very similar interests to those of the United States in terms of wishing to promote a liberal world trading system; there was also the constant factor that the Bonn government, not wishing to incur American displeasure during the difficult negotiations on Ostpolitik, was careful not to create difficulties for the United States even in the field of monetary affairs, where the convergence of interests was by no means such an automatic one.

The negotiations leading to Britain's signature of the treaty of accession to the European Communities in January 1972 were begun, as we have seen, by the Labour government early in 1970, and their most serious difficulties were overcome in May-June 1971 after the new Conservative Prime Minister, Edward Heath, visited President Pompidou.[29]

From the beginning of the process, at the conference at The Hague in December 1969, the German government was strongly in favour of British entry. At the same time, Germany was determined to ensure that the problems in Atlantic relations which the enlargement entailed did not become a source of intolerable conflict with the United States. The creation of a commercial bloc controlling a very large percentage of the world's trade, and possessing preferential agreements with a number of Mediterranean and African countries which somewhat limited American export prospects, was naturally a factor of some concern to the United States. Again, the European Communities' adoption in March 1971 of the so-called Werner Plan, a project for economic and monetary union in which European exchange parities would be firmly linked and a European currency developed, was a potential threat to the position of the dollar in the world monetary system in a period of acute strain on the American balance of payments.

The German position on all these issues was consistently friendly towards the United States. On the issues arising from the EEC's enlargement, Bonn's influence was exerted on the side of liberal trade policies and a limitation of preferential agreements that were likely to damage American interests. On the problems of economic and monetary union, the German position—often against French opposition—was clearly in favour of monetary policies that did not add to the problems of the dollar.

These problems became acute in 1971 in a form which was certainly unforeseen at the start of the year. President Nixon's 'state of the world message' issued in February proudly recorded, in opening its consideration of international economic affairs, that 1970 'was one of the most tranquil years for the international monetary system in a decade'.[30] The dollar was, however, in renewed difficulties within less than a month of this statement. In March, when the flow of dollars from the United States to Europe was accelerating alarmingly, the *Bundesbank* cut its discount rate in an attempt to discourage more transfers from dollars into Marks.

In the next phase of the crisis, the unprecedented inflow of funds into Germany in the first few days of May, the German action—the floating of the Mark—was again one which helped the dollar at the expense of antagonizing Germany's EEC partners, since it created difficulties both for the Common Agricultural Policy and for the proposed economic and monetary union.[31]

At an international banking conference from 23 to 28 May in Munich (a reflection of Germany's powerful position in international monetary affairs) German spokesmen, notably Wilhelm Hankel, Assistant Secretary for Money and Credit Policy in the Ministry of Economics and Finances, proposed international monetary reforms including a collective float of European currencies (a compromise between an 'Atlantic' and a 'European' position), and an extension of the IMF's Special Drawing Rights to replace the dollar as the main reserve currency.[32] US spokesmen, however, and notably the Secretary of the Treasury John Connally, insisted that the proper course for Europeans to follow was to increase their contribution to American defence costs, take in more American exports, and help the American position on monetary matters;[33] no agreement was reached.

The next phase of the crisis came with the package of measures announced by President Nixon on 15 August, including a surcharge of 10 per cent on foreign imports into

America, and the suspension of the dollar's convertibility into gold.[34] Throughout all the international negotiations that followed this dramatic move it was clear that the Germans—again, often in conflict with France—were making every effort to help the Americans: in particular, the continued floating of the Mark was a source of support to the dollar. It is true, however, that part of the background to the August measures was American irritation with her foreign partners as a whole, in which Germany was to some degree included. In the words of one commentator:

> The toughness of the U.S. bargaining position during the post-August 15 international monetary negotiations reflects the American popular mood of populism and nationalism—itself a threat to free international trade. It also reflects the understandable American feeling that the U.S. has been paying for most of the defense of Western Europe and Japan, to their profit, and that its worsened economic situation requires increased burden-sharing in the defense field. Finally, and not surprisingly, the rise to economic super-power status of America's two major enemies in World War II, Germany and Japan, initially with U.S. help but now at U.S. expense, does not endear them to many American hearts.[35]

However, America had much more reason for irritation with Japan—the principal inundator of the American market with low-priced goods—than with Germany. As the Secretary of State put it in his review of the year's events, 'The Germans were understanding of our dollar problem and the objectives of our new economic policy,'[36] and at one stage in the negotiations of autumn 1971, the Secretary of the Treasury went so far as publicly to envisage exempting German imports from the surcharge announced in August, in reward for this helpful attitude.[37]

The months leading up to the Smithsonian Agreement of 18 December 1971 when new parities were agreed, including an up-valued Mark and a devalued dollar, were in general marked by continued agreement between Bonn and Washington. This was also a feature of the trade negotiations conducted during the winter of 1971–2 between the EEC (represented by its Commissioner for External Relations, Ralf Dahrendorf) and the American President's Special Representative, William Eberle.[38]

The pattern in Atlantic economic affairs, where Germany consistently tried to guide Europe's emerging structure and the outcome of substantive problems in a direction favourable to good European-American relations, was similar to the pattern in the military affairs of the region. The West German Defence Ministry under Helmut Schmidt remained strongly attached to 'Atlantic' rather than 'European' policies. In the developing structures of the alliance—the 'Eurogroup', the European Defence Improvement Programme adopted late in 1970, and the refurbishing of Western European Union—Germany's influence was placed firmly on the side of solidarity with the United States.

NATO's organizational structure, strategic posture, and arrangements for the ownership and disposition of 'hardware' were now vastly less important, as scenes or sources of American-German tension, than they had been in any previous phase of the alliance.

The main origin of such German-American tension as did make itself felt in the NATO context was far less the affairs of the alliance iself than the 'external' question of the attitudes of NATO's members towards the presumed adversary, as the 'Era of Negotiation' came to justify the appellation President Nixon had given it.

Relations with the Adversary: Washington's SALT and Bonn's Ostpolitik

The strong interest of the Nixon administration in making a reality of the 'Era of Negotiation' was confirmed by the emphasis given to East-West détente in the annual 'state of the world' messages and by the President's extensive travels. In 1969 he visited Rumania—the first time an American president had been in a Communist country since Roosevelt went to Yalta; in 1970 he went to Yugoslavia, and in 1971 President Tito went to the United States; constant diplomatic negotiations were pursued with Communist countries on a wide range of subjects including Vietnam, Berlin, and the Middle East; and the dramatic culmination of the process came with the President's visits to Peking and Moscow in 1972, and the signature of the SALT Agreement.

As for Bonn, the Brandt government's determination to

conduct an active Ostpolitik reflected a distinct shift in German perceptions of the relationship between détente and reunification, in marked contrast to earlier years. Under Adenauer the watchword had been 'no détente without progress on the German problem'; by the time of Erhard and Schröder, the word had become 'we must press ahead with détente at the same time as we seek progress on the German problem'; with the Grand Coalition of Kiesinger and Brandt, the decisive shift had occurred to 'détente is so fundamental to subsequent progress on the German problem that we are ready to make unilateral concessions so as to make progress towards a détente, and we agree to the resolution of the German problem coming much later.'[39] With the Brandt-Scheel government, the readiness for unilateral concessions became more pronounced, and the acceptable delay in the solution of the German problem became much longer. The old linkage between arms-control agreements and progress towards reunification was now finally broken.

The scene was thus set for an active pursuit of détente both by Washington and by Bonn. The first step forward, after Brandt's accession to the chancellorship, concerned the Non-Proliferation Treaty on which the new Soviet Ambassador to Bonn, Semyon K. Tsarapkin, was qualified by long years as a disarmament negotiator to explain the Soviet viewpoint. As we have seen,[40] a compromise acceptable both to Bonn and to Washington was evolved within a few weeks of the change of government: Washington and Moscow proceeded with their ratification of the treaty; while Bonn's signature of it in November was to be followed by ratification only after certain important issues had been clarified.

The main focus of interest in arms-control policy had by now become the Soviet-American SALT talks. Originally expected to start in 1968, these were delayed until November 1969, and even then their opening phase was distinctly exploratory, being limited to an exchange of views on general problems of strategic weaponry, questions of inspection and verification, and the agenda for the remaining discussions.[41]

As the dialogue between the super-powers proceeded in 1970 and 1971 fears were occasionally expressed by America's European allies that the resulting agreement might damage Western Europe's security, for instance, by bringing about a reduction in the number of American missiles 'covering' the

Soviet missiles targeted on Europe. However, the American negotiators in SALT appear to have taken exceptional pains to keep their allies fully consulted on each phase of the negotiations, and no inter-allied tension remotely comparable to that provoked by the Test Ban Treaty or the Non-Proliferation Treaty negotiations was to be detected. One of the reasons for this, particularly as far as Bonn was concerned, was that the German government itself was simultaneously engaged in its own branch of détente diplomacy—the Ostpolitik negotiations with Eastern capitals, leading in the direction of a European Security Conference—which it saw as complementary to the SALT undertaking at the super-power level.[42]

The SALT Agreement signed by Nixon and Brezhnev in Moscow in May 1972 in fact contained little to cause alarm in Europe, even in West Germany.[43] More disturbing, though it was hard to say precisely why, was the growing awareness of Europeans that Washington's obvious rapprochement with Moscow, coming as it did at the same time as American overtures to Peking, clearly downgraded the importance of Western Europe in American concerns. The promulgation of the notion that bipolarity was giving way to pentapolarity, the indications that American withdrawal from Vietnam (' Vietnamization ') must be followed by a certain disengagement from Europe too, and the mounting signs of American irritation with the European Economic Community and with Europeans in general all confirmed the fact that transatlantic relations had entered a new phase. German concern about the risk of a total American withdrawal from Europe was graphically expressed in the title of a tract published by a leading CDU politician in the spring of 1972—*Goodbye America: and What Then?*;[44] more academic analyses also dwelt pessimistically on the decline of America's interest in West Europe's defence, the strength of her preoccupation with détente, and even a disturbing increase in her propensity to engage in dealings with the GDR.[45]

One symptom of a certain malaise in transatlantic relations, induced by President Nixon's discussions in Moscow, was a press report six weeks after his visit that European members of NATO were deeply perturbed at the administration's action in negotiating with the Soviet government on general principles of coexistence without informing them. At the very time when the NATO Council had been working on a joint statement of principles to guide Western relations with Moscow, it appeared that Washington had been engaged in private bilateral discussions of the same subject with Moscow, whose results—embodied in the twelve-point declaration signed by Nixon in Moscow—included concessions which the West Europeans found hard to accept.[46]

The reports of dissension in NATO were officially denied,[47] and in fact the Western alliance, within a few days of the President's signature of the SALT Agreement on 25 May, was able to agree on further collective steps towards East-West détente, including both the planning of a conference on security and co-operation in Europe and also the discussion, now accepted in principle by the Soviet side, of mutual and balanced force reductions. Both Washington's signature of the SALT Agreement and Bonn's treaties with the Soviet Union and Poland, as well as the Berlin agreements which concerned both capitals, were regarded as necessary preliminary steps for this next phase of détente diplomacy, and the underlying harmony between the views of Washington and Bonn was thus confirmed.[48]

If the direction and speed of Washington's rapprochement with the Communist world thus caused only passing concern in Bonn, the same appeared hardly to be true—at least superficially—of Washington's reactions to the Ostpolitik pursued by Bonn. As Chancellor, Brandt was in a position to seek agreement with the East much more actively than during his period as Foreign Minister, when his freedom of action had been continually limited by Chancellor Kiesinger.[49] Together with Egon Bahr, who moved with him from the Foreign Ministry to the Chancellor's office, Brandt quickly initiated active exploratory talks at all three of the relevant levels of Bonn's Eastern relationships: within a few months of his accession to office, his government was consulting intensively with Moscow, with Warsaw, and with East Berlin.

From the beginning, there were press reports that the independent spirit of Brandt's approaches to the East was causing concern in Washington. For instance, the *New York Times* reported on 5 December 1969 that the deputy chief of the United States Embassy in Bonn had delivered a memorandum of complaint at the German government's action in preparing to discuss an agreement on the renunciation of force with Moscow without consulting Washington: this was said to reflect particularly the concern of Dr Kissinger rather than that of the State Department. Although the alleged démarche was denied,[50] the rumour was not wholly implausible: Washington was not used to dealing with a German government which initiated lines of policy without exhaustively clearing them first with its ally.

In itself, as has already been pointed out, the Ostpolitik of the Brandt government contained little that did not reflect American sentiments about the need to face the realities of Germany's division.[51] The main American concern was lest, by making premature concessions that might remain unreciprocated, the new German government might not provoke a public reaction violent enough to endanger both the policy of détente and the whole West German regime. Concern about some of the Ostpolitik's possible consequences, however, could at times look to its German supporters like opposition to the policy itself.

The Bonn government's initiative in dealing directly with the East German state—symbolized by Brandt's visit to Erfurt in March 1970 and the invitation to the GDR's Prime Minister Willi Stoph to Kassel two months later—was certainly not an action likely to arouse American misgivings: as we have seen, American policy-makers from John Foster Dulles onwards had been urging Bonn to believe that only the West German side could gain by an increase in contact between the two Germanies.[52] Again, Bonn's soundings for an agreement with Warsaw, which would have to be based on German acceptance of the Oder-Neisse Line, were thoroughly welcome to Washington. The element of concern about Ostpolitik arose mainly in relation to Bonn's dealings with Moscow, where it was feared that the German government, despite its good intentions, might be led into making unwise concessions. Chancellor Brandt, looking back at the beginning of 1971 on German exchanges of view with the American government during the previous year, inadvertently made a revealing distinction between the constant, detailed, and effective consultation on matters concerning Berlin and the treatment of other aspects of Ostpolitik: on these—including essentially relations with the Soviet Union—he stated merely that he had had 'very good discussions' with President Nixon during his 1970 visit.[53]

When Bonn's intensive negotiations with the Soviet Union culminated in the signature of a treaty of friendship in Moscow in August 1970 the American response was basically one of approval. The Assistant Secretary of State for European Affairs, Martin Hillenbrand, had told a Senate Committee on 24 June, 'we approve the efforts of the German Government in Bonn to normalize its relations with the countries of Eastern Europe, including the Soviet Union',[54] and this was confirmed in numerous public statements. However, an underlying current of concern that Bonn might be moving too fast, and particularly that the apparent Soviet readiness for a serious move towards détente might be illusory (particularly with regard to Berlin) continued to be perceptible.

The Secretary of State, William Rogers, in his formal public endorsement of the German-Soviet treaty, made a point of underlining the importance of successful progress on the related issue of the future of Berlin: the West would now expect, he sternly stated, 'tangible evidence of Soviet cooperation towards bringing about substantial practical improvements for the people of Berlin'.[55]

Misgivings about Ostpolitik in Washington appear to have reached their peak in the closing weeks of 1970, when the Moscow treaty had been followed by Brandt's visit to Warsaw to sign the German-Polish treaty of friendship (7 December), and when his government was beginning to put troublesome pressure on Washington to move faster in the Soviet-Western negotiations on the future of Berlin: by now it had been decided that the German-Soviet and German-Polish treaties would be submitted for parliamentary ratification only if a satisfactory agreement guaranteeing the position of West Berlin were reached first, and the Bonn government, eager for ratification, was pressing Washington, as well as London and Paris, to accept a less exacting definition of 'satisfactory' than they were inclined to. Bonn's wish foi quicker progress on Berlin was expressed, for instance, by Brandt's close Ministerial colleague Horst Ehmke in discussions with State Department and White House staff in Washington in December 1970.[56]

The background to Ehmke's visit was in fact an atmosphere of suspicion in Bonn that Ostpolitik was opposed not only by such eminent 'founding fathers' of the Federal Republic as General Clay, John J. McCloy, Thomas Dewey, and Dean

Acheson (the last-mentioned of whom, emerging from a meeting with President Nixon, publicly condemned Brandt's 'mad race to Moscow') but also by powerful officials of the Nixon administration: according to German press reports, even such men as Henry Kissinger in the White House, Melvin Laird in the Pentagon, and Martin Hillenbrand in the State Department, were all privately more sceptical about Ostpolitik than their public statements of support would suggest.[57] Although a State Department spokesman described these rumours as 'stupefying', and emphatically reaffirmed American support for the Brandt government's policies—which was also reiterated by Kissinger to Ehmke[58]—German doubts about the strength of this support remained very much alive. Even though the opposition of Acheson, Clay, McCloy, and others to Ostpolitik was castigated in an article by Arthur Goldberg, former United States Ambassador to the United Nations and Supreme Court justice,[59] the reply to Goldberg by George Ball, Under Secretary of State under Kennedy and Johnson, gave a strong reminder that distrust of German power and independence was still widely felt in the American foreign policy establishment.[60]

There was indeed a serious divergence of perception between the government in Bonn, for whom Ostpolitik during 1970 meant essentially the negotiation of general treaties of friendship and force-renunciation with the Soviet Union and Poland, and the administration in Washington, faced with the vastly more intractable problem of negotiating a viable agreement concerning Berlin. Whereas the treaties with Moscow and Warsaw could not be unfairly described as a series of unilateral acceptances by West Germany of the frontiers insisted on by her Eastern interlocutors (acceptances which made agreement relatively easy), a worthwhile agreement on Berlin necessarily entailed hard pressure by the Western negotiators, if satisfactory Soviet concessions were to be forthcoming.

For this reason, although President Nixon accepted the idea of seeking a Berlin settlement in principle as early as February 1969,[61] the actual negotiations between the four powers concerned began only thirteen months later, and expectations of success among Western officials were very low.[62] Several of the professional diplomats in the State Department, the American Embassy in Bonn, and the American Mission in Berlin believed that it was a mistake for the West even to seek an agreement with the Soviet Union, since the present situation guaranteed essential Western interests more effectively than any likely agreement would do.[63] This view led to a very cautious approach to the negotiations—it should also be said that the Soviet Union, under strong pressure from East Germany, was also highly non-conciliatory towards any suggestion of strengthening West Berlin's ties with the West—and their pace was distinctly slow throughout 1970. (A further distinction between the perspectives of Washington and Bonn was that the American administration, as befitted the government of a superpower, linked concessions on Berlin with demands for reciprocal Soviet concessions on such issues as the Middle East and the presence of Soviet submarines in Cuba—concerns naturally remote from those of Bonn, though very pressing for Washington.) On two occasions, American delay appears to have particularly irritated the German government, increasingly anxious to attain an agreement to restore its waning popularity: in the summer of 1970 an adjournment of ten weeks occurred just after the German-Soviet treaty had appeared to offer a hope of progress; and in December a ten-week interruption, occurring this time after the German-Polish treaty, provoked considerable German-American tension, whose symptoms included the Washington visit of conciliation by Ehmke, already mentioned.[64]

It was only several weeks after the beginning of 1971 that harmony was restored between Washington's and Bonn's views on the desirable negotiating tactics and final conditions for the Berlin Agreement.

Although President Nixon appears to have decided in the late summer of 1970 that more active negotiating efforts should be made—a decision reflected in his discussion of Berlin with Gromyko on 22 October, and in concerted reassessments of the position with West Germany and other allies—the new Western proposals took some time to work out, and were not submitted until February 1971.[65] West German and American views on Ostpolitik were now again closely aligned, since both Bonn and Washington wanted to achieve a Berlin agreement in order to take further steps towards détente: just as Brandt could not submit the Soviet and Polish treaties to the Bundestag without a satisfactory Berlin agreement, it was by now clear that, for the United States, a Berlin agreement was an indication of

Soviet goodwill which must be given before any progress could be made in discussing a conference on security in Europe. A series of Soviet concessions in the spring of 1971 brought agreement nearer: in April and May a successful breakthrough in reaching a compromise in the SALT negotiations was announced; early in May, Walter Ulbricht was replaced by Erich Honecker in the leadership of the German Democratic Republic; and later in the month Leonid Brezhnev's announcement that the Soviet Union was willing to discuss mutual and balanced force reductions in the context of a European Security Conference appeared to indicate not only the Soviet leadership's willingness to help President Nixon defeat the Mansfield Resolution but also to accept an important point in the Western view of the desirable agenda for East-West security negotiations.[66]

A further, and decisive, impetus to the Berlin negotiations came in mid-July, from a quite unexpected direction: this was the development of relations between Washington and Peking, culminating in the announcement on 15 July that President Nixon was to visit Peking early in 1972. It appears that just as Moscow was induced by this development to be more responsive to Western views on Berlin, so as to bring about an agreement which would prevent a dangerous degree of isolation, so the decision-makers in Washington redoubled their efforts to reach agreement on Berlin, to counter the accusation that rapprochement with Peking would necessarily disrupt détente with Moscow.[67]

Thanks in part to this fortuitous conjunction in Sino-American relations, American objections to certain Soviet demands concerning Berlin were dropped—for instance, Washington accepted the presence of a Soviet Consulate in West Berlin, which had been urged by Moscow and by Bonn for several months—and after gruelling negotiations throughout August a four-power agreement on Berlin was signed on 3 September 1971.[68] There is no doubt that the close relations between President Nixon and the American Ambassador in Bonn, Kenneth Rush, greatly facilitated American decision-making in the final phase of the negotiations, when very close harmony between Washington and Bonn was restored.[69] This harmony was only superficially disturbed by Brandt's independent action later in September in visiting Brezhnev in the

Crimea without giving sufficient advance warning to Washington.

The next step after the signature of the four-power agreement, was the negotiation of supplementary arrangements concerning Berlin between the two German governments. This process was completed by December,[70] and the way was clear for the Bonn government to present the Moscow and Warsaw treaties to the Bundestag for ratification. As we have seen, a great deal depended on this, since neither the coming into effect of the Berlin Agreement, nor the final conclusion of a SALT Agreement (by now expected to occur when Nixon visited Moscow at the end of May) could be counted on unless the treaties were ratified. The German government's parliamentary majority was in process of being eroded virtually to nothing by defections to the Opposition: it was finally lost in April 1972 [71] and the American administration had to act with great caution and discretion in helping Brandt to secure a majority for ratification. The Christian Democratic Opposition in Bonn did its utmost to exploit every hint of American reservations about Ostpolitik to discredit or overthrow the Brandt government—Barzel visited Washington in January 1972 in the hope of winning support, but was disappointed [72]—and rumours of such reservations were constantly reported by the Opposition press.[73]

The American administration was strongly urged both by Germans and by Americans to give all possible support to Brandt, if necessary by bringing 'strong pressure quietly but firmly on the Christian Democrats, making plain . . . that if they come into power by blocking the treaties this will adversely affect our relations '.[74] This advice does not appear to have been taken,[75] and in the event, the Christian Democrat Opposition, realizing spontaneously that further hostility to the treaties would isolate them not only from Germany's allies but also from the majority of German opinion, decided to abstain in the critical votes on 17 May, which allowed the treaties to be ratified.[76] By the beginning of June 1972, when Brandt gave his Marshall Plan anniversary address at Harvard,[77] the Eastern treaties had been ratified, the Berlin Agreement had come into force, Nixon and Brezhnev had signed the SALT Agreement, and the NATO Ministerial meeting had agreed on the next steps towards a conference on security in Europe and negotiations on MBFR.[78]

Close harmony had thus been restored to relations between Washington and Bonn, which since 1969 had occasionally appeared likely to incur the danger of considerable strain through the development of Bonn's Ostpolitik. It is worth repeating the general conclusion that, as in the period of much more severe discord in the relationship during the Kennedy period, by far the greatest source of tension had been the dealings of one of the allies with their presumed adversary: the main difference—apart from the striking improvement in the containment of tension by effective consultation—was that this time the initiatives which gave rise to the trouble included some emanating from Bonn as well as from Washington.

NOTES

1 *U.S. Foreign Policy for the 1970s: a New Strategy for Peace. A Report to the Congress by Richard Nixon, President of the United States, February 18, 1970*, esp. pp. 133 ff.

2 Quoted from *Time*, 1 Jan. 1972, by Alastair Buchan, 'A World Restored?", *For. Aff.*, 50/4 (1972), p. 644.

3 Buchan, ibid. and S. Hoffman, 'Weighing the Balance of Power', ibid. pp. 618–43.

4 See above, pp. 2–3.

5 See the article by Marion, Countess Dönhoff, in *Die Zeit*, 25 Feb. 1972; when Rush returned to Washington in Feb. 1972, he was succeeded by Hillenbrand.

6 *International Herald Tribune*, 20 May 1971.

7 See above, p. 177.

8 See below, p. 207.

9 See above, pp. 106–10, 126–31.

10 On Bahr, see above, p. 161, n. 50.

11 See the author's analyses 'The 1969 Election in West Germany' and 'Political Prospects in Bonn', *The World Today*, Nov. 1969 and Aug. 1972 respectively.

12 Brandt, 'Germany's "Westpolitik"', *For. Aff.*, 50/4 (1972), p. 416.

13 See above, p. 172.

14 See Stanley.

15 *Orbis*, Fall 1971, p. 735.

16 *Congressional Record*, 20 Apr. 1970, cited by Newhouse and others, *U.S. Troops in Europe*, p. 16.

17 *Congressional Record*, 19 May 1971, cited by Newhouse and others, ibid. p. 17.

18 On the background, see *Orbis*, Fall 1971, pp. 733–8.

[19] Address on Western Europe and NATO (wireless bulletin from Washington, 21 Jan. 1970, Bonn-Bad Godesberg, US Embassy), p. 4.

[20] *Evening Standard*, 4 Apr. 1970.

[21] *NYT*, 11 and 12 Apr. 1970.

[22] Ibid. 14 Apr. 1970.

[23] Leslie H. Gelb and Morton H. Halperin, 'Why Europe needs 300,000 GIs', *Washington Post*, 20 Dec. 1970.

[24] *International Herald Tribune*, 12 Mar. 17 Apr., 12 May, 30 June, and *The Times*, 29 June 1971; Elke Thiel, 'Devisenausgleich und Lastenteilung im Atlantischen Bündnis', *Europa-Archiv*, 26/10 (1971), pp. 353–62.

[25] Newhouse and others, *U.S. Troops in Europe*, p. 165.

[26] *Financial Times*, 11 Dec.; *International Herald Tribune*, 11 and 12 Dec. 1971.

[27] See pp. 106–10, 126–31, above. The parallel is not quite accurate, since one prominent actor in the economic issues, Japan, had played no part in NATO's troubles in the Kennedy era; the general resemblances, however, are striking.

[28] For more comprehensive analyses, see Calleo; and Ian Davidson and Gordon L. Weil, *The Gold War* (1970), among others.

[29] For details, see the author's article 'Anglo-French Relations Today', *The World Today*, July 1971.

[30] *U.S. Foreign Policy for the 1970s: Building for Peace. A Report to the Congress by Richard Nixon, President of the United States, February 25, 1971*, p. 135.

[31] Susan Strange, 'The Dollar Crisis 1971', *Int. Aff.*, Apr. 1972, pp. 200–2.

[32] *Orbis*, Fall 1971, pp. 735–6.

[33] Strange, p. 203.

[34] *U.S. Foreign Policy for the 1970s: the Emerging Structure of Peace. A Report to the Congress by Richard Nixon, President of the United States, February 9, 1972*, pp. 60–5.

[35] William E. Griffith, *The Great Globe Transformed*, cited by Peter Christian Ludz, 'Amerikanische Haltungen zur deutschen Frage', *Deutschland Archiv*, 5/6 (1972), p. 578.

[36] William P. Rogers, cited by Ludz, ibid. p. 586.

[37] *The Times* and *Financial Times*, 18 Oct.; *NYT*, 19 Oct. 1971. Germany declined this offer, which was probably not intended as more than a friendly gesture by Connally to Schiller, and, if accepted, would have created serious conflicts with Germany's European partners.

[38] On the US-EEC agreement of 4 Feb. 1972, see *The Times* and *NYT*, 5 Feb. 1972.

[39] These formulations are taken from Alfred Grosser's perceptive article 'France and Germany: less divergent outlooks', *For. Aff.*, 48/2 (1970), p. 241.

[40] See above, pp. 183–4.

[41] Only the barest outline of the SALT talks can be given here: an article in *Orbis*, 15/2 (1971), pp. 469–72, gives a useful survey of their progress up to spring 1971; and the concluding phase (1971–2) is analysed by Andrew Pierre in 'The SALT Agreement and Europe', *The World Today*, July 1972; and in documents and articles in *Survival*, July-Aug. 1972, pp. 188–99, and Sept.-Oct. 1972, pp. 210–19.

[42] This view is well reflected in German publications of the period, including particularly the articles of Theo Sommer (Director of the Defence Ministry Planning Staff from 1969 to 1970) in *Die Zeit*. See also his chapter ' Kriterien und Instrumente der europaischen Sicherheit ' in K. Birrenbach and others, *Aussenpolitik nach der Wahl des 6. Bundestages* (1969), pp. 23–37.

[43] See Pierre, *The World Today*, July 1972, esp. pp. 287–8.

[44] Walther Leisler Kiep, *Goodbye Amerika: Was Dann?* (1972): the book's main theme is the need for Europe to act so as to prevent a total American withdrawal, and to mitigate the consequences of a partial one.

[45] See in particular Ludz, *Deutschland Archiv*, 5/6 (1972), pp. 573–94.

[46] *NYT*, 26 July 1972. The concessions which Kissinger and Hillenbrand, among others, were said to have hidden from the West Europeans included the omission of a Western demand for ' self-determination ' as a principle of coexistence in Europe.

[47] *NYT*, 27 July 1972.

[48] North Atlantic Council communiqué, 31 May 1972, reproduced in *Survival*, Sept.-Oct. 1972, pp. 243–5. A certain symbolism might be seen in the fact that the Council's annual spring meeting was held, in this critical year, in Bonn.

[49] Private information, Bonn. A comprehensive study of Germany's Eastern policy up to early 1971 is given by Lawrence L. Whetten, *Germany's Ostpolitik: Relations between the Federal Republic and the Warsaw Pact Countries* (1971). On American views of Ostpolitik, see pp. 138, 140, 180–1, 196–7.

[50] *NYT*, 6 Dec. 1969, confirmed by private information, Washington.

[51] See above, p. 199.

[52] See above, p. 185.

[53] C. L. Sulzberger, *NYT*, 29 Jan. 1971; see the leading article ibid. 20 July 1970.

[54] US Senate, Cttee on Foreign Relations, Subcttee on US Security Agreements and Commitments Abroad, *US Security Agreements and Commitments Abroad*, Hearings, 91st Congress, 2nd sess., vol. 2, pts 5–11 (1971), p. 2197.

[55] Quoted in *NYT*, 13 Aug. 1970, with the apt comment that American reservations about Ostpolitik could be explained by its effect in weakening the position of the US in Europe. See the emphasis placed by Hillenbrand on the continuing rights and responsibilities of the Allies in Berlin: as n. 54 above, pp. 2270.

[56] *Washington Post*, 22 Dec. 1970, supplemented by private information relating also to the question of a ' satisfactory ' Berlin agreement.

[57] *NYT*, 20 Dec. 1970 and German press sources quoted by Whetten, pp. 180–1.

[58] *NYT*, 22 Dec. 1970.

[59] ' The Cold Warriors versus Willy Brandt ', *NYT*, 5 Jan. 1971.

[60] George Ball, ' A Reply to Arthur Goldberg ', *NYT*, 8 Jan. 1971; Ball argued that Germany's Ostpolitik indicated a dangerous turning away from the West.

[61] US Information Service press release of Nixon's Berlin speech of 27 Feb. 1969.

62 *The Guardian*, 26 Mar. 1970. See Dieter Mahncke's articles on the Berlin negotiations in *The World Today*, Apr. 1970 and Dec. 1971.

63 Private information. This attitude reflected the normal phenomenon whereby ' the bureaucracy prefers the known dangers of an existing course to the uncertain costs and gains of change ', Francis E. Rourke, *Bureaucracy and Foreign Policy* (1972), p. 60, quoting M. Halperin and Tang Tson, ' United States Policy toward the Offshore Islands ', *Public Policy*, 15/37 (1966).

64 Robert Kleiman, ' Mr Nixon and Berlin ', *NYT*, 4 Sept. 1971. According to sources in Washington, Ehmke tried to persuade senior American officials that a quicker negotiating tempo would favour the West, since the Russian leadership would wish to conclude an agreement before the forthcoming 24th Party Conference, but his interlocutors did not share this assessment.

65 Ibid. and Kenneth A. Myers, *Ostpolitik and American Security Interests in Europe* (1972), pp. 42 ff., which gives a very illuminating analysis of the Berlin negotiations.

66 See Myers, pp. 52–60 for a fuller analysis.

67 Private information, Washington.

68 For analyses of the agreement, see Myers, esp. pp. 48–65, and Mahncke's articles in *The World Today*, Apr. 1970 and Dec. 1971.

69 Private information, Washington, Bonn, and Berlin.

70 Texts in *Europa-Archiv*, 27/3 (1972), pp. D51–82.

71 See the author's analysis ' Political Prospects in Bonn ', *The World Today*, Aug. 1972, esp. pp. 351–3.

72 Myers, p. 88, note.

73 See, as one example among many—particularly in the Springer press—the report of congressional opposition to Ostpolitik in *Die Welt*, 21 Mar. 1972. CDU politicians engaged in intensive lobbying in Washington throughout this period.

74 Averell Harriman, ' Giving Brandt a Chance ', *NYT*, 2 May 1972.

75 Private information, Bonn.

76 See Morgan, ' Political Prospects in Bonn ', *The World Today*, Aug. 1972, p. 356.

77 *NYT*, 6 June 1972.

78 See above, pp. 192–3.

CHAPTER ELEVEN

Stability under Pressure 1972–1973

Background: the Ambiguous World System

THE summer of 1972 saw both Nixon and Brandt electioneering: the American president starting his campaign for re-election in November, after his first four-year term, and the German chancellor working towards an election he had called for the same month, after unexpectedly losing his parliamentary majority. Both leaders were to be triumphantly re-elected to office, but their political fortunes were to take radically different courses thereafter: whereas Brandt successfully defended his government against the accusations of bribing opposition parliamentarians in order to secure ratification of his Eastern treaties, Nixon was accused during 1973 of responsibility for much more serious crimes committed in aid of his own re-election, and by the end of the year his failure to disprove his involvement in the Watergate affair and other incidents had threatened him with impeachment and removal from office.

The world scene against which these dramas were played out was one of dynamic movement, often in ambiguous and contradictory directions. One of the basic trends of the late Sixties and early Seventies, the movement towards détente between major powers, appeared to continue unabated. In the Far East, China's entry into the United Nations late in 1972 confirmed the seriousness of the new American 'open door' policy expressed during Nixon's visit to China in the spring. It also prepared the way for a cease-fire agreement in Vietnam, signed in January 1973, which brought about the withdrawal of the last American combat forces from the war-ravaged country. The growing understanding between the United States and the Soviet Union continued after the conclusion of the first SALT agreement in 1972. Nixon's visit to Moscow in 1972 was followed in June 1973 by Brezhnev's visit to Washington, when the two leaders committed themselves to a series of far-reaching declarations expressing their determination not to use nuclear weapons or to allow local conflicts to escalate into general wars. The two super-powers also continued their SALT conversations, of which this second phase concerned several issues, including that of forward-based systems (largely American nuclear forces based in Western Europe), which appeared considerably harder to resolve than those covered by the first agreement of 1972. Although the American president stoutly defended his policy of détente with the USSR—including large shipments of American wheat to Russia, which compensated for the poor harvest of 1972—the policy came under increasingly strong criticism from some of his opponents in Congress. Senator Henry Jackson, for instance, won considerable support during 1973 for a proposal that the USSR should be denied most-favoured-nation treatment in commerce unless it allowed Soviet Jews to emigrate freely to Israel.

The Soviet leader also paid a visit in May 1973 to West Germany, thus setting a formal seal on Chancellor Brandt's Ostpolitik and also preparing the way for considerable economic transactions. The European Community of which West Germany was part had by this time grown in membership from six states to nine with the accession of the United Kingdom, Denmark, and Ireland in January 1973, the expected tenth member, Norway, having refused to join as the result of a referendum the previous November. The enlarged Community began its life in a period of considerable turbulence in the economic and monetary affairs of the Western world: the Smithsonian Agreement of December 1971, by which new currency parities were fixed after the crisis of that summer, finally broke down in the spring of 1973, when several of the Community currencies were linked in a collective float from which Britain and Italy remained apart, a situation which created renewed difficulties for the dollar. The year 1973 saw complicated negotiations aimed both at rebuilding the world monetary system (the official IMF negotiations on this began in Nairobi in September) and at laying the foundations for an improved system of commercial rules (for which the GATT negotiations began in October in Tokyo).

The enlarged European Community thus had to define its position, as a leading entity in the economic life of the non-Communist world, in relation to the United States and Japan. At the same time, the Community and its member states were forced to work out what position to take on the pressing questions of Western Europe's relations with the Eastern part of the continent. As soon as the package of major East-West agreements of 1972 was ratified—notably West Germany's Eastern treaties, the four-power agreement on Berlin, and the bilateral SALT agreement—the way was clear for progress towards East-West negotiations on a multilateral basis and with a very extensive subject-matter. The year 1973 saw the formal opening of two long-announced sets of East-West negotiations, the Conference on Security and Co-operation in Europe and the talks on Mutual and Balanced Force Reductions. The former of these undertakings, a conference of thirty-four states, known for short as CSCE, began in July with formal speeches by a large number of foreign ministers in Helsinki, then reconvened in the autumn in Geneva for work in a series of specialized committees which were expected to produce results for decision at a higher level, either foreign ministers or heads of governments, early in 1974. The negotiations on military force levels (MBFR for short) involved a smaller number of participants, since only nineteen members of NATO and the Warsaw Pact were involved. These talks opened in Vienna in October 1973, and were expected, in view of their sensitive subject-matter, to take several years to reach conclusive results. One of the interesting features of the preparation for both of these East-West negotiations, notably the CSCE, was that the nine states of the European Community worked very effectively in co-ordinating their views on the subjects to be discussed with the East, so that the nine-member 'Davignon Committee' of the Community's member states became a focal point of the attempt to develop a co-ordinated foreign policy for Western Europe.

Geneva, Helsinki, and Vienna were not, however, the only centres of active East-West diplomacy as the 'Era of Negotiation' went ahead: the United Nations Organization not only incorporated the People's Republic of China in 1972; it also, a year later, welcomed into membership the two German republics, after they had agreed to recognize each other's statehood and to regulate their future relations by the Basic Treaty which they signed in December 1972. The appearance in the September 1973 General Assembly of Willy Brandt and his East German opposite number was a sign that the two German states were now formally taking their places in the complex and conflict-ridden world of international politics.

Conflict was not to be long in manifesting itself. There had been occasional moments of drama in the Middle East, including the mass dismissal of Egypt's Soviet military advisers in July 1972 by President Sadat, the successor of Colonel Nasser. Again, the countries of the capitalist world, including Japan as well as the United States and those of Western Europe, had become uncomfortably aware by early 1973 how much they depended on oil from the Arab states of the Middle East, and talk of a more or less imminent ' energy crisis ' was widespread. Against this background the renewed outbreak of warfare between Israel and her Arab neighbours, in October 1973, posed acute problems for the outside world. Western Europe, in particular, was confronted with a serious threat of the total cut-off of her essential energy supplies, and took a distinctly pro-Arab position, while the United States continued to give substantial support to Israel. After two weeks of heavy fighting a temporary settlement was reached, in part through the efforts of the new American Secretary of State Henry Kissinger, but not before the Middle East crisis had seriously affected America's relations with Europe, including particularly, and quite unexpectedly, those with West Germany.

The Middle East crisis of 1973 showed that the two superpowers understood each other well enough to prevent even very acute local conflicts from escalating into all-out wars (a point that was also illustrated by Soviet non-intervention in the simultaneous crisis in Chile), but that the process of overall détente did not spare the world from some very unpleasant moments. It was this ambiguous world of simultaneous détente and crisis in which the American and German governments—particularly the former—were to undergo some severe internal convulsions in 1972–3.

Internal Politics: the Shadow of Watergate

From the point of view of good American-German relations, President Nixon's crushing defeat of Senator George McGovern in November 1972 was undoubtedly an encouraging sign. The fact that the Democratic candidate belonged to the left wing of his party, and held views on many issues which were similar to those of European social democracy, would have brought a McGovern administration close in many ways to the Brandt government. It was, however, much more important that McGovern represented forces in the Democratic Party which were in conflict with many of the interests of West Germany as perceived by Brandt and his colleagues. It was not merely that a McGovern victory would undoubtedly have strengthened the hand of Senator Mansfield and others who wished to cut America's military strength in Europe: McGovern's election slogan 'Come home, America' reflected a much deeper inclination, of which the issue of troops in Europe was only a part, for America to reduce its burdensome commitments in all parts of the world and to concentrate on solving very demanding problems at home. It would go too far to say that McGovern and his advisers were in the strict sense isolationists, but there were distinctly isolationist elements in the policies and moods they represented.[1]

Nixon's triumphant re-election was thus a matter for relief in Bonn. Even though Nixon was committed to the 'Vietnamization' of the military effort in South Vietnam by withdrawing all American forces, it was by now clear that his administration was firmly opposed to any comparable 'Europeanization' of the NATO effort in Europe. The European allies, it was clear, would be expected to make an increasing defence contribution commensurate with the growing economic strength of the enlarged Community, but they could be sure that the administration in Washington saw a continued American presence of a substantial size as being in the interest of the United States as well as their own. In trade matters again, Nixon and the Republicans appeared more likely than the Democrats to resist the protectionist pressures exerted by many sections of American society, including the labour unions, and to ensure a more favourable outcome for Europe in the impending GATT negotiations.

In the event the year 1973, the first year of Nixon's second term, was to see the administration so embroiled in the conflicts and confusions arising from the Watergate affair that its capacity to uphold its original lines of foreign policy was seriously impaired, and the forces represented by McGovern seemed after all likely to gain the upper hand.

The responsibility of some elements in the Republican Party for the Watergate incident—the breaking into the Democrats' Washington office in June 1972, early in the election campaign—became clear quite soon after the participants had been arrested. It was only in February 1973, however, that responsibility could clearly be traced higher up the Republican hierarchy, within the President's closest entourage at the White House, and that a Senate investigating committee under Senator Sam Ervin was established. By the summer the inquiries of the committee had indicated strong evidence that the President himself might be implicated in the affair, even though responsibility was taken by his senior White House subordinates, H. R. Haldeman and John Ehrlichman, who resigned from office at the end of April together with Nixon's Attorney-General, Richard G. Kleindienst. In October, after months of escalating drama involving destroyed White House files, missing tape-recordings, and deadlock between a defiant President and a suspicious Congress, Nixon also lost the services of Elliott Richardson, the upright Bostonian who had replaced Kleindienst as Attorney-General, and who resigned in protest at the President's dismissal of Archibald Cox, the Special Prosecutor appointed to investigate the Watergate affair.

Turmoil of this order at the highest level in Washington—turmoil which included legal proceedings against Nixon's leading associates and former cabinet members Harold Stans and John Mitchell, and in October the enforced resignation of his Vice President Spiro Agnew under charges of bribery and corruption—inevitably affected the conduct of American foreign policy. Brezhnev, it is true, visited Washington for a week of important talks in June 1973, and Nixon's new Secretary of State Henry Kissinger (who formally took over from William Rogers in August 1973 the powers he had long exercised from the White House) played a very active role in the Middle Eastern conflict in the autumn.

Kissinger also tried to make a reality of the much-heralded

'Year of Europe' in American foreign policy: the slogan was meant to imply that in 1973 the administration would turn towards consolidating its relations with its European allies, after achieving a breakthrough in rapprochement with the Soviet Union and China in 1972. However, Kissinger's resounding appeal to America's allies to join in drafting a new 'Atlantic Charter'—made in a speech delivered in April, four months before he became Secretary of State—appeared to many Europeans suspiciously like an attempt to distract attention from Nixon's domestic difficulties and received, as will be seen, a less than sympathetic response.

In general, the paralysis of the administration by Watergate hampered its attempts at holding back forces which threatened to endanger America's relations with Western Europe. Most conspicuous among these forces was the powerful group of Democrats in Congress, led by Senators Mansfield and Symington, who saw their chance in the administration's moment of weakness to renew their demands for the reduction of American troops in Europe. In March 1973, as the Watergate drama developed, Mansfield induced the Democratic members of the Senate, in a private caucus meeting, to pass by an overwhelming majority a resolution demanding the halving of American ground forces in Europe within eighteen months.[2] This advance by the supporters of troop cuts was followed by active debate in Congressional committees during July, and the Senate voted on the issue on 26 September. The situation was in fact highly confused, since the Senate expressed two contradictory votes on the same day: Mansfield's resolution calling for a 40 per cent cut was passed by 49 votes to 46, but then—after strong intervention by officials of the administration—the Senate in effect revoked that vote by resolving, by 51 votes to 44, not to attach the earlier resolution to the bill authorizing the defence budget.[3] The following day, however, the Senate reverted towards the Mansfield position by voting 48 to 36 in favour of a cut of 40,000 American troops abroad by mid-1974, to be followed by a further 70,000 (out of an estimated total of 470,000, i.e. a cut of 23 per cent) by the end of 1975.[4] In a further reversal the administration succeeded in obtaining a vote by a committee of the two Houses of Congress, on 12 October, which nullified the Senator's resolution of 26 September.[5] Thus although American troop levels in Europe would be maintained at least during the early phases of the East-West talks on Mutual and Balanced Force Reductions, due to open at the end of the month, it was by now abundantly clear that America's European allies could not expect her force levels to be kept up indefinitely. Furthermore, it was also clear that the Europeans would be expected to pay a larger share of the cost.

Another sector of Congressional opinion which now created difficulties in the administration's relations with Europe was located much further to the Right. The 'hawkish' Democratic Senator Henry Jackson, as we have noted, was perturbed by the administration's zealous pursuit of détente with the Soviet Union at a time when Soviet intellectuals were being flagrantly persecuted and Soviet Jews prevented from emigrating to Israel. His response, shared by other influential members of both Houses of Congress, was to propose denying the Soviet Union most-favoured-nation treatment for its exports until its emigration policies for Jews wishing to emigrate were substantially liberalized. By November 1973, after this principle had been written by Congress into the President's Trade Bill (the basic document authorizing him to negotiate a new set of GATT rules with Europe, Japan, and other partners) the international situation had seriously worsened, and the demands of the Congressional 'hawks' had been increased by the Soviet-American clash of interests in the Middle East. On 7 November Nixon announced that he was abandoning the attempt to seek Congressional approval for the Trade Bill as a whole since this approval would have been granted only on terms which seriously damaged the administration's pursuit of détente with the Soviet Union. Specifically, it was clear that Congress would have used the Bill to enforce the denial of any commercial credits to the Russians unless all restrictions on the emigration of Soviet Jews were removed. Rather than face such a limitation of his existing rights, the President asked for indefinite postponement of Congressional consideration of the Trade Bill as a whole.[6] European reactions to the postponement of the Bill—which meant that full-scale GATT negotiations were most unlikely to start until the second half of 1974—were mixed: some members of the European Community had in any case not been anxious to press for early negotiations. However, the prevailing European view, strongly shared in Germany, was that the postponement represented a victory for American political forces which might quite seriously damage Europe's interests.[7]

If the American political scene was marked by an increase in the influence of forces unwelcome to West Germany, American policy-makers, as they considered the state of political life in Germany, saw the same phenomenon in reverse. Chancellor Brandt and his leading colleagues in the victorious coalition of 1972 were of course strongly pro-American: neither the Chancellor nor his Vice-Chancellor Walter Scheel, nor Helmut Schmidt (who had replaced Karl Schiller as Finance Minister in the summer), nor Georg Leber (Schmidt's replacement as Defence Minister) could possibly be considered anti-American, and the same was true of their diplomatic and other officials. However, when Helmut Schmidt, in a speech in Washington in January 1973, uttered a carefully worded expression of regret at America's Christmastime bombing of North Vietnam, he was reflecting disapproval of American policy which was felt with considerable intensity by growing sections of German opinion. The Youth Section of the Social Democratic Party—the *Jungsozialisten* or '*Jusos*'—were particularly outspoken, condemning not only America's Vietnam policy but also the continued American military presence in Europe. By mid-April, when the Social Democratic Party Congress met in Hanover to lay down the party's long-term strategy, the Young Socialists had formally adopted a resolution demanding the cutting-off of Germany's contribution to the cost of American troops, and there were other signs of anti-American feeling in the country: public opinion polls showed a marked decline in German admiration for the United States, and extensive protests in the Nuremberg area against American use of land for military manoeuvres were widely reported by American television networks as evidence of deep-seated anti-American feelings.[8] The German opposition spokesman, Franz Josef Strauss, in the budget debate in the Bundestag on 3 April, accused Schmidt and other Social Democratic leaders of fomenting anti-Americanism, quoting as evidence Schmidt's Washington speech and a widely reported American article which suggested that Egon Bahr, Brandt's principal adviser on Ostpolitik, was intending to neutralize the Federal Republic and to remove it from NATO.[9] Accusations of this kind, coming from Strauss, could be discounted as political manoeuvres, but it was generally held that the SPD's Hanover Congress would be a serious trial of strength between the party leadership and a powerful left-wing opposition. The latter's attack at Hanover on Brandt and his colleagues included a strong dose of anti-Americanism, including the argument that the growth of East-West détente made military pacts obsolete, and that American forces should be withdrawn from Europe, but Brandt and his colleagues were able to hold their own without any real difficulty. The Congress, by voting in support of Germany's continued membership of the Western alliance, and also by re-electing Brandt as party chairman by a majority of over 400 to 20, gave a clear demonstration that the Social Democrats, like the rest of German opinion, were still basically pro-American.[10] The position of Brandt's government, and its capacity to conduct a clearly defined foreign policy, were shortly to be strengthened by the internal disputes of the Christian Democratic opposition, which led to Rainer Barzel's removal in July from their parliamentary leadership and his replacement by Karl Carstens.

There was a certain air of improvisation about the visit Chancellor Brandt paid to President Nixon at the beginning of May, two weeks after his triumph at the party conference. Government spokesmen in Bonn first denied that the Chancellor was planning to visit Washington, then suddenly announced a change of plan. An impression was given that Nixon himself had somewhat imperiously requested a visit from Brandt in order to estimate the likely strength of European support for American policies—including demands for increased offset-payments and the proposal for a 'new Atlantic Charter' which was about to be launched by Dr Kissinger—but it was also clear that Brandt himself welcomed an opportunity to allay Washington's apprehensions of a wave of anti-American sentiment in Germany.

Although the Nixon-Brandt talks of May 1–2 revealed certain differences of approach, particularly to the problems of American relations with the European Community, there was little doubt that the two governments, each confronted with considerable difficulties, actively wished to approach them in a co-operative and friendly spirit. Both Brandt and Nixon were due to meet the Soviet leader Leonid Brezhnev within the next few weeks; each of them faced the problem of inflation and the challenge of re-ordering the economic arrangements of the Western world; both wished to find an agreed solution to the important problem of paying for America's continued military presence in Europe; and each of them was assured of the support of considerable sections of his public opinion in trying to find mutually acceptable solutions to these problems.[11]

As far as German dispositions towards America were concerned, Brandt accurately summed up the situation in an interview which an American journal published shortly before his visit to Washington: 'What is called anti-Americanism has been produced by exaggeration on my side of the ocean, and that, in turn, has resulted in a reaction on your side.'[12]

On the American side, there were in fact more serious forces which threatened to disrupt good relations with Bonn. As we have seen, different sections of these forces were represented by Senators Mansfield and Jackson but the precise degree of their impact was still difficult to judge as the year 1973 approached its end.

Bilateral Relations: the Continued Problem of Offset Costs

One of the problems discussed by Brandt and Nixon in May and considered in more detail by their Defence Ministers Georg Leber and James Schlesinger in mid-July, was the perennial issue of troop-stationing costs. By the time the two-year agreement signed in 1971 expired at the end of June, the problem had been made more acute by the devaluation of the dollar in February, which meant that goods and services (for instance, housing) cost the American forces in Germany 25 per cent more in German currency than before the devaluation. The American response was to press the German government for increased contributions to offset the difference, but the Germans countered with the argument that the devaluation had already cost them dearly through cutting the value of their immense dollar deposits, and in the end the extra costs resulting from devaluation were met from the American side.[13]

More serious for the longer-term future of offset arrangements was the American demand that the new agreement for the two years to mid-1975 should cover the entire dollar costs of keeping American forces in Germany, instead of only 80 per cent of these costs as in the agreement for 1971–3. This would entail

Germany's paying 8,000 million Marks, an increase of 1,500 million on the previous figure.[14] The German government responded, predictably, by reviving a previous proposal that the cost of American troops in Germany should be paid not by Germany alone, but also by the United Kingdom and other European states whose security was enhanced by the American presence. Britain's reaction to such a ' multilateralization ' of offset costs was negative, on the grounds that Britain herself was already paying substantially towards the cost of her own forces in Germany.[15]

The issue of American troops in Europe was naturally one of concern to the whole alliance, particularly in view of the insistent congressional demands for their diminution and the prospect that the East-West talks on force reductions, due to open in Vienna late in October, would lead in the first instance to cuts in American and Soviet forces rather than in those of Western Europe. The question was clearly one which would preoccupy the alliance as a whole as the attempt to work out a ' new Atlantic Charter ' was painfully resumed after the Middle East crisis of October 1973, but in its essence the problem was still a bilateral one in German-American relations: the bulk of America's troops in Europe were still stationed in Germany, and although their presence there served the interests of both governments, it was understood that the burden to the American balance of payments should be largely offset by Germany. When the discussions for a new agreement began in October 1973 with talks in Bonn between Brandt and the American Secretary of the Treasury George P. Schultz, there were signs that the bargaining would be fairly hard: in response to the American demands for a total offset of balance of payments costs, the German government produced arguments already used in earlier years, that Germany's own budget was severely strained and that her need for American military ' hardware ' was limited, particularly as her own armaments industry was now better developed.[16] It appeared likely, however, that Germany's acute need of American protection, especially in the uncertain phase of ongoing détente, would induce her as usual to pay a very large share of the cost. The United States appeared all the more likely to press for the renewal of such an arrangement as the obvious direct measurement of the bilateral German-American relationship, the size of their trade with each other, showed a mounting surplus on the German side: $528 million in the first half of 1973, compared with $349 million in the corresponding period in 1972.[17]

Alliance Politics: the 'Year of Europe'

Dr Rolf Pauls, the Brandt administration's able Ambassador to Washington, observed quite accurately, in an article he wrote before leaving for a new post in Peking early in 1973: 'There would be less reason for concern about US-EEC relations if we could reach the same high level of consultation and cooperation between Europe and the US in economic matters that over the last four years has been achieved in co-ordinating German and American foreign policy'.[18] This was not merely a justified comment on a phase of bilateral diplomacy in which Pauls had played an important part: it also reflected the fact that German-American relations by 1973 were strongly influenced by Germany's membership of an enlarged European Community which had numerous points of friction with the United States.

The problem was not new in itself: its essence, which had been clear for several years, was that although Europe's integration was undoubtedly a political interest of the United States, as a stabilizing factor in the international system, some of its economic consequences were clearly detrimental to American interests. The enlargement of the Community in 1973—a further development which the United States had long desired for political reasons—meant that Americans faced the prospect of paying a higher economic price for political gains which were still uncertain, at the very moment when their own economy was running into increased difficulties. This background explains the vigour with which the United States tried, during 1973, to induce the European Community to adopt policies which would do the minimum damage to American commercial, industrial and agricultural interests, and the particular zeal of American officials in attempting to obtain the maximum support from their German allies for this objective.

On 8 March 1973 the American Ambassador to Bonn, Martin Hillenbrand, in a speech in Dusseldorf which began with an allusion to 'the special relationship which has existed between our two countries over the last 25 years', offered a tactful but firm exposition of American apprehensions about the European Community. Noting that the Community's summit conference of October 1972 had laid down objectives of improved commercial and monetary arrangements which President Nixon heartily endorsed, the Ambassador went on to outline some of the specific European-American differences which the forthcoming GATT and IMF talks would have to resolve.

There was first the problem of non-tariff barriers to international trade, which, as the Ambassador remarked, had in many cases become greater impediments to the free flow of goods and services than customs duties themselves: without going into details, Hillenbrand hinted that European governments, by their policies on standards and specifications, public procurement regulations, and quota arrangements, were creating difficulties for American exporters. In a second major area of disagreement, agricultural trade, he advanced the American argument that the Common Agricultural Policy of the European Community, by guaranteeing European farmers high prices for grain, as well as meat, was discriminating against American exports of grain in which the United States had a natural competitive advantage, and impeding an economically advantageous division of labour by which European farmers should concentrate on livestock production, leaving America to supply the necessary feedgrain. Turning finally to a third issue of concern to the United States, Hillenbrand argued that the European Community's preferential agreements with Mediterranean and EFTA countries also created discrimination against American exports, and that their effects should be reduced by all-round tariff cuts in the GATT negotiations.[19]

All these arguments were by now familiar components of the American attitude to the European Community—they had been eloquently voiced by Robert Schaetzel, America's Ambassador to the Community from 1966 to 1972 [20]—and the European answers to them were equally familiar. As it happened, they had been summarized by Ambassador Rolf Pauls in the article of January 1973 which has already been quoted. As Pauls reminded his American readers, their country's trade balance with the European Community showed a healthy surplus on the side of American exports, which suggested that European integration had so far helped rather than hindered American trade, and that America's trade deficit in 1971 was due to Japanese competition, not European. Even in the sensitive area of agriculture, the EEC, according to the figures quoted by Pauls, was the biggest foreign market for American products: American farm exports to the EEC had risen since 1964 almost twice as fast as to other markets, resulting in a record American surplus in agricultural trade with the EEC in 1971–2. Again, in those developing countries where Americans complained of discriminatory preferential agreements concluded by the EEC, American exports had grown faster than exports to other developing countries, so that Europe's economic support was producing beneficial results for the United States in those cases also.[21]

These conflicting assessments of European-American economic relations cannot be analysed in more detail here.[22] The contrast between the two versions, however, indicates the potentially acute nature of the problems imparted into Bonn's relations with Washington in a period when the Federal Republic was developing new links within the enlarged European Community and the United States was facing unprecedented economic and political difficulties.

The economic issues which troubled America's relations with the Community were intimately bound up with the strategic question of NATO's future role in an era of East-West détente. The links between the commercial, monetary, and strategic aspects of European-American relations, which had long been apparent, were spelled out with unusual directness by Dr Kissinger in a speech in April 1973, four months before he became Secretary of State in name as well as in substance. This speech, which marked the belated opening of America's 'Year of Europe'—originally promised for early 1973 but delayed by several factors, not least Europe's disapproval of America's bombing of North Vietnam in December 1972—called on the Europeans to co-operate in working out 'a new Atlantic Charter setting the goals for the future—a blueprint that . . . creates for the Atlantic nations a new relationship in whose progress Japan can share.'[23]

This ambitious programme (Kissinger called for the text of the new 'charter' to be completed by the time of President Nixon's visit to Europe which was then expected to take place in autumn 1973) placed the German government in a certain degree of difficulty. On the one hand, Brandt and his colleagues clearly wished to carry out their usual role as America's most faithful allies in Europe, and the Federal Republic had indeed been conspicuously active in approaching the linkage between economics and strategy in a constructive spirit; [24] but on the other hand Germany wished to remain closely aligned with her partners in the European Community. Although the British response to Kissinger's initiative was on the whole favourable, the French government saw in his linkage of economics and strategy an attempt to extort commercial and monetary concessions from the Europeans by threatening to reduce America's military support for them.[25]

Brandt's first response to Kissinger's speech, when he visited Washington ten days later, was thus a judicious compromise between welcome and reserve: he accepted the principle of redefining the aims of the Atlantic alliance, including the economic relations between America and the Community, but insisted that the European states must carefully work out their own position rather than uncritically accept the American view.[26]

During the ensuing months, the German government actively encouraged the governments of the European Community, as they prepared their response to Kissinger and their reception for Nixon, to try to reconcile American and European interests to the maximum. By mid-September, after a series of meetings of Community Foreign Ministers in Copenhagen (Denmark holding the chairmanship of the EEC Council of Ministers for the second half of 1973), agreement was reported to have been reached on a series of principles likely to commend themselves to Europe's American interlocutors.[27]

This promising situation—in which Washington and Bonn appeared to be working harmoniously together to resolve difficulties posed by their common membership of the Western economic and political system—was abruptly transformed by the Middle East crisis of October, whose repercussions profoundly affected the two governments' relations with each other as well as with the Soviet bloc.

Relations with the Adversary: Ostpolitik becomes Multilateral

In the speech of April 1973 in which he called for renewed efforts to make 1973 ' the Year of Europe ', Dr Kissinger made the challenging comparison that whereas 1972 had been the year in which ‘ the President transformed relations with our adversaries ’, 1973 must be the year in which the United States reinvigorated ‘ shared deals and common purposes with our friends ’.[28] The prescription for 1973 was to remain notably unfulfilled, but the judgement on 1972 was accurate enough. Relations with the Soviet bloc had indeed been transformed, at least outwardly, by the group of agreements concluded not only by the United States but by the West German government too, in the early summer of 1972. As we have seen, these included, essentially, the first SALT agreement between Washington and Moscow, the ratification of Bonn's treaties with Moscow and Warsaw, and the coming into force of the 1971 four-power agreement governing the future of Berlin.[29] June 1972 thus represented the successful conclusion of a phase of East-West relations in which the principal initiatives had of necessity been taken individually by the major Western states: only Washington could negotiate the SALT agreement, and only Bonn could bring about the treaties with Moscow and Warsaw by which the Federal Republic's relations with her major Eastern neighbours were regularized. At the same time there were parallel East-West negotiations on other issues affecting the Western allies as a whole, notably Berlin, and in any case the co-ordination of Western diplomatic efforts during the whole dramatic period from 1969 to 1972 remained, as we have seen, impressively effective. This, however, did not affect the central fact that the main activity in East-West diplomacy was of a bilateral kind.

During the next phase, from mid-1972 until late 1973, there were still some strands of bilateral diplomacy to be pursued—agreement on the Basic Treaty between the two German states, the beginnings of the second phase of SALT talks, and the joint economic enterprises which Brezhnev discussed on his visits to individual Western capitals—but the main focus of attention now became the large multilateral conferences in which East-West issues affecting considerable numbers of states were under discussion.

In terms of stress on the Western alliance, and specifically between Washington and Bonn, this phase of multilateral diplomacy, at least until the Middle East crisis of October 1973, raised remarkably few problems. The negotiations between the two German states, which led to the signing of the Basic Treaty in December 1972 and the entry of the two Germanies into the United Nations the following September, created no difficulties for the United States once the Berlin agreement had confirmed American rights and Soviet obligations in that city. The Basic Treaty itself, although it was not approved in West Germany without some controversy over its significance for the future of the German nation, in fact marked West Germany's acceptance of the division of the country into two states, a division which Americans had accepted in practice for years.[30] This tying-up of a loose end in Germany's Ostpolitik, coming in the form and context of 1972, caused no friction with the United States.

America's own bilateral Ostpolitik, in contrast, had some features which caused mild concern in the Federal Republic, though they aroused no serious alarm in the Brandt government. It was difficult for America's European allies to be sure that they were fully informed about the second phase of the SALT talks, which Washington and Moscow pursued in an exploratory way from the latter part of 1972 onwards. According to the reports available, the Soviet side heavily emphasized the need to negotiate on the reduction of 'forward based systems' (i.e. American missiles stationed in Western Europe), and this naturally caused some concern in European capitals including Bonn. By the end of 1973, however, it was clear that the Soviet-American talks were going forward very slowly, and that Europe need not fear dramatic surprises from this source.[31]

A further aspect of arms control, which made a new appearance at this stage, was the treaty on the non-proliferation of nuclear weapons negotiated in the mid-1960s. As we have seen, the Brandt government had signed the treaty at the end of 1969, but its ratification had been delayed until Bonn was satisfied that the respective control rights of Euratom and the International Atomic Energy Authority had been clarified.[32] Early in April 1973 agreement on the rights of these two bodies was reached,[33] and the process of ratification by the West German parliament was set in motion. The Christian Democratic opposition in Bonn showed signs of wishing to make a major political issue out of the treaty's alleged discrimination against Germany, but early in 1974 it was in fact ratified without great friction.[34] In any case, the successful conclusion of a treaty which had originally led to a considerable degree of conflict between Washington and Bonn was a further sign of how close the two governments now were as the ' Era of Negotiation ' proceeded.

The two broader and much more substantial series of negotiations of the Conference on Security and Co-operation in Europe and the talks on Mutual and Balanced Force Reductions, both of which formally opened in 1973, posed more delicate problems of alliance cohesion, and certain indications of German-American tension were clearly visible. Briefly summarized, these arose from the fact that Washington attached much greater importance to the MBFR negotiations, which held out a prospect of mutual force-cuts and thus gave the administration a valuable weapon against Senator Mansfield and other supporters of unilateral American cuts, whereas Bonn was more interested in the CSCE: like other West European governments, the Federal German government hoped to use the CSCE to press the Soviet bloc to make substantial improvements in the freer movement of people and ideas across European frontiers—a point which was naturally of particular importance to the divided German nation.

This difference between American and German priorities was exploited by the Soviet Union during the preliminary discussions of both the MBFR and the CSCE timetables in 1972–3. The Soviet government tried to use America's active interest in the MBFR talks to achieve a bargain by which the American government would get an early start to these negotiations only in exchange for the acceptance of Soviet demands concerning the CSCE: these were that the CSCE should be of short duration, should concentrate on general principles of coexistence rather than the embarrassing issues of liberalization, and should conclude with a session at the ' summit ' level at which a large congregation of heads of state and government would formally confirm the territorial and political status quo in Europe.[35]

When Nixon and Brezhnev met in Washington in June 1973 they reached agreement on the general timetable for the various East-West negotiations, and it was apparent that the United States had moved some distance towards the Soviet position. The passage of their communiqué dealing with CSCE, in which both governments pledged themselves to ' make efforts to bring the Conference to a successful conclusion at the earliest possible time ' and envisaged ' possibilities for completing it at the highest level', reflected partial American acceptance of the Soviet viewpoint. So also did the omission at Soviet insistence of the word 'balanced' from the plans agreed for the talks on Mutual and Balanced Force Reductions, which now became 'negotiations on the mutual reduction of forces and armaments and associated measures in Central Europe'.[36]

America's European allies, especially West Germany, made it clear that they were dissatisfied with the inadequate degree of consultation offered them by the American administration before the conclusion of this agreement, and of a separate Soviet-American agreement on the prevention of nuclear war, which somewhat affected the interests of the allies.[37]

The course of the actual negotiations in the second half of 1973—the CSCE in Helsinki and Geneva from July onwards, and the force reduction talks in Vienna from the end of October—showed evidence of close and effective consultations between the American, West German, and other allied governments, but the mild discord of the early summer had clearly shown how the process of détente could raise certain difficulties between Washington and Bonn.

If some features of Washington's super-power diplomacy caused disquiet in Bonn, there were still certain aspects of Bonn's Ostpolitik which aroused a degree of concern in America. In the spring of 1973 something of a sensation was caused by the publication, in an article in an American journal, of an off-the-record interview given by Egon Bahr in January 1969, to the author of the article Walter Hahn. In this, Brandt's adviser (at the time of the conversation, Head of the Planning Staff in the German Foreign Ministry) intimated that the ultimate goal of Ostpolitik was a pan-European collective security system in which the two German states would come closer together and NATO and the Warsaw Pact would be 'dissolved'.[38] The politicians and press of the German opposition, who had been given advance notice of the publication of the article, exploited to the maximum the argument that the Ostpolitik of the Brandt government now stood revealed as a dangerous enterprise directed towards neutralizing Germany and destroying the Western alliance.[39] There was some evidence that some Americans critically disposed towards the Brandt government, in Congress and elsewhere, were influenced by the 'revelations' about Bahr's ultimate intentions, but those responsible for American foreign policy knew better, and were immediately reassured by the German explanation that the remarks attributed to Bahr represented only the theoretical speculations of a foreign policy planner, and not the policy of the Bonn government. The incident thus did nothing to disrupt the close working partnership between Washington and Bonn on the question of Ostpolitik which had evolved during the whole period of Brandt's chancellorship.[40]

By the autumn of 1973 the German-American relationship appeared fundamentally in a very harmonious condition, despite all the potential sources of friction in America's domestic troubles, the worsening problem of troop offset-costs, the sad state of European-American relations, and the inevitable strains of détente diplomacy.

The mid-September meeting of EEC Foreign Ministers in Copenhagen marked a step in the direction of a European response to Dr Kissinger's proposal for a 'new Atlantic Charter', and it appeared that Nixon might after all come to Europe before the end of the year for a visit in which Brandt would clearly play a leading role.

This hopeful prospect was abruptly overshadowed by the Middle East crisis of October, which brought to the surface a remarkable degree of resentment between the United States and Europe, including West Germany. The American commitment to Israel, when the Arab-Israeli war started in October, was clearly very pronounced, whereas the West European countries, largely because of their heavier dependence on Middle East oil, took a much more pro-Arab position. The mounting crisis led to unprecedentedly outspoken recriminations between America and her European allies, with mutual accusations of egoism and lack of solidarity. The West German government was alarmed, as were other European governments, by America's unilateral decision to place all her nuclear forces on alert, and by the subsequent degree of bilateral American-Soviet diplomatic co-operation. The issue on which particularly acute tension arose between Washington and Bonn, however, was a more limited one. During the early days of the conflict, although the Federal Republic maintained a strictly neutral attitude between Israel and the Arabs, the German authorities turned a blind eye to the American use of bases in Germany for deliveries of war material to Israel to replace the weapons lost in the fighting. However, when these deliveries continued after the cease-fire agreement on October 22—Israeli cargo-boats were being loaded with howitzers, jeeps, and other equipment in the port of Bremerhaven—the German government became seriously concerned about its relations with the Arab states, and asked that the American deliveries of weapons cease. The American Ambassador in Bonn, Martin Hillenbrand, is reported to have stated in reply that the United States regarded West Germany's sovereignty as limited, and reserved the right to take any action which it regarded as right and necessary in the interests of international security. A similar view was reportedly expressed by Dr Kissinger to the German Ambassador in Washington, Bernd von Staden.[41]

Relations between Washington and Bonn had clearly reached a stage of fairly acute tension, but press comments to the effect that 'the relationship reached its lowest point in many years, some say since the Second World War'[42] were patently exaggerated. The degree of indignation with which Adenauer had learned of America's use of German bases for operations in the Lebanon in 1958 was greater than that expressed by Brandt and his colleagues (the two occasions were closely parallel in many ways),[43] and Germany's good relations with Washington, once the immediate anger of the episode was over, were seen to be fundamentally unimpaired.

Differences between Bonn and Washington clearly remained, but the most impressive feature of the situation at the end of 1973 was the capacity of both partners to deal constructively with the great variety of problems raised by their domestic political systems, by Germany's membership of the enlarged European Community, and by the on-going process of East-West détente in which they were both actively involved.

NOTES

1 The American debate on isolationism at this time is well reflected in two tracts with contradictory theses: Robert W. Tucker, *The New Isolationism: Threat or Promise?* (1972) and Walter Lacqueur, *Neo-Isolationism and the World of the Seventies* (1972).

2 *Daily Telegraph*, 16 Mar. 1973, *International Herald Tribune*, 31 Mar. 1973.

3 *International Herald Tribune*, 27 Sept. 1973.

[4] *The Guardian*, 29 Sept. 1973.
[5] *The Times*, 13 Oct. 1973.
[6] *The Guardian*, 8 and 9 Nov. 1973.
[7] *Daily Telegraph* and *Financial Times*, 9 Nov. 1973.
[8] Useful assessments of the situation are given by Theo Sommer in *Die Zeit*, 19 Jan. 1973 and John M. Goshko in the *Washington Post*, 24 Mar. 1973.
[9] Report of Strauss's speech in *Das Parlament*, 14 Apr. 1973, and of Rainer Barzel's use of the theme of governmental anti-Americanism in *FAZ*, 6 Apr. 1973. The article concerning Bahr in the review *Orbis* is referred to at n. 38 below.
[10] *The Times*, 10 Apr. 1973 and following days.
[11] Brandt's Washington visit is well assessed in *Suddeutsche Zeitung*, 5 May and *Der Spiegel*, 7 May 1973.
[12] 'What Europe wants from U.S.: Interview with West Germany's Chancellor Willy Brandt', *U.S. News and World Report*, 30 Apr. 1973.
[13] *NYT*, 10 May; *International Herald Tribune*, 28 July; *Christian Science Monitor* (London edn), 11 Oct. 1973.
[14] *Die Zeit*, 23 Mar.; *Financial Times*, 21 Sept. 1973.
[15] *The Guardian*, 3 Oct. 1973.
[16] *Christian Science Monitor* (London edn), 11 Oct. 1973.
[17] *The Guardian*, 16 Aug. 1973.
[18] Rolf Friedemann Pauls, 'On German-American Relations', *Aussenpolitik* (English-language edn), Jan. 1973, p. 11. Pauls' successor in Washington, Bernd von Staden, had served there in the 1960s before representing the Federal Republic in the 'Davignon Committee' of senior West European officials. He was thus admirably qualified to explain Germany's European policy in America.
[19] For Hillenbrand's speech, 'German-American Commercial and Economic Relations in the Atlantic Community', see *DOSB*, 67/1764 (1973), pp. 462–8.
[20] J. Robert Schaetzel, 'A Dialogue of the Deaf across the Atlantic', *Fortune*, Nov. 1972.
[21] Pauls, as n. 18 above.
[22] For detailed discussion, see Karl Kaiser, *Europe and the United States: the Future of the Relationship* (1972), pp. 10–57.
[23] Speech to Associated Press in New York, 23 April 1973; text in *NYT*, 24 Apr. 1974.
[24] See e.g. Brandt's article 'Germany's "Westpolitik"' in *For. Aff.*, Apr. 1972, which supports his often-repeated suggestion of a more institutionalized European-American dialogue.
[25] European reactions to Kissinger's speech are summarized by Ian Smart, 'The New Atlantic Charter', *The World Today*, June 1973, pp. 238–43.
[26] *Der Spiegel*, 7 May 1973.
[27] *Financial Times*, 11 and 12 Sept. 1973. See also Roger Morgan, 'Can Europe Have a Foreign Policy?', *The World Today*, Feb. 1974, pp. 43–50. For a strongly worded plea for the US to 'look to Bonn rather than to Brussels', in view of Germany's economic and political weight, see C. Fred Bergsten, 'Die amerikanische Europa-Politik angesichts der

Stagnation des Gemeinsamen Marktes. Ein Plädoyer für Konzentration auf die Bundesrepublik ', *Europa-Archiv*, 25 Feb. 1974, pp. 115–22.

28 *NYT*, 24 Apr. 1973.

29 See above, pp. 191–2.

30 For the text of the Basic Treaty, see *Survival*, 15/1 (1973), pp. 31–2. The situation of Berlin up to 1972 is admirably analysed by Dieter Mahncke, *Berlin im geteilten Deutschland* (1973).

31 See Ian Smart, ' Perspective from Europe ', in M. Willrich and J. B. Rhinelander, eds, *SALT: the Moscow Agreements and Beyond* (1974).

32 See above, pp. 183–4.

33 *FAZ* and *Die Zeit*, 6 Apr. 1973.

34 *FAZ* and *The Times*, 21 Feb. 1974. See also Kohler; and Uwe Nerlich's *Der NV-Vertrag in der Politik der BRD* (1973) and ' Vor der Bonner Entscheidung über den Nichtverbreitungsvertrag ', *Europa-Archiv*, 28/21 (1973), pp. 729–38.

35 Press reports, including *FAZ*, 7 Apr. 1973, and private information, Washington and Bonn.

36 *To Build Peace: a Summary of Agreements and Statements during the Visit to the United States of General Secretary Leonid Brezhnev of the Soviet Union, June 18–25, 1973* (US Information Service, n.d.), p. 33.

37 Ibid. pp. 22–3; private information on German reactions.

38 Hahn, ' West Germany's Ostpolitik: the Grand Design of Egon Bahr ', *Orbis*, 16/4 (1973), pp. 59–80.

39 See Strauss's speech in the Bundestag, *Das Parlament*, 14 Apr. 1973, and *Die Welt* for March and April 1973.

40 See above, pp. 208–18.

41 *Der Spiegel*, 29 Oct. and *Die Zeit*, 2 Nov. 1973; and private information, Bonn.

42 *The Times*, 31 Oct. 1973.

43 On the 1958 episode, see above, pp. 71–2.

Conclusion

THE most striking theme running through German-American relations in the period of more than a quarter of a century surveyed in this book is the high degree of harmony established between two nations which during the previous generation had twice been enemies in war. Despite the frequent incidents involving disagreement or friction which are recorded in these pages, the partnership as a whole showed a degree of mutual confidence rare in the history of relations between two major states, to the point where the American Ambassador, addressing a German audience in 1973, could refer without exaggeration to a ' special relationship ' uniting them for more than twenty years.

The underlying cause of this remarkable and lasting rapprochement between two ex-enemies was their common interest in withstanding the power of the Soviet Union—the source of pressure at the fourth of the levels of analysis in this study. Washington's perception of the nature and gravity of the Soviet threat throughout the period was, of course, different in many ways from that of Bonn: the super-power always had to take serious account of events throughout the world, from Korea to Cuba, while West German eyes were usually as firmly riveted on the barbed wire of the intra-German frontier as French eyes before 1914 had been on the blue line of the Vosges. Despite such natural differences in perspective between a super-power and its protégé, however, the governments of Washington and Bonn remained constantly aware of a profound and durable core of common interests in the life-and-death question of their relations with the East.

It follows from this that the moments of greatest tension between the two capitals were those when one or the other dealt or appeared to deal unilaterally with the adversary in a way which the partner saw as potentially damaging to its own interests. When Kennedy appeared to soften America's attitude on the question of access to Berlin, or on arms control, or on recognition of the German Democratic Republic Adenauer's reaction was one of alarm and obstructiveness. A decade later, when Brandt's Ostpolitik appeared to be going faster than Washington thought prudent, and with insufficient regard for America's global interests, the corresponding American reaction was one of irritation (much less acute than Adenauer's irritation with Kennedy, but still clearly perceptible). The comparison between Kennedy's policy and Brandt's, and the respective impact of the policies on the German-American relationship, in fact needs to be made with considerable care, since one of the most remarkable feaures of this relationship in the 1970s has been the high degree of understanding which the two governments have maintained amid all the complex pressures of the ' Era of Negotiation '. It is scarcely an exaggeration to say that whereas close harmony was maintained under Adenauer and Dulles by their firm rejection of any dealings with the Soviet Union, and was dramatically disturbed by Kennedy's unilateral deviation from this principle, the degree of mutual confidence prevailing in the 1950s has since been recovered and maintained by the acceptance that both Washington and Bonn have an active interest in détente with the East. The unity of the 1950s rested on a deep mutual attachment to immobilism; the discord of the early 1960s resulted from an asymmetrical progression towards a diplomacy of movement, Washington moving several years ahead of Bonn; and the renewed harmony of the 1970s has rested on joint acceptance of détente diplomacy, both Washington and Bonn dealing actively with the East and normally consulting each other closely and effectively.

What has just been said does not, of course, imply that the level of activity related to the Soviet bloc—the fourth level of our analysis—has been the only one to produce powerful sources of change in the relationship. At the first level, the marked rapprochement of the two ex-enemies was due to profound forces at work within the two societies—the affinity for Germany felt by many Americans, and the widespread impulse of Germans after the war to model their new society on America—as well as to similarities in their approach to economic policy. It has also been a fact that the two governments have normally succeeded very effectively in overcoming differences both in their bilateral relations and in the range of strategic and economic issues confronting them as members of the West European/Atlantic system (the second and third levels of our analysis): their notable success at these levels has been due not only to the absence of any differences of intrinsically overwhelming proportions, but also to the way in which the two governments were powerfully impelled in the direction of compromise at these levels by their compatibility at the 'domestic' level and by their overriding common interest at the East-West level.

Again, it should not be assumed that the harmony of interests, which is a constant theme of these pages, developed entirely automatically. As with agreement between two entities in any social system (whether states, social groups, or individuals), harmony resulted in part from one partner's acceptance of the point of view of the other. In the case of the harmony between Washington and Bonn, it can be said that on the critical question of the future of Germany (the prospect or non-prospect of reunification, as it changed over time, being the central issue in East-West relations in Europe) the situation was that Washington outwardly accepted Bonn's point of view for many years, during which Bonn gradually came round to that of Washington. West Germany began by firmly refusing to recognize either the division of the country or the legitimacy of the East German state; and the United States, though naturally not fully sharing West German concern on these points, appreciated the need not to dissent from it in public. It was only two decades or so after the founding of the Federal Republic that West German opinion evolved sufficiently to allow the formal recognition of the division of Germany into two states, which American official opinion had accepted—tacitly, of course—since the beginning. Only when West Germany had established formal relations with the GDR did the United States move towards doing so.

At another critical level of the American-German relationship, that of their dealings within the framework of the Western economic system, harmony was again brought about largely by German concessions to the American viewpoint. These concessions included German readiness to settle for relatively disadvantageous bargains on the offsetting of troop-costs, to tolerate a certain degree of inflation caused by the influx of dollars through the American forces, and on more than one occasion to devalue the German currency in order to help the American balance of payments. These conciliatory gestures were of course motivated in part by self-interest, and they were accompanied by many instances, discussed in these pages, of a stout defence of German positions against pressure from Washington. The prevailing pattern, however, has more often been one of German compliance with American demands than of American concessions to Germany.

The evidence of the 1970s so far is that it is possible for Washington and Bonn to maintain an impressive degree of unity in a phase of potentially divisive pressures resulting from rapid changes in international relationships both at the East-West and at the 'West-West' levels. There has been nothing comparable, in recent years, to the tension of the Kennedy-Adenauer period, when Adenauer was confronted with America's determination both to deal actively about international security questions with the Russians (when Adenauer still regarded them as mortal enemies), and also to take steps to remedy a balance of payments deficit (which meant imposing demands on a Germany whose economic strength was still only partially recovered). There is thus a reasonable chance that the harmony of the Nixon-Brandt phase can be maintained into the mid-1970s and later, though our analysis of the post-war period as a whole suggests two main potential sources of conflict. These do *not* include violent changes of direction in the internal political life of either partner: not only are extreme changes unlikely, but the evidence of twenty years suggests that the kind of changes which *do* occur—even when the leftward transition from Kiesinger to Brandt coincided in time with the rightward shift from Johnson to Nixon—can be readily absorbed into the existing pattern of co-operation. What is more likely is some disruption from one or both of two other sources: firstly, a divergence in American and German views on the future of their relations with the Soviet bloc; secondly, growing friction on economic issues, including competition for scarce energy resources, between the United States and the enlarged EEC of which Germany is the most important member.

On the question of the West's Ostpolitik, a great deal depends on whether Washington and Bonn continue to interpret Bonn's Eastern treaties, particularly the relationship with the other German state, in the same way. By establishing relations with the GDR, West Germany has in fact accepted the division of the country into two states for an indefinite period, though Chancellor Brandt and his colleagues constantly reaffirm that they see the acceptance of two German states as a means of 'preserving the substance of the German nation' by facilitating freer contact between them. The territorial status quo is accepted as a means of changing the human status quo. If the West Germans continue to base their policy on this principle they will remain in close agreement with the American and other Western governments, who see nothing wrong with freer connections between the two Germanies but would be most unwilling to see the vast resources of the two German states—the second largest economic power in the Western world, and the second largest in the Eastern—united under a single political authority, geographically a resurrected German *Reich*. On the other hand, any future German government which attempted to move from reunifying the nation to reunifying the state—unless the whole system of East-West European relations were improved beyond recognition—would provoke the kind of reaction induced by Brandt's accelerated Ostpolitik of 1970, although this time on a dangerously heightened scale. Another way in which German-American harmony might be disrupted by East-West relations would be if the United States government were to press ahead with American-Soviet agreements on arms control or other matters in ways which appeared to infringe West Germany's interests or threaten her security: there have been some indications of the dangers of such bilateral dealings in SALT II and also in the whole American approach to the CSCE and MBFR negotiations of 1973.

The situation by the mid-1970s, however, will clearly be one in which excessive American-Soviet bilateralism will be regarded as a potential threat not only in Germany but throughout Western Europe, and the problem is thus linked to the second main source of possible tension between Bonn and Washington, the evolution of economic relations between the

United States and the European Community. As the Western world advances through the 1970s, with mounting difficulties caused by rising prices, the problems of reaching agreement on trade and monetary matters (including the increasingly intractible issue of non-tariff barriers), and probably direct competition for scarce energy resources, it is hard to escape the conclusion that European-American relations will undergo very considerable stress. In future, moreover, it will not always be so easy as in the past for West Germany to play the role of mediator —in some degree America's 'Trojan horse' inside the Community—nor will she necessarily wish to do so. There have already been several issues on which Germany has consulted her own or Europe's interests rather than America's: to take only one instance, German insistence on a high EEC price for cereals. An inclination to pursue such lines more strongly in future can be detected in one aspect of Germany's reactions to the Middle East oil crisis of 1973: in addition to repairing the damaged links with Washington, Bonn has moved to strengthen Europe's cohesion in the face of a clear divergence between European and American interests.

The future of German-American relations will thus be marked by considerable uncertainties arising at two of the four levels we have identified for analysis: first at the all-important level of relations with the Soviet bloc, and secondly at the level of relations within the Western grouping in the larger sense. Much will depend on the performance of the two nations at the remaining two levels of activity: on their capacity to produce and sustain governments responsive to each other's interests and to resolve their more strictly bilateral problems. The success of their efforts will not only be vital for the future of American-German relations; it will also illuminate the prospects for harmony in other bilateral relationships in the increasingly interdependent world system of the 1970s.

Postscript July 1974

By the time Chancellor Helmut Schmidt and Henry Kissinger watched the final of the world football championship together in Munich on 7 July 1974 (West Germany beat the Netherlands 2–1), the political configuration of the world was different in many ways from what it had been at the start of the year. The most important new development, as far as the West German and American governments were concerned, was certainly the dramatic change in the leadership of the Federal Republic. Whereas it had appeared increasingly likely during the winter of 1973–4 that President Nixon would succumb to the consequences of Watergate, leaving Chancellor Brandt to survive his minor 'local difficulties' in Bonn with ease, July 1974 saw Nixon still holding on to power (although he was to lose it in August), while Brandt, amid general astonishment, had fallen from office. The actual occasion of Brandt's resignation in May—the discovery that an East German spy had been operating in the office of the Chancellor who was devoted to reconciliation with the East—was in its way as ironical as the downfall of the architect of the 'economic miracle' as a result of the recession of 1966. It was clear, however, that the deeper reasons why Brandt chose to take full responsibility for this episode, and to resign, included his weariness with the strains of coalition politics in Bonn, his distress at the threatened disintegration of the European Community, and his disillusionment at the failure of East-West détente to progress as he had hoped. In Brandt's successor, Helmut Schmidt, the United States was dealing with a man whose keen appreciation of the need for the closest possible relations with Washington would ensure that these would be untrammelled by either the preoccupation with the European Community or the concern with Ostpolitik which had created passing difficulties in the time of Brandt.

Chancellor Schmidt had already, while still Finance Minister, used the opportunity of the Washington energy conference in February to discuss the perennial question of offset costs with his American counterpart George P. Schultz. The new agreement on this issue, finally signed on 25 April 1974, provided for German payments of $2.24 million during the two years from mid-1973 to mid-1975. Even though the devaluation of the dollar since 1971 meant that this payment actually represented a smaller sum in German currency than under the 1971–3 agreement, the American administration expressed itself satisfied with a contribution to the burdens of the alliance which helped to appease congressional critics of America's military presence in Europe.

In the framework of the Western alliance more generally, relations between Washington and Bonn recovered during the first half of 1974 from the blow they had suffered during the Middle East war of the previous October. The labyrinthine negotiations for an 'Atlantic Declaration' bore fruit of a kind at the end of June—fourteen months after Kissinger's original appeal—in a ceremony in Brussels at which Nixon, Schmidt, and other Western heads of government signed a document pledging the alliance to more effective consultation in future. Agreement on this text had been facilitated by a change of government in France, where the new administration of President Giscard d'Estaing was distinctly less anti-American than its predecessor. A new element of uncertainty had also developed through the unexpected change in London, where the scepticism of the new Wilson government towards the European Community's economic and political aspirations contrasted unhappily with the objectives frequently proclaimed by Germans. The new West German government used its influence in this delicate situation to guide its European Community partners towards better relations with the United States, an attitude which also found expression in the Community's successful negotiation in late May of an agreement to compensate the United States, under Article 24/6 of the General Agreement on Tariffs and Trade, for the effects of the

Community's enlargement. German influence was again visible in the agreement reached in Luxemburg on 10 June that member-governments of the Nine, collectively or severally, should take pains to consult the United States on matters of mutual concern.

An important dimension of these common concerns continued to be the West's dealings with the East, in the various conferences and other dialogues which had already been under way at the end of 1973. The continued unity of the West, despite the intensification of these East-West negotiations, was facilitated by almost complete lack of progress in the latter. By July 1974, when Nixon and Brezhnev came together in Moscow for their third summit meeting, the situation was characterized not only by a marked failure to reach any substantial agreement in the Strategic Arms Limitation Talks, but also by a state of deadlock in relations between Bonn and East Berlin, to which the unmasking of an East German spy in Brandt's entourage had contributed only the final detail. Neither Washington nor Bonn thus appeared likely to be tempted easily into any Eastern relationships which might cast a shadow over their alliance: even the fear that Nixon might accept the Soviet demand for an early and high-level conclusion of the Conference on Security and Co-operation in Europe, which had concerned Germans and other Europeans in the spring, proved groundless.

The East-West dimension of international affairs thus imposed few strains on the German-American relationship. It remained to be seen how well this relationship would stand up to the economic pressures which increasingly assailed the Western world as the year 1974 advanced. There was great significance in the warning given by Schmidt at the signing of the 'Atlantic Declaration' at the NATO meeting in June, that 'it is not possible to settle the political problems without stabilizing the economies.' This reminder of the inescapable interconnections between economics, politics, and defence indicated the type of problem most likely to determine the course of German-American relations in the later 1970s.

Bibliography

1. Unpublished Sources

Dulles Oral History Project, Princeton University Library.
A collection of transcripts of interviews, by Professor Gordon A. Craig and others, with individuals who knew John Foster Dulles. Many of the interviews are quite short: page references are given only when quotations are made from the longer ones.

John Foster Dulles Papers, Princeton University Library.
These documents, the private papers of Mr Dulles, are classified in several categories—e.g. 'Correspondence,' 'Additional Papers,' 'Conference Dossiers and Files on Special Subjects'—to which reference is made when a document is quoted.

2. Official Publications

France

Gaulle, Charles de. *Major addresses, statements and press conferences of General Charles de Gaulle, May 19, 1958—January 31, 1964.* New York, French Embassy, Press and Information Division [1964].

German Federal Republic

Auswärtiges Amt. *Die auswärtige Politik der Bundesrepublik Deutschland.* Cologne, Verlag Wissenschaft und Politik, 1972.

—— *Die Bemühungen der deutschen Regierung und ihrer Verbündeten um die Einheit Deutschlands 1955–1966.* Bonn, 1966.

Presse- und Informationsamt, ed. *Bulletin.* Bonn.

United Nations

Yearbook of international trade statistics. New York.

United States of America

Dept of Commerce. *Survey of current business.* Washington, DC.

Dept of State. *The Department of State Bulletin.* Washington, DC.

President. *Public papers of the presidents of the United States: John F. Kennedy, containing the public messages, speeches, and statements of the President, January 20 to December 31, 1961.* Washington, DC, 1962.

—— *Public papers of the presidents . . . John F. Kennedy . . . January 1 to November 22, 1963.* Washington, DC, 1964.

—— *U.S. foreign policy for the 1970s: a new strategy for peace. A report to the Congress by Richard Nixon, President of the United States, February 18, 1970.* Washington, DC, 1970.

—— *U.S. foreign policy for the 1970s: building for peace. A report to the Congress by Richard Nixon, President of the United States, February 25, 1971.* Washington, DC, 1971.

—— *U.S. foreign policy for the 1970s: the emerging structure of peace. A report to the Congress by Richard Nixon, President of the United States, February 9, 1972.* Washington, DC, 1972.

—— *U.S. foreign policy for the 1970s: shaping a durable peace. A report to the Congress by Richard Nixon, President of the United States, May 3, 1973.* Washington, DC, 1973.

Senate. Cttee on Foreign Relations, Subcttee on US Security Agreements and Commitments Abroad. *United States security agreements and commitments abroad*, Hearings, 91st Congress, 2nd sess., vol. 2, pts 5–11. Washington, DC, 1971.

US Information Service. *To build peace: a summary of agreements and statements during the visit to the United States of General Secretary Leonid Brezhnev of the Soviet Union, June 18–25, 1973.* Washington, DC, 1973.

3. Periodicals and Newspapers

L'Année Politique, Economique, Sociale et Diplomatique en France; Aussenpolitik; The Christian Science Monitor; The Daily Telegraph; Deutschland-Archiv; The Economist; Europa-Archiv; Foreign Affairs; Frankfurter Allgemeine Zeitung; The Financial Times; Foreign Policy; The Guardian; International Affairs; International Herald Tribune; International Organization; Journal of International Affairs; Le Monde; Neue Zürcher Zeitung; New Left Review; New York Times; Orbis; Das Parlament; Der Spiegel; Süddeutsche Zeitung; Survival; The Times; U.S. News and World Report; The Washington Post; Die Welt; World Politics; The World Today; Die Zeit.

4. Books and Articles

Acheson, Dean. *Present at the creation: my years in the State department.* Paperback edn. New York, New American Library, 1970.

—— 'The illusion of disengagement'. *Foreign Affairs*, 36/3 (1958).

Adenauer, Konrad. *Erinnerungen*, i: *1945–1953*; ii: *1953–1955*; iii: *1955–1959* (these three volumes in paperback edn, Frankfurt am Main, Fischer, 1967–9); iv: *1959–1963* (hard-cover edn, Stuttgart, Deutsche Verlags-Anstalt, 1968).

Aron, Raymond and D. Lerner, eds. *La querelle de la CED.* Paris, A. Colin, 1956.

Ashkenazi, A. *Reformpartei und Aussenpolitik.* Cologne, Westdeutscher Verlag, 1968.

Ausland, John C. 'Crisis management: Berlin, Cyprus, Laos'. *Foreign Affairs*, Jan. 1966.

Backer, John H. *Priming the German economy, American occupational policies 1945–1948.* Durham, NC, Duke UP, 1971.

Bader, William B. *The United States and the spread of nuclear weapons.* New York, Pegasus, 1968.

Balabkins, N. *Germany under direct control.* New Brunswick, NJ, Rutgers UP, 1964.

Bandulet, Bruno. *Adenauer zwischen West und Ost: Alternativen der deutschen Aussenpolitik.* Munich, Weltforum, 1970.

Baring, Arnulf. *Aussenpolitik in Adenauers Kanzlerdemokratie.* Munich, R. Oldenbourg Verlag, 1969.

Barraclough, G. and R. F. Wall. *Survey of international affairs 1955–1956.* London, OUP for RIIA, 1960.

Barraclough, G. *Survey of international affairs 1959–1960.* London, OUP for RIIA, 1964.

Bechtoldt, H. 'Deutschland und das Moskauer Abkommen'. *Aussenpolitik*, 14/19 (1963).

Bell, Coral. *Negotiation from strength: a study in the politics of power.* London, Chatto & Windus, 1962.

—— *The debatable alliance: an essay in Anglo-American relations.* London, OUP for RIIA, 1964.

—— *Survey of international affairs 1954.* London, OUP for RIIA, 1957.

Beloff, Max. *The United States and the unity of Europe.* Washington, DC, Brookings Institution, 1963.

Bergsten, C. Fred. 'Die amerikanische Europa-Politik angesichts der Stagnation des Gemeinsamen Marktes. Ein Plädoyer für Konzentration auf die Bundesrepublik', *Europa-Archiv*, 29/4 (1974).

Besson, Waldemar. *Die Aussenpolitik der Bundesrepublik.* Munich, Piper, 1972.

Besson, Waldemar. 'The conflict of traditions', in K. Kaiser and R. Morgan, eds, *Britain and West Germany: changing societies and the future of foreign policy*. London, OUP for RIIA, 1971.

Beugel, E. van der. *From Marshall aid to Atlantic partnership*. Amsterdam, Elsevier, 1971.

Blauhorn, Kurt. *Ausverkauf in Germany?* 3rd edn. Munich, Moderne Verlags, 1967.

Borch, Herbert von. ' Für die Amerikaner '. *Der Monat*, May 1965.

—— ' Anatomie einer Entzweiung '. *Aussenpolitik*, 13/6 (1962).

—— ' Amerika und der europäische Status Quo '. *Aussenpolitik*, 15/2 (1964).

—— *Friede trotz Krieg: Spannungsfelder der Weltpolitik seit 1950*. Munich, Piper, 1966.

Brandt, Willy. 'Germany's Westpolitik'. *Foreign Affairs*, 50/4 (1972).

Buchan, Alastair. *The multilateral force: an historical perspective*. London, ISS, 1964. (Adelphi Paper no. 13.)

—— ' A world restored? '. *Foreign Affairs*, 50/4 (1972).

—— ed. *A world of nuclear powers?* Englewood Cliffs, NJ, Prentice-Hall, 1966.

Bunn, Ronald F. *German politics and the Spiegel affair*. Bâton Rouge, Louisiana State UP, 1968.

Calleo, David. *The Atlantic fantasy: the US, NATO and Europe*. Baltimore, Md, Johns Hopkins UP, 1970.

Camps, Miriam. *Britain and the European Community, 1955–1963*. Princeton, NJ, Princeton UP, 1964.

Carr, E. H. *What is history?* London, Macmillan, 1961.

Cleveland, Harlan. *NATO: the transatlantic bargain*. New York, Harper & Row, 1970.

Conze, W. *Jakob Kaiser, Politiker zwischen Ost und West. 1945–1949*. Stuttgart, Kohlhammer, 1967.

Cromwell, W. C., ed. *Political problems of alliance partnership*. Bruges, College of Europe, 1969.

Czempiel, E.-O. *Das amerikanische Sicherheitssystem, 1945–1949*. Berlin, De Gruyter, 1966.

Davidson, Ian and Gordon L. Weill. *The cold war*. London, Secker & Warburg, 1970.

Deutsch, Karl W. and Lewis J. Edinger. *Germany rejoins the powers: mass opinions, interest groups, and elites in contemporary German foreign policy*. Stanford, Calif., Stanford UP, 1959. (This work contains a chronology up to May 1959.)

Dulles, Eleanor Lansing. *John Foster Dulles, the last year*. New York, Harcourt, Brace & World, 1963.

—— *One Germany or two: the struggle at the heart of Europe*. Stanford, Calif., Hoover Institution Press, 1970.

Eckhardt, Felix von. *Ein unordentliches Leben.* Dusseldorf, Econ-Verlag, 1967.

Edinger, Lewis J. *Kurt Schumacher: a study in personality and political behaviour.* Stanford, Calif., Stanford UP, 1965.

Eisenhower, Dwight D. *The White House years,* ii: *Waging peace 1956–1961.* London, Heinemann, 1963.

Epstein, Leon D. *Britain—uneasy ally.* Chicago, University of Chicago Press, 1954.

Foster, William C. 'New directions in arms control and disarmament', *Foreign Affairs,* 43/4 (1965).

Freund, G. *Germany between two worlds.* New York, Harcourt Brace, 1961.

—— *Unholy alliance: Russian-German relations from the treaty of Brest-Litovsk to the treaty of Berlin.* London, Chatto & Windus, 1957.

Friedman, Julian R., Christopher Bladen, and Steven Rosen, eds. *Alliance in international politics.* Boston, Allyn & Bacon, 1970.

Furniss, Edgar. *France, troubled ally.* New York, Harper, 1960.

Gaitskell, Hugh. *The challenge of co-existence.* (Godkin Lectures, Harvard University.) London, Methuen, 1957.

Galbraith, J. Kenneth. *Ambassador's journal.* London, Hamish Hamilton, 1969.

Gasteyger, Curt. *The American dilemma: bipolarity or Atlantic cohesion?* London, ISS, 1966. (Adelphi Paper no. 24.)

Gaulle, Charles de. *Mémoires d'espoir,* i: *Le renouveau 1958–1962.* Paris, Plon, 1970.

Gimbel, E. J. *The American occupation of Germany: politics and the military, 1945–1949.* Stanford, Calif., Stanford UP, 1968.

Golay, F. *The founding of the Federal Republic of Germany.* Chicago, Univ. of Chicago Press, 1958.

Goold-Adams, Richard. *The time of power.* London, Weidenfeld & Nicolson, 1962.

Gordon, Kermit, ed. *Agenda for the nation.* Washington, DC, Brookings Instn, 1968.

Griffith, William E. 'Die Bundesrepublik in Amerikanischer Sicht'. *Aussenpolitik,* 13/3 (1962).

—— 'The German problem and American policy'. *Survey,* no. 61, Oct. 1966.

Grosser, Alfred. *Germany in our time.* New York, Praeger, 1971.

—— 'France and Germany: less divergent outlooks'. *Foreign Affairs,* 48/2 (1970).

Guttenberg, Baron K. T. von und zu. *Wenn der Westen Will: Plädoyer für eine mutige Politik.* 2nd edn. Stuttgart, Seewald, 1965.

Hahn, Walter F. 'West Germany's Ostpolitik: the grand design of Egon Bahr'. *Orbis,* 16/4 (1973).

Hammond, Paul Y. 'Directives for the occupation of Germany: the Washington controversy', in Harold Stein, ed., *American civil-military decisions: a book of case studies*. Birmingham, Ala., Univ. of Alabama Press for Twentieth Century Fund, 1963.

Hanrieder, Wolfram F. *West German foreign policy 1949–1963*. Stanford, Calif., Stanford UP, 1967.

—— *The stable crisis: two decades of German foreign policy*. New York, Harper & Row, 1970.

Hassner, Pierre. 'German and European reunification'. *Survey*, no. 61, Oct. 1966.

Heath, Edward. *Old world, new horizons*. Cambridge, Mass., Harvard UP, 1970.

Hilger, Gustav and A. G. Meyer. *The incompatible allies: a memoir-history of German-Soviet relations 1918–1941*. New York, Macmillan, 1953.

Hillenbrand, Martin J. 'German-American commercial and economic relations in the Atlantic community'. *DOSB*, 67/1764 (1973).

Hoffmann, S. 'Weighing the balance of power'. *Foreign Affairs*, 50/4 (1972).

Jackson, Henry M., ed. *The Atlantic alliance: Jackson subcommittee hearings and findings*. New York, Praeger, 1967.

Joffe, J. 'Germany and the Atlantic alliance: the politics of dependence 1961–68', in W. C. Cromwell, ed., *Political problems of alliance partnership*. Bruges, College of Europe, 1969.

Johnson, Lyndon B. *The vantage point*. New York, Holt, Rinehart & Winston, 1971.

Kahin, George McTurnan and J. Wilson Lewis. *The United States in Vietnam*. Rev. edn. New York, Dial Press, 1969.

Kaiser, Karl. *German foreign policy in transition: Bonn between East and West*. London, OUP for RIIA, 1968.

—— *Europe and the United States: the future of the relationship*. Washington, DC, Columbia Books, 1973.

—— and R. Morgan, eds. *Britain and West Germany: changing societies and the future of foreign policy*. London, OUP for RIIA, 1971.

Kennan, George. *Memoirs: 1925–1950*. London, Hutchinson, 1968.

—— *Memoirs: 1950–1963*, Boston, Mass., Atlantic-Little Brown, 1972.

— *Russia, the atom and the West*. (Reith Lectures, BBC, 1957.) London, OUP, 1958.

Kennedy, J. F. 'A Democrat looks at foreign policy'. *Foreign Affairs*, 36/1 (1959).

Kiep, Walther Leisler. *Goodbye Amerika: Was dann?* Stuttgart, Seewald, 1972.

King, Gillian, ed. *Documents on international affairs 1958*. London, OUP for RIIA, 1962.

Kissinger, Henry A. *The troubled partnership*. New York, McGraw-Hill, 1965.

—— ' Central issues of American foreign policy ', in K. Gordon, ed., *Agenda for the nation*. Washington, DC, Brookings Instn, 1968.

Kleiman, Robert. *Atlantic crisis*. London, Sidgwick & Jackson, 1965.

Knapp, Manfred. ' Amerikanische Besatzungspolitik in Deutschland '. *Politische Vierteljahresschrift*, 13/4 (1972).

—— ' Zusammenhänge zwischen der Ostpolitik der BRD und den deutsch-amerikanischen Beziehungen '. Unpublished paper presented to the conference of the Deutsche Vereinigung für politische Wissenschaft, Hamburg, Oct. 1973 (duplicated, 34 pp.).

Kohler, Beate. *Der Vertrag über die Nichtverbreitung von Kernwaffen und das Problem der Sicherheitsgarantien*. Frankfurt, Alfred Metzner Verlag, 1972.

Kramish, Arnold. *The watched and the unwatched*. London, ISS, 196. (Adelphi Paper no. 36.)

—— *Die Zukunft der Nichtatomaren*. Opladen, Leske Verlag, 1970.

Krause, Lawrence. ' Private international finance ', in R. O. Keohane and J. S. Nye, Jr, eds, *Transnational relations and world politics*. Cambridge, Mass., Harvard UP, 1972.

Kuklick, Bruce. *American policy and the division of Germany: the clash with Russia over reparations*. London, Cornell UP, 1972.

Lacquer, Walter. *Neo-isolationism and the world of the seventies*. New York, Library Press, 1972.

Latour, Conrad F. and Thilo Vogelsang. *Okkupation und Wiederaufbau. Die Tätigkeit der Militärregierung in der amerikanischen Besatzungszone Deutschlands, 1944–1947*. Stuttgart, Deutsche Verlags-Anstalt, 1973.

Ludz, Peter Christian. ' Amerikanische Haltungen zur deutschen Frage ', *Deutschland Archiv*, 5/6 (1972).

McGeehan, Robert. *The German rearmament question*. Urbana, Univ. of Illinois Press, 1971.

Macmillan, Harold. *Memoirs*, iv: *Riding the storm 1956–1959*. London, Macmillan, 1971.

Macridis, Roy C. *De Gaulle—implacable ally*. New York, Harper & Row, 1966.

Mahncke, Dieter. *Berlin im geteilten Deutschland*. Munich, Oldenbourg Verlag, 1973.

—— *Nukleare Mitwirkung*. New York, de Gruyter, 1972.

Marshall, Charles Burton. *The exercise of sovereignty*. Baltimore, Md, Johns Hopkins Press, 1965.

Martin, L. W. 'The American decision to rearm Germany', in Harold Stein, ed., *American civil-military decisions: a book of case studies*. Birmingham, Ala., Univ. of Alabama Press for Twentieth Century Fund, 1963.

Mendershausen, Horst. *Troop stationing in Germany: value and cost*. Santa Monica, Calif., Rand Corpn for US Air Force, Dec. 1968. (Memorandum RM-5881-PR.)

Merkl, Peter H. *The origin of the West German republic*. New York, OUP, 1963.

—— *Germany: yesterday and tomorrow*. New York, OUP, 1965.

Morgan, Roger. *West European politics since 1945*. London, Batsford, 1972.

—— 'The writing and teaching of contemporary history', in J. L. Henderson, ed., *Since 1945: aspects of contemporary world history*. 2nd edn. London, Methuen, 1971.

—— 'Washington and Bonn: a case study in alliance politics', *International Affairs*, 47/3 (1971).

—— 'The Federal Republic of Germany', in S. Henig and J. Pinder, eds, *European political parties*. London, Allen & Unwin for PEP, 1969.

—— 'The scope of German foreign policy'. *Yearbook of World Affairs 1966*. London, Stevens, 1966.

—— 'The 1969 election in West Germany'. *The World Today*, Nov. 1969.

—— 'Political prospects in Bonn'. *The World Today*, Aug. 1972.

—— 'Anglo-French relations today'. *The World Today*, July 1971.

—— 'Can Europe have a foreign policy?', *The World Today*, Feb. 1974.

Morgenthau, Henry, Jr. *Germany is our problem*. London, Harper & Brothers, 1945.

Morse, Edward L. 'Crisis diplomacy, interdependence, and the politics of international economic relations', in R. Tanter and R. Ullman, eds, *Theory and policy in international relations*. Princeton, NJ, Princeton UP, 1972.

Murphy, Robert. *Diplomat among warriors*. Paperback edn. New York, Pyramid Books, 1965.

Myers, Kenneth A. *Ostpolitik and American security interests in Europe*. Washington, DC, Center for Strategic and International Studies, Georgetown University, 1972.

Nerlich, U. 'Die nuklearen Dilemmas der Bundesrepublik'. *Europa-Archiv*, 20/17 (1965).

—— *Der NV-Vertrag in der Politik der BRD: zur Struktur eines aussenpolitischen Prioritätskonflikts*. Eggenberg, Stiftung Wissenschaft und Politik, 1973.

Nerlich, U, 'Vor der Bonner Entscheidung über den Nichtverbreitungsvertrag'. *Europa-Archiv*, 28/21 (1973).

Neustadt, Richard E. *Presidential power: the politics of leadership*. New York, John Wiley, 1968.

—— *Alliance politics*. New York, Columbia UP, 1970.

—— 'Memorandum on the British Labour party and the MLF'. *New Left Review*, Sept.–Oct. 1968.

Newhouse, John. *De Gaulle and the Anglo-Saxons*. London, Andre Deutsch, 1970.

—— and others. *U.S. troops in Europe: issues, costs, and choices*. Washington, DC, Brookings Instn, 1971.

Osgood, Robert E. *Alliances and American foreign policy*. Baltimore, Md, Johns Hopkins Press, 1968.

—— *NATO, the entangling alliance*. Chicago, Univ. of Chicago Press, 1962.

Pauls, Rolf Friedemann, 'On German-American relations'. *Aussenpolitik* (English-language edn), Jan. 1973.

Pierre, Andrew J. 'The SALT agreement and Europe'. *The World Today*, July 1972.

Pirker, Theo. *Die SPD nach Hitler*. Munich, Rütten & Loening, 1965.

Planck, Charles R. *The changing status of German reunification in Western diplomacy 1955–1966*. Baltimore, Md, Johns Hopkins Press, 1967.

Prittie, Terence. *Adenauer: a study in fortitude*. London, Tom Stacey, 1972.

Quester, George. *The politics of nuclear proliferation*. Baltimore, Md, Johns Hopkins UP, 1973.

—— 'The nonproliferation treaty and the International Atomic Energy Agency'. *International Organization*, 24/2 (1970).

Richardson, Elliott. Address 'Western Europe and NATO'. *Wireless bulletin from Washington*, 21 Jan. 1970. Bonn, US Embassy.

Richardson, J. L. *Germany and the Atlantic alliance*. Cambridge, Mass., Harvard UP, 1966.

Rostow, Walter W. *View from the seventh floor*. New York, Harper & Row, 1964.

Rourke, Francis E. *Bureaucracy and foreign policy*. Baltimore, Md, Johns Hopkins UP, 1972.

Ruhm von Oppen, B., ed. *Documents on Germany under occupation, 1945–1954*. London, OUP for RIIA, 1955.

Saeter, Martin. *Okkupation, integration, gleichberechtigung*. Oslo, Norsk Utenrikspolitisk Institutt, 1967.

Sattler, J. F. 'The transformation of German-American relations as a strategic problem'. Unpublished Ph.D. thesis, Univ. of Alberta, Edmonton, 1971.

Schaetzel, J. Robert. 'A dialogue of the deaf across the Atlantic'. *Fortune*, Nov. 1972.

Schlesinger, Arthur, Jr. *A thousand days*. Boston, Mass., Houghton Mifflin, 1965.

Schmidt, Helmut. *The balance of power*. London, William Kimber, 1971.

Schwarz, Hans-Peter. *Vom Reich zur Bundesrepublik*. Neuwied, Luchterhand, 1966.

Siegler, H. von. *Dokumentation zur Deutschlandfrage*, vol. 2. Bonn, Verlag für Zeitarchive, 1961.

Silj, Alessandro. *Europe's political puzzle: a study of the Fouchet negotiations and the 1963 veto*. Cambridge, Mass., Harvard Center for International Affairs, 1967.

Smart, Ian. 'The new Atlantic charter', *The World Today*, June 1973.

—— 'Perspective from Europe', in M. Willrich and J. B. Rhinelander, eds, *SALT: the Moscow agreements and beyond*. New York, Free Press, 1974.

Smith, Jean Edward. *The defense of Berlin*. Baltimore, Md, Johns Hopkins UP, 1963.

Sommer, Theo. 'The objectives of Germany', in A. Buchan, ed., *A world of nuclear powers?* Englewood Cliffs, NJ, Prentice Hall, 1966.

—— 'Bonn changes course'. *Foreign Affairs*, 43/3 (1967).

—— 'Germany's reservations'. *Survival*, May 1967.

—— 'Bonn's new Ostpolitik'. *Journal of International Affairs*, 22/1 (1968).

—— 'Kriterien und Instrumente der europäischen Sicherheit', in K. Birrenbach and others, *Aussenpolitik nach der Wahl des 6. Bundestages*. Bonn, Leske Verlag for Deutsche Gesellschaft für Auswärtige Politik, 1969.

Sorensen, Theodore C. *Kennedy*. New York, Harper & Row, 1965.

Speier, H. *German rearmament and atomic war*. Evanston, Ill., Row, Paterson, 1957.

Stanley, Timothy, 'Atlantic security in the seventies'. Paper presented to 17th Assembly of the Atlantic Treaty Association, London, Sept. 1971.

Stebbins, Richard M. *The United States in world affairs 1962*. New York, Random House, 1963.

Strange, Susan. 'The dollar crisis 1971'. *International Affairs*, Apr. 1972.

Strauss, Franz Josef. 'An alliance of continents'. *International Affairs*, Apr. 1965.

Stützle, Walter. *Kennedy und Adenauer in der Berlin-Krise 1961–1962.* Bonn—Bad Godesberg, Verlag Neue Gesellschaft, 1973.

Tabor, George M. *John F. Kennedy and a uniting Europe: the politics of partnership.* Bruges, College of Europe, 1969.

Thiel, Elke. 'Truppenstationierung und Devisenausgleich'. *Europa-Archiv*, 24/7 (1969).

—— 'Devisenausgleich und Lastenteilung im Atlantischen Bündnis'. *Europa-Archiv*, 26/10 (1971).

Tucker, Robert W. *The new isolationism: threat or promise?* New York, Universe Books, 1972.

Vandenberg, Arthur H. *The private papers of Senator Vendenberg.* Ed. Arthur H. Vandenberg, jr, with the collaboration of Joe Alex Morris. Boston, Mass., Houghton Mifflin, 1952.

Wagner, Wolfgang. *Die Bundespräsidentenwahl 1959.* Mainz, Mathias Grünewald-Verlag for Kommission für Zeitgeschichte, Katholische Akademie in Bayern, 1972. (No. II in series Adenauer Studien.)

Watt, D. C. *Survey of international affairs 1961.* London, OUP for RIIA, 1965.

—— *Survey of international affairs 1962.* London, OUP for RIIA, 1970.

—— ed. *Documents on international affairs 1961.* London, OUP for RIIA, 1965.

—— ed. *Documents on international affairs 1962.* London, OUP for RIIA, 1971.

Weizsäcker, Carl von. 'Nuclear inspections'. *Survival*, May 1967.

Wettig, G. *Entmilitarisierung und Wiederbewaffnung in Deutschland 1943–1955.* Munich, R. Oldenbourg Verlag, 1967.

Whetten, Lawrence L. *Germany's Ostpolitik: relations between the Federal Republic and the Warsaw Pact countries.* London, OUP for RIIA, 1971.

Willis, F. R. *France, Germany and the new Europe 1945–1967.* 2nd edn. Stanford, Calif., Stanford UP, 1968.

Wilson, Harold. *The Labour government 1964–70.* London, Weidenfeld & Nicolson; Michael Joseph, 1971.

Windsor, Philip. *Germany and the management of détente.* London, Chatto & Windus for ISS, 1971.

Wolfe, Thomas W. *Soviet power and Europe, 1945–1970.* Baltimore, Md, Johns Hopkins UP, 1970.

Zink, Harold. *The United States in Germany, 1944–1955.* New York, D. Van Nostrand, 1957.

Index